THE ROGUE'S YARN

'Rogue's yarn' - a piece of coloured yarn inserted in each strand of any rope issued by HM Dockyard to distinguish it from material of inferior quality.

THE ROGUE'S YARN

by
H.K. Oram

Edited by
Wendy Harris

LEO COOPER
LONDON

First published in Great Britain in 1993 by
LEO COOPER,
190 Shaftesbury Avenue, London WC2H 8JL
an imprint of Pen & Sword Books Ltd., 47 Church Street,
Barnsley, S. Yorks S70 2AS

Copyright ©

The Executors of the late Captain H.K. Oram
and Wendy Harris

A CIP catalogue record for this book is available from the British Library

ISBN: 0 85052 285 4

Printed by
Redwood Press,
Melksham, Wiltshire

For Peter

CONTENTS

ACKNOWLEDGEMENTS

I would like to thank Mrs E. Mills and Mrs K.N. Duncan for effecting the introduction which enabled this book to be written, and encouraging Captain Oram to proceed with the work. I am particularly indebted to Commander John Oram RN Rtd. for his generosity in allowing free access to family papers, also to Mr and Mrs W. Rowntree for their help in the early stages of the project, and to Charles Owen for his continued advice and support throughout.

Thanks are also due to Admiral R. Heaslip; the crew of HM Submarine *Onslaught* under their CO, Lieutenant-Commander David Cooke, and especially Lieutenant Stephen Backhouse, Lieutenant-Commander B.S. Jones, Captain (SM) First Submarine Squadron, HMS *Dolphin*, and Second Officer Helen Brown.

The preparation of the manuscript could not have been undertaken without the kind assistance of the Submarine Museum Archive, Gosport, all those ex-service personnel who responded so fully and warmly to requests for personal memoirs of Captain Oram in *The Navy News* and *The Cape Horner Magazine*, Mrs Brenda Gore-Brown and Lieutenant-Commander Brian Head RNR Rtd. who advised on communications systems.

Photographs appear courtesy of Captain Oram's Estate, the Submarine Museum Archive and the Imperial War Museum. I would particularly like to thank Gus Britton, ex-signalman, at the Submarine Museum, who supplied captions for the photographs and provided invaluable guidance during the preparation of the text.

Wendy Harris

1

An Independent Spirit

AT ABOUT THE TIME Napoleon was stowing his gear for Elba my great-grandfather, Thomas Bate Crowther, launched himself down the vertiginous slipway of life in southern England.

Everybody, at some time or another, has been curious about their forbears — and with good reason because it is from antecedents that we have inherited the genes which determine our own personalities. It is quite natural to assume that we feel the way we do and behave in the peculiar way that seems right to us because one of our many ancestors had similar emotions. It would certainly be revealing to journey back in time and meet those relatives whose distant lives have made their contribution to our own complex characters.

In times gone by, before the dubious advantages of modern systems of communication were placed at our disposal, the jigsaw of past generations could be fairly accurately reconstructed from contemporary correspondence. The habit of informal, chatty letter-writing all but disappeared in my lifetime. The environment inhabited by my own antecedents is difficult to recreate and there remain many blanks in the picture, for neither line from which I am descended was characterized by its desire or ability to communicate. We were not fluent correspondents nor, generally speaking, demonstrative with our affections. There is little to go on save disconnected nursery stories, snippets of family gossip and legends told to me by my elders and betters, pieced together with recollections of my own far-distanced childhood. Occasionally one catches a fleeting glimpse, real or imagined, of an ancestor with whom one had some vague fellow-feeling. Such are the ephemeral way-points of heredity.

Thomas eventually married Jane Strong, a girl from Cumbrian farming stock, in the same year that Queen Victoria married her Prince Albert — 1840. The Queen and her Prince Consort then got on with the happy business of reproducing themselves. Jane and Thomas, whose union was not blessed by the Crowther parents who felt their son had rather married beneath himself, followed the Royal example but decided to stop at six little Crowthers — a son and five daughters, one of whom, Margaret, was my maternal grandmother.

Thomas Crowther saw to it that all his brood were well-educated, beginning in a nearby primary school founded, with meagre financial support from the Anglican church, by himself and a like-minded group of friends who were keen to give their children a good start in life. Thus, perhaps, one of the first strands was laid in the genetic warp of my own character, for education and training became abiding interests not only throughout my professional life as a sailor but later in the wider and wilder world of discontented youth when I became a member of Kurt Hahn's Outward Bound School Board in Wales, working with, among others, Vic Feather. The Outward Bound philosophy of enabling psychologically malnourished youngsters to discover undreamt of potential through exposure to challenges which were, apparently, tinged with danger was a far cry from my great-grandfather's educational theories. He must, nevertheless, have been something of an innovator in his own time.

Margaret and her four younger sisters attended this school, by all accounts a chilly alma mater whose more delicate students were often, for want of an adequate heating system, excused lessons and sent home in wintertime, their raw red knees knocking with the cold. Thomas prevailed once more upon the Church Commissioners, this time for funds to provide a stove but his request fell upon deaf ears and the local community eventually raised the grand sum of six guineas which furnished the equipment. Thomas himself contributed ten shillings and sixpence, possibly reflecting the proportion of the school roll occupied by his own family! Blessed warmth trickled across the schoolroom floor and rose to thaw the numbed brains of its pupils, sending the lifeblood of curiosity racing once more about their perished little beings.

John, the eldest child, was sent further afield to Greenlea School in Abbeytown within sight of the Solway Firth. He became friendly with a boy called Henry Sewell whom he invited home for the Christmas holidays one year. Margaret Crowther was just fifteen. Henry was clearly smitten and sent her a Valentine card the following February, thanking her for making the holidays so enjoyable.

Margaret was a proper Victorian. Born in 1845, just ahead of the tumultuous social revolution heralded by the repeal of the Corn Laws, she was brought up under the old, strict régime. It plainly did her no harm. She had a back as straight as a ramrod and lived to be ninety-nine. By then I was a Captain at the Admiralty but this exalted station in life did nothing to diminish my respectful fear of Grandmother Sewell. She was a tall woman with a rather long face — a characteristic shared by the Sewells. She enunciated, rather than spoke, through habitually pursed lips — a mannerism which persists in certain branches of the Sewell line to this day. I found this very precise articulation uncomfortably intimidating. It forestalled any spontaneous conversational exchange and childish demonstrative urges gradually died in the breast so that by the time the Sewells reached adulthood, they were, broadly speaking, an uncommunicative lot bound by the many taboos proscribed by those pursed lips.

My wife and I visited Grandmother Sewell shortly before her death. Her crinkled skin, dried and yellowed under the Jamaican sun, reminded me of an Egyptian mummy. Her dignified stillness all but completed the illusion. She was sitting bolt upright in her chair, but the minute those resolutely pursed lips parted it was clear that life beat tenaciously on from deep within the aged frame. Apart from getting a bit mixed up with the family generations who had come to tea with her, she still ruled the roost. Many a poor rating had come face to face with me across the defaulter's table by this late stage in my career. At Grandmother Sewell's tea-table the roles were definitely reversed!

When we left she tucked a pound note and a bar of chocolate into my hand. Both very useful. The pound note helped to pay for the taxi and the chocolate, in wartime, was a wanton luxury. Where she laid her hands on it I cannot imagine but this careful talent for always having 'a little something put by' may very well have been inherited from her father, a careful man to the last. One day in 1861 he went off to the local station and bought a train ticket. Rail travel was still in its infancy and it was possible to buy a personal insurance, together with one's ticket, against an accident on the journey. Thomas had never bothered with insurance before but on this particular day he did, and stuck the ticket in his waistcoat pocket. Sure enough, the train went off the rails and he was trapped in the wreckage. He might well have survived had the rescue services not folded him in half to extricate him from the mangled débris. He was still breathing on arrival at hospital but an inquest revealed that he died from a punctured lung which must have occurred as the result of a rib piercing it during his ungainly exit from the carriage.

Back to this young Victorian Miss then, whose father died when she was barely sixteen. This was a great shock to the family and young Margaret found herself shouldering a considerable burden of responsibility. Her mother later married again so there was someone to provide for them all and supplement poor Thomas's insurance money, but life did not feel as secure as before and there were five daughters to be married off.

Henry Sewell, hearing of the family tragedy and undoubtedly feeling great sympathy for Margaret, kept in touch. Margaret was certainly not beautiful. 'Handsome' would have best described her. She was a tall, self-contained young woman with a rather stilted manner of speech. It may have been her natural air of reserve which fascinated Henry, or perhaps he detected a hidden streak of adventure and unconventionality. She was certainly able to run a household quite competently. For her part,

Margaret may have been looking for a way out of her family situation. The relationship between daughter and step-father is often a difficult one.

The Sewells were pioneering colonials, starting from scratch and creating their fortune from plantations in Jamaica. Henry's father William must have employed freed slaves – possibly his own father's – looking after them in a patrician sort of way as he rode about his estates in Nankeen trousers, managing sugar-cane and pineapple harvesting with great determination while maintaining strict discipline among his negro labour force. The friendship between Margaret and Henry ripened over the years. Henry would one day be a man of property, even if the property was to all intents and purposes on the other side of the world. Margaret by this time was getting on for twenty-five. No time to lose. The following year they were married.

There must have been a sharp intake of breath from the Crowthers when Margaret announced her intention to set sail for Jamaica with her new husband. Whether it came from relief at the marriage of one of the five financial liabilities or anxiety at her extraordinary choice of domicile in a foreign land one can only hazard a guess. Her own Victorian countenance must surely, though, have concealed an emotional turmoil as she stepped aboard the ship which was to carry her across the Atlantic.

The newly-weds became the next generation of landowners in Jamaica, inheriting from Henry's father. Margaret lost no time in getting on with her family responsibilities. Between 1870 and 1881 she in her turn gave birth to six children. The first of these was my mother, Alice Maude Mary. She made an unexpectedly early appearance one storm-torn night as the fringe of a hurricane clawed noisily at the island. The story goes that there were no clothes ready for the new baby so Marjie the nursemaid ripped up one of my grandfather's nightshirts and wrapped her in it. This somewhat unconventional arrival set the pattern for Alice's life, which was hardly one of conformity. Her birth so delighted old William Sewell, Henry's father, that he remade his will leaving all the estates in trust to her and any siblings she might acquire in the future. Perhaps William had glimpsed into the crystal ball. On Alice's second birthday, a Sunday, he suddenly died of a stroke.

Henry found himself in sole charge of a substantial business. Margaret, in the early years of her marriage, criss-crossed the Atlantic to bear the rest of her children. The next one after my mother, a boy was born in Cumbria almost five years later. Several miscarriages had sapped Margaret's considerable mental and physical resources. After William's death the family returned to England for a time and Jane wept as she beheld her eldest daughter, the rosy bloom now gone from her cheeks. Health and strength gradually returned, however, bringing with it another child, this time a girl.

Then, with the newest arrival barely able to walk, back to Jamaica for another boy. Hardly fifteen months went by before the family was on the move again, this time to a house in Wales from which Henry could indulge his passion for terrier hunting, a pastime which fully engaged his attention while his long-suffering wife gave birth to the last two members of his family.

But Alice had been the first. Alice had been the pioneer. Alice had changed her old grandfather's mind — a stroke of financial good fortune which brushed my boyhood and enabled me to embark on my own career. Alice had made her first Atlantic crossing before she could properly read or write. Another strand laid perhaps. She entered into a well-established family which continued to thrive and prosper. The Sewells must have seen the end of the slave trade in Jamaica and when I eventually visited the island after the end of the Second World War, I found a village shop on the way to Montego Bay with the name 'Sewell' over the door. My uncle — one of my mother's younger brothers with whom I was staying — informed me that slaves would often take the name of their employer when they were freed. His words sent a shiver of ghastly fascination down my spine.

Henry and Margaret carried on the sugar business which grew until the Sewell family owned eight or ten different properties on the island. The principal estate was called Vale Royal and every year Henry chartered a small sailing ship to bring the produce back to England. Eventually she was renamed the *Vale Royal* and would arrive off Ventnor each summer, with a case or two of pineapples for the family.

Sugar was a very profitable business in the late nineteenth century. My grandfather worked hard and became a wealthy man. He redesigned the estate house, 'Arcadia', adding a second storey to accommodate his growing family and an elaborate wrought-iron verandah which was made in Glasgow and shipped out. In the summer the family would congregate in England where, if they were not lodged with Henry's uncomplaining mother-in-law in Cumbria, they would rent quite grand houses for the holidays. Balls were given, receptions were held. My grandmother did not have a particularly close relationship with any of her children and they inherited her natural reserve with the exception of Alice who, though outwardly guarded in her dealings with others, possessed the most affectionate nature of them all. She was educated at first by governesses but then, being five years older than her nearest sibling, was sent to boarding school in London. She developed into a sophisticated young woman of quiet charm, although she could let her hair down when the occasion merited it. One summer when the little *Vale Royal* had sailed into the Western Approaches laden with the fruits of the Caribbean, the Sewells threw a costume party at Steephill Castle, Ventnor. Henry had chosen Steephill that year so that he could indulge one of his other passions — sailing. Another strand. The theme the family chose was

Gilbert and Sullivan's *The Gondoliers* and Grandmother Sewell sent to a theatrical costumier in Covent Garden for the dresses. The party was a riot and my mother captivated everyone by posing at the top of the grand staircase in full regalia and then dancing the 'kachoucha fandango bolero' all the way down. She was quite tall, although her brothers and sisters passed her as they grew up. Nevertheless she had 'presence' and was once mistaken on a train journey to Lyon in France for Sarah Bernhardt. When the train stopped, she was mobbed!

In addition to the family income from the estates, Grandmother Sewell suddenly found herself the benefactress of a close friend's will. Life was good and my mother and her five brothers and sisters grew up in some luxury. Nevertheless, Henry was a strict father, as men who like to indulge their own pleasures often are. He most likely recognized his eldest daughter's affectionate and attractive nature and therefore kept her on a particularly short rein. He was a bit of a Barrett of Wimpole Street when it came to young gentlemen admirers. This jealousy caused him, on one occasion, to warn a young man — of whom Alice had become rather fond — off the premises. Alice, with something of her mother's spirit and tenacity, stood her ground and pleaded her suitor's cause. That was her downfall. Within the month she had been packed off on a cruise. Although Alice was the apple of his eye, Henry was determined to sever the bond between his daughter and her admirer once and for all. A young lady could not, of course, in those days travel unaccompanied so the faithful Marjie, who had assisted at her birth, acted as chaperone. The inevitable happened. On board ship Alice met a good looking young man called Harry Kendall Oram. He was acting as a member of the crew in some capacity whilst deciding what to do with his life. One of the first things he did, according to Marjie, was to disappear behind the funnel with Alice. A complementary strand was spliced! This quickly led to elopement, marriage, excommunication from the Sewell family and the start of a new life for my mother in London.

It was 1892. My father, who had been educated at Clifton College and whose family ran a successful business in Bristol, eventually joined the Militia, the 19th century equivalent of the Territorials. The newly-weds set up home in a spacious flat in Bayswater. They were able to live relatively comfortably although the luxury my mother had grown accustomed to as a girl was gone. I was born on the twenty-third of October, 1894, in Clifton, near my father's home. When I was still a very small boy my parents went off to Malta where my father had been posted with his regiment. I was farmed out to relatives near Winchester. It must have been quite a long tour because I apparently failed to recognize my mother when she and my father returned.

Visits to my Oram grandparents were rare occurrences. In fact I do not remember meeting my Oram grandfather at all. It was Grandmother who met me off the puffing GWR from London as I peered apprehensively through the billowing clouds of steam condensing under the great arc of Temple Meads Station roof. The high spots of those visits were arrival and departure when I could, for a few precious moments, clear a tiny smudged porthole in the steamy carriage window and indulge in secret fantasies of exotic and tantalizingly scarifying destinations.

Reality, in the shape of Grandmother Oram, was somewhat different. In summer she would greet me stiffly in the Arrival Hall, well away from flying smuts. With reluctant steps I disembarked and trailed across the platform, resigned to the very unexotic inevitable. Grandmother was encased in a complicated harness of black jet beads and smelled of medicated lozenges.

One dust-laden July afternoon I was, by way of diversion, to be taken to the shop which my grandparents owned. It sold ladies' clothes and items of haberdashery. It was on the first floor of a large house half-way up a steep hill. On the way there I fell and grazed my bony knees which became painfully caked with grit. Somebody must have cleaned me up and administered gentian violet to the damaged parts. I presented myself to my disapproving relative with a pair of bright blue knees and was then almost frightened out of my wits by the headless torso of a naked dummy used for displaying ladies' dresses.

My sister Peggy was born in 1898 and that completed our little family.

Being in the Militia was only a part-time job for a soldier. I was not aware of my father being in any kind of permanent employment when I was small. He enjoyed a full social life, he was very fond of the races and he had a large moustache. This was stuffed into a moustache corset at night to keep it flat and was a source of some wonder to my sister Peggy and me.

When the Boer War broke out in 1899 my father went off to serve his country. A soldier's pay was precious little and a part-time soldier's pay was even less. I suppose my father had had some money of his own when he married but, for one reason or another, our financial health deteriorated to such an extent that by the time he went away we were in some difficulty. Grandmother Sewell's legacy was to be our salvation. The terms of the bequest were that the major part of the money be held in trust for the Sewell children when they came of age.

My uncles in Jamaica, noting mother's straitened circumstances and, I suspect, a less than happy marriage, decided that she should be given her share of the money to enable her to bring up her two young children. They then discovered that all the extravagant childhood summers in England, all the fine country houses and balls, had been financed by Grandfather Sewell's liberal interpretation of the terms of the trust fund to include himself! The boys turfed him out from the management of the estates after that and took over themselves. But all the money which should have come to them and to mother through Grandmother Sewell was gone. Peggy and I were the children of a born-again Micawber father and a genuinely affectionate mother who was catapulted, partly by her own stubbornness, into a chaotic world of Alice in Blunderland.

We moved to Fulham, into a mansion block – a rare thing in those days. We had a top floor flat and I used to bowl my hoop past a mulberry tree and along a path which led around to the tennis courts at the back. Peggy and I were a strange, self-contained little pair. We didn't seem to need other children, which was very convenient since there was little money for parties and outings. We amused ourselves by going on train rides. The District Line and the Inner Circle were steam trains then and our idea of heavenly joy was to scamper off to Putney Bridge Station clasping the few pennies that mother had managed to find for us. In ecstasy, we would then descend, clutching our tickets in our hands, to breathe in great gulps of sulphurous fumes on the journey up to Sloane Square, where we would turn around and come back again!

Another favourite jaunt was the music hall. We used to go week after week and saw George Robey, Vesta Tilley, Marie Lloyd – all the great entertainers. We must have presented an odd picture, this solemn little boy holding his small sister firmly by the hand and creeping into the back row at the Victoria Palace. Perhaps the front of house people thought we were orphans! But it was a happy childhood. It didn't seem at all odd to Peggy and I that father was sometimes there and sometimes not. Very often, the only way that we knew he had come home was when we were sitting in the kitchen with Marjie, who continued to look after us and rub in the camphorated oil. Heavy footfalls would be heard whereupon Marjie's expression underwent a sea change as she admonished us to 'Pay attention! There's the Major!'

When it came to education, Peggy and I pretty much educated ourselves on our endless train rides and visits to the theatre. A tram clanked and trundled its way up and down the Fulham Palace Road for our delight. We were left to our own devices and although that's not a thing one could really recommend these days, we came to no harm and certainly developed an early sense of self-confidence and self-reliance as a result. I am still very much a believer in the value of practical skills, but that may be because I was never much of an academic and could only cope with theoretical learning by slogging away in a rather pedestrian manner. Formal schooling had to come of course and I was eventually sent to the prep school for St Paul's as a day boy. There seemed to be some feeling that I would eventually go to Jamaica and take my part in running the estates when I grew up.

Three terms later we were on the move again. Fortunes had plunged still further and we went to the sea, to a tiny cottage at Goring near Worthing in Sussex. I went to a prep school in Worthing as a day boy and there received the only real education I had in my life, in the sense that I was taught subjects like Latin, geometry, mathematics, English and all the usual stuff. It had remarkably little effect on my subsequent career but I did enjoy the choir where I sang lustily and with great commitment. I dawdled my way home, as boys always do, banging a stick against the knobby pebbles in the sea wall. I lost all track of time, scanning the vast horizon for pirate ships and clippers running before the wind. I became absorbed in the quietly satisfying domestic chores of the local fishermen, bent over their nets with time and yarns to share. It was an unremarkable boyhood, laced with an accidental salty tang. Who knows what effects such influences spawn in later life? I should, by rights, have been a soldier, following in my father's footsteps and fired by his tales of derring-do as he led me by the hand through lines of troops under canvas in Hyde Park.

The year was 1901, the Boer War recently ended, and my father, together with thousands of others, returned to the home of Empire for the coronation of Edward VII. Through a haze of smouldering campfire smoke and steaming drizzle the veldt materialized and I rode like the wind behind Father who cut the darkness at a gallop in search of a column of our Yeomanry which had gone off in the wrong direction. The rendezvous was a farm. Intelligence reports told of Boers holed up there. Orders were to surround them but by the time we arrived the birds had flown − not far, though, for the embers were still warm. Father flung himself exhausted on the floor of the farmhouse. I flung myself by his side. No sooner had we closed our dust-caked eyelids than a furious din broke out all around us − big guns, Pom-Poms and rifles. As the dawn streaked round the horizon Boers opened fire on us from three nearby ridges. It took only half a minute for our fifteen pounders to go into action. 'Oram!' barked the Colonel, 'Tell the 10th Infantry to take the left ridge and the Yeomanry the right!' Father leapt into the saddle and jammed in his spurs. I leapt up after him. We rode like the devil scattering loose stones to the wind, gaping potholes nearly unseating us. Orders safely delivered, we were back in next to no time to find the guns limbered up and instructions to follow the Colonel up to the central ridge. Then came the orderlies with the bodyguard next in line and the guns and escort thundering after us. It was wildly exciting and we breasted the ridge at a gallop to find the Boers streaming away to the north. Six prisoners were taken but our horses were done up so we pulled back to rest them at the farm and revive ourselves with fresh-brewed coffee and biscuits. What great adventure! I had no idea where Africa was but it thrilled me to the core.

Father's presence became less and less evident as I grew up. The moves we made did not seem particularly ominous to Peggy or I. We were protected in our cocoon of childish ignorance by our own self-sufficiency and Mother's unfailing affection. Our sojourn in Goring took on the aspect of a prolonged summer holiday. I would occasionally arrive home from school to find Mother pouring tea for a most sympathetic gentleman who I later learned was the Bailiff. Then the Jamaican Uncles appeared on the scene telling me it was time to make the first of life's great decisions. They had obviously discussed my future with Mother, who was acquainted with the perilous state of the family economy in Jamaica, and they offered to help her educate her son so that he would in time, be able to support himself. The choice offered to me was Bedford Grammar School or the Merchant Navy.

Both options involved leaving home. Self-reliant though I had become, this seemed a huge step to a twelve-year old. A young friend I had made at Goring was going to Bedford so, rather than be alone and friendless in this new semi-adult world I was being forced to enter, I elected to go with him. Mother and the Uncles, on the other hand, clearly had Jamaica in their sights and felt that the ability to sail a ship would come in handy. Thus it was one chilly autumn morning in 1908 that I found myself reporting aboard the sail training ship *Worcester* for embarkation on the next leg of life's voyage.

2

Learning My Trade

THE EXCITEMENT OF finding myself aboard a First Rate Ship, a wooden waller with a hundred and ten guns, went some way to distracting me from the cold porridgey lump of nerves firmly wedged just below my ribcage. The *Worcester* smelt of the sea. It is an indescribable perfume, unique and instantly recognizable – hemp, old oak soaked in the brine of the oceans, capstan grease and sailcloth.

Boys were taken on between the ages of eleven and sixteen. I was already nearly a year older than the most junior recruit so I had a lot to catch up on and a lot of scornful remarks to parry from the younger but infinitely less lubberly cadets with whom I was berthed. I envied their nonchalant confidence. I gasped in awe at their monkey-like agility. I pretended with serious nods to know exactly where belfry and snatch block were and what the topsail sheet bitts did. Secretly I despaired. Would I ever master this strange new language?

The Thames Nautical Training College, of which I was now a part, had been established in 1862. Two years earlier the training ship aboard which I was now a cadet had been laid down as the *Frederick Royal*. By the time she came to be launched she was renamed the *Frederick William*. She was lent to the Nautical Training College in 1875 where she replaced the original *Worcester* which was sold ten years later. Her three lines of gunports were ranged along a length of two hundred and four feet, the heavier guns on the lower deck. I scrambled up and down companion ladders, barking my shins and marvelling at this impressive fire-power. Suddenly the taut, dry discipline of schoolboy history sprang to life. The *Worcester* became the *Victory* leading the *Fighting Témeraire* into battle at the head of the line. Nelson paced his quarterdeck while all about me Trafalgar seethed and boomed. I determined, with all my heart, to do my duty!

The *Worcester* carried six 68-pounders, a hundred 32-pounders and four 18-pounders to pick off the small fry with. She was constructed along traditional lines but was unusual in that she had a screw added. She was a 'transitional' ship, the Navy itself then being in a state of technological and social transition from sail to steam, from wooden wallers to ironclads. This change carried with it social implications of some magnitude for the Royal Navy, hitherto something of an élitist 'club' which had suffered over the years from a certain amount of inbreeding. The long-term consequences of this social and professional snobbery were to become swiftly and painfully apparent during the course of two world wars.

The *Worcester* had a 60-foot beam and displaced 4,725 tons. She'd been built at Portsmouth dockyard and launched on 24 March, 1860. Trouble was brewing across the Atlantic that year and soon America was at war with herself. By 1864 the Federal Fleet was under serious threat of attack from a dastardly new weapon. The Confederates were going under water to sabotage the Unionists and they did it with the CSS *Hunley*. She was the earliest submersible to be engaged with an enemy surface ship in time of war. The Confederate Navy scored a direct hit against the 1,264-ton frigate *Housatonic* of the Union Fleet, courtesy of *Hunley*'s primitive but effective armament. This was a 30-foot spar torpedo discharged underwater while the vessel itself was only partially submerged. The explosive charge was activated by the commanding officer who, bravely bracing himself against the *Hunley*'s casing, pulled a lanyard. Nearly a hundred and fifty pounds of gunpowder went off bang. The spar shot through the water into the USS *Housatonic*, holing her below the waterline and causing her to sink rapidly. The *Hunley* herself was flooded through an open hatch and sucked into the hole she had blown in her quarry's side. She went down with all hands.

Thus the first naval submarine was lost on active service at almost the same time that my training ship made sail on her maiden voyage as a sailing warship charged with the defence of her island nation. In 1908 I, of course, was quite ignorant of this timely coincidence half a century earlier and totally unaware, as my tender and clumsy fingers struggled hour after hour with reeving and bousing, what a significant part submarines were to play in my own life when I later joined the Royal Navy. First I had to learn my trade.

The vessel aboard which I set about this daunting task was the second of three *Worcesters*, the last one starting life as the *Exmouth* and being built specifically as a training ship. The reason they all took the same name was that once a vessel had established herself at a particular job, subsequent vessels took on her name. The first vessel to be used as a training ship had been the *Worcester*, moored at Blackwall Reach when the College was founded. The name became the name of the job rather than the name of the ship although it obviously still applied to whichever vessel happened to be in commission at the time. Thus the old *Frederick William* became the *Worcester* of my day and was permanently moored in the Thames at Greenhythe for the education of little boys who had the idea of becoming sailors.

It was a bruising experience, this business of becoming a sailor. The blue and yellow patches in which I seemed to be covered for the first few weeks were not the result of floggings, although there was a cat and discipline was severe. They were the concrete evidence of my early aspirations towards a naval life — learning how to get in and out of my hammock! We were turned out each morning at seven and required to wash, in bone-chilling water, under inspection. I still think this is probably one of the fastest and most accurate manoeuvres any of us was to carry out in his entire naval career. Failure to scour under any hidden parts resulted in a severe tongue-lashing and a double douche of freezing water.

To get the blood circulating again and bring some feeling back to our deadened limbs we had twenty minutes of P.E. from half past seven until ten to eight. Then it was divisions for inspection and at eight o'clock prayers and breakfast. Half an hour later we scurried below to stow our hammocks and then laid hold of huge brooms and began to sweep the decks. We quickly learned that nothing was wasted on board ship — neither time nor artefact. Every second was crammed with at least three things to be done and every piece of gear we touched seemed to have at least three functions. Our hammocks, for example, were not simply blessed resting places for our exhausted little bodies at the end of a long hard day. In time of war they could be rolled and packed into the hammock netting strung on either side of the poop deck as protection against enemy fire. If any poor unfortunate did get seriously in the way of stray shot or perhaps fall prey to some deadly illness on a voyage, his mortal remains would be sewn into his hammock, together with a largish cannonball for ballast. Before the ceremonial burial at sea, the final stitch in his shroud was passed through his nose, just to make sure there had been no mistake!

The forenoon was devoted to formal education and from nine until midday we sat in the schoolroom assiduously learning our lessons. These were more or less normal school subjects for small boys but with a nautical bias which became more pronounced as the course progressed. We learned the anatomy of our ship from keel to bulwarks. We crawled through her from sternpost to hawse-holes learning the outlandish terminology of our new domain. We barked our shins on hatch coamings and rubbed our fingers raw bending on prickly, unyielding ropes. We began to identify sections of the great web of rigging aloft and to understand what happened to a bit of cloth when the wind blew against it from different directions. Our elementary mathematics lessons led into basic navigation — and so on until the empty lockers of our minds started to fill with gear needed on the voyage.

We grasped at our scant periods of recess, cramming them with lively chatter and irreligious imitation of our 'chalkies.' It all helped to let off steam. Between the start of morning school and dinner at one o'clock we were allowed twenty-four minutes' freedom precisely. There was a ten-minute break at eleven, another at twelve and four minutes to get cleaned up and ship-shape for dinner. The time between the end of morning school and dinner — which hardly touched the sides as we wolfed it down after our long morning's exertions — was taken up with seamanship and drills. Drills were a nightmare until we got the hang of them, but somehow, in a remarkably short span of time, our totally unco-ordinated young limbs were tamed from flailing chaos into a disciplined and accurate response to command. After dinner it was back to school again until half past four when we were dismissed to clean up the decks. We went below for refuelling an hour later and then, after tea, we actually had a choice! The library and gym were both open until ten to eight so we could blow off any remaining energy or pass a sedentary couple of hours before bedtime. We were given hot chocolate and biscuits or bread and butter to last us through the night and at eight fifteen hammocks were hung. Half past eight was prayers and cadets turn in. More bruises! Fat boys firmed up under this hectic régime and thin ones quickly developed muscle. Irregular bowels performed like clockwork. In the navy, we learned, everything happens on time!

The strangeness of those early days in a ship going nowhere had a lasting effect. We were still landsmen at the outset, tethered to our shore-based lives by the short halters of our infant experience and comforted by the regularity of a shore-based routine and familiar language. Afloat, we were in a totally different element. The language was incomprehensible and time was measured in watches by bells. This mysterious sequence of four-hourly turns started, for some obscure reason, at eight o'clock in the evening with the First Watch and progressed through the Middle or 'graveyard' Watch to Morning, Forenoon, Afternoon, First Dog and Last Dog before coming round again to First.

We discovered that the four-hour turn immediately before the First Watch was split into 'dog' watches to give a total of seven turns in twenty-four hours. Thus the mens' duty periods could be varied each day. We heard, and tried hard to remember, how the passage of a watch was marked in half hours by the sounding of the ship's bell, starting with one stroke after the first half hour and culminating in eight at the end. This seemed straightforward enough and pretty soon we were able to tell the time by the bell without resorting to our fingers!

The use of half-hour sandglasses to record the passage of time at sea was within the direct experience of some of the more encrusted old salts charged with our education. It didn't go out of the Navy until fairly late in the nineteenth century and one of our more colourful instructors, steeped in the brine of ancient naval tradition, persisted in admonishing us to 'Look lively, boy and get that job done in two glasses.' It was he who took me aside to explain a verbal blunder I had made when being tested on my timekeeping. 'Never strike five bells in a dog-watch, Boy,' he growled, 'Tis, the signal for Mutiny!' I had no idea I was about to perpetrate a capital offence and listened all agape as he related the events leading up to the Nore Mutiny of 1797. Thereafter only one bell was struck at 1830, with two at 1900, three at 1930 and eight at 2000 to signify the end of the watch. The custom is still followed today, even by foreign warships.

Little by little we started to become seamen. We no longer ate, we messed – much after the inelegant fashion, I imagine, of the sailors of Queen Elizabeth I's time who 'messed from the common pot' so naming the sailor's eating and sleeping space once and for all. We all aspired to be 'taut hands'. It was hard but it was never unbearable. Life was so busy we never felt homesick and some of the old Mates who taught us our seamanship livened things up with a yarn or two. We were an odd collection of little boys, learning how to become men under the watchful and fatherly eyes of sailors whose only family was the sea and her creatures.

My time aboard the *Worcester* fairly flew past. We were constantly being put through our paces and examined verbally to ascertain how much of the vast store of knowledge imparted by our schoolmasters and naval instructors was being absorbed into our lubberly heads. We never actually went anywhere in the *Worcester*, of course. She was permanently moored. But we did get in a fair amount of small boat drill and learned how to row, steer, go alongside without taking chunks out of anything, handle ropes and to swim!

Every year several prizes were given in the *Worcester*. One of these was called The King's Medal. Four or five boys were put up for it and it went to the one considered to be 'Cadet of the Year.' I didn't win the medal in 1911 but I was one of the five. On prize day, Sir Philip Devitt of Devitt and Moore, an old-established shipping company, gave the awards. Devitt and Moore was exceptional among shipowners at that time for making special provision for training cadets in its cargo-carrying fleet. The King's Medallist was automatically offered a place on board the *Port Jackson*, a D and M iron-clad wool clipper plying the Australia run. The boy who won the King's Medal in my year already had a place in another ship and the *Port Jackson* cadetship was offered to me.

Once again Fate had intervened in life's unpredictable game of snakes and ladders and thrown me a six. In order to qualify for a Second Mate's Certificate in those days you had to spend three years at sea. There was an examination to be passed and candidates were not accepted until they had done their sea time.

Cadetships aboard commercial vessels cost money. It was evident from my holidays at home that money was, as always, in short supply. The *Port Jackson* cadetship was being offered to me under exactly the same conditions as if I had won the Medal. There would be no fee to pay and my accommodation was all found. In just three years' time I would be able to sit for my Second Mate's Certificate and then I should be able to start earning my own living. Independence — and adventure — beckoned. The smell of caulking was firmly in my nostrils. I could hardly wait for the sound of filling sails.

It was scarcely two years after topping this ladder that I plunged headlong down a snake. To be more precise I plunged backwards into the *Port Jackson*'s hold which I had been cleaning out as we lay in Sydney Harbour preparing her for the voyage home. Wool is a greasy cargo and as I clambered up the vertical ladder to haul myself out for a breath of fresh air on deck, my well-oiled fingers slipped on the hatch coaming and back I went. It was a forty-foot drop and as the wind whistled past my ears I had the presence of mind to raise my right arm behind my head. As luck would have it, I landed on a hatch cover which broke my fall somewhat. It was the only piece of wood in the entire hold! My arm cushioned my head all right, but at the cost of a badly dislocated shoulder. After a brief spell in a Sydney hospital I was back on board with my arm in a sling and paralysed down one side. Once back home in England I had to go into hospital again because the arm had not responded very well and so I missed my ship.

It would have been my third voyage, and my third year, in the *PJ*. This was a bitter disappointment to me and I tried to persuade the owners to send me out by steamer to rejoin her, but no. Two circumnavigations, twice round the Horn under canvas in a merchant ship, was obviously all I had in my sailing orders for the time being.

The year was 1913. I was almost nineteen. It was time to heave to for a while and wait for wind and tide to carry me off on a new course.

3

Turned Over From RNR

DURING THE NEXT five years the final chapters of one part of world history were written and a new volume was begun. The changes wrought during and after the Great War signalled far more than mere adjustments to national boundaries or shifts in political allegiance. A different social order struggled to emerge from the turmoil of conflict and loss. Moral, economic and religious values suffered searing reappraisal. Technology started to make itself felt as a primary force for change throughout society.

Change was in the wind for me too. Indeed so rapid and complete was it that in the months between the autumn of 1913 and the outbreak of war on 4 August the following year, my future career was determined. Any aspirations I might have had toward life as a sailorman were firmly scotched. Whatever family ambitions existed on my behalf in the direction of Jamaica vanished without trace.

I had been one of four cadets who, on leaving the *Worcester*, had been enrolled as Midshipmen, Royal Naval Reserve, and under a new scheme that had just been announced I was eligible for a year's training in the Fleet.

With my ambitions firmly centred on sitting for my 'Square Rig Certificate Examination' as soon as practicable it seemed to me to be a waste of time to spend a year in a warship when I could have been finishing my three-year period of qualifying sea-time in the *Port Jackson*. My arguments were unavailing and, in October, 1913, I received an impressive-looking document from the Lords Commissioners of the Admiralty directing me to proceed to Portsmouth forthwith for service in the Home Fleet. Though it still rankled that my plans had been capsized, I set about rigging myself out with new uniform gear, including a dirk which seemed to me to be a peculiarly anachronistic weapon for twentieth century warfare.

Boarding a taxi and looking at my instructions for the hundredth time, I told the driver to take me to HMS *Orion* at the South Railway Jetty.

Accustomed to vessels of modest size I found the dark grey mass of the giant battleship intimidating and strangely unreal. Crossing the brow I was acutely conscious that I was stepping over the threshold into a new and unfamiliar world. The prospect, though exciting, was unnerving. I was formally saluted by the Officer of the Watch in a frock coat and a Midshipman in a bumfreezer with white patches on the collar. I introduced myself and was taken below by the Midshipman through a warren of passages bright with lights and gleaming paintwork to the Gunroom which, he told me, would be my home from home shared with nine sub-lieutenants and thirteen midshipmen.

In the Mess I encountered a Maltese steward and three recumbent sub-lieutenants, to one of whom I was presented. He was, I gathered, the Sub of the Gunroom, the ruler and arbiter of midshipmens' fortunes. He gave me a friendly greeting and, leading the way to the head of the table, called for tea, over which he probed my professional history. Hearing that I had been at sea for two years he relieved my apprehensions by saying that after a month to get acclimatized he would accord me the status of Senior Midshipman. This was welcome news because I had heard disturbing yarns about the Navy's treatment of junior 'snotties.' Those who ventured to set foot on the hallowed decks after boarding from sail training ships like the *Worcester* or the *Conway* were rumoured to be less 'equal' than graduates of the conventional passage via Osborne and Dartmouth.

The rumours were well-founded, describing a prejudice which more often than not percolated down from aloft. This was confirmed on my first interview with the 'Bloke', an awesome figure in a ship's hierarchy. Answering a summons delivered by a breathless Snotty I entered my Commander's cabin to find myself face to face with a malarial countenance framed by a trim black beard which quivered with suppressed impatience. No time was wasted on formalities and I was promptly catechized with disconcerting directness. I was beginning to feel under stress when the Commander, alerted by a distant bugle, ceased fire and brought the inquisition to an end with, 'As you have been round the Horn I suppose you think you know it all, but you have a hell of a lot to learn so get busy and, as a start, go and see the Snotties' nurse.'

The Snotties' nurse, a senior lieutenant-commander who carried responsibility for organizing and supervising midshipmen's instruction, was a 'salt horse' who offered sound counsel. 'Get to know your ship first,' he said, 'ferret around on your own, be inquisitive about the whys and wherefores of everything that happens until you can see the patterns in the organization.'

It was sound advice. 'Nursie's' words of wisdom echoed down the next thirty years and crept unbidden into my mind each time I found myself appointed to a new job, full of boundless enthusiasm and all too keen to go full ahead, bent on subjecting my unsuspecting shipmates to some newly devised scheme or other. It is no bad thing to throttle back and take a bearing or two before sweeping in with revolutionary 'reforms.' There are times when a change of course is necessary but these are rarer than a zealous 'new boy' might think!

Following my 'nurse's' advice I set out on a questioning campaign and, in the course of my amateur research, collected information on *Orion*'s vital statistics. She was the name ship of a class of four battleships of 25,000 tons displacement. Her battle honours were impressive, starting with the Glorious First of June, 1794*, and including St Vincent, the Nile and Trafalgar. She had a main armament of ten 13.5″ guns in five twin-gunned turrets; a secondary armament of sixteen 4″ guns and two 21″ submerged torpedo tubes. She had an overall length of 545′ a beam of 88′ and, in common with all battleships, was fitted with heavy armour protection.

The four ships of the *Orion* class which cost £2,000,000 apiece were the first capital ships to be fitted with 13.5″ guns which, as the turrets were all mounted on the centre line, could fire a 5.5 ton broadside. The eighteen coal-fired boilers provided power for four steam turbine units giving a designed full speed of 21 knots and a full stowage of 3,300 tons of coal enabled them to cover about 4,000 miles at 19 knots. *Orion* had a complement of 900 officers and men. Compared with the *PJ*'s slender company of 47, this seemed to me to be the entire British Navy miraculously berthed aboard a single battleship.

My delusion was soon reinforced when this impressive array of Naval might, among which company I now numbered myself an insignificant and awestruck member, was told off to appear in full rig for the ceremonial pomp and circumstance surrounding a change of flag. The 2nd Battle Squadron to which we belonged was commanded by Vice-Admiral Sir George Warrender flying his flag† in *King George V. Orion* was the designated Flagship of the Rear-Admiral of the squadron. We were to embark Rear-Admiral Sir Robert Arbuthnot, a noted disciplinarian with a reputation for being 'an 'oly terror of an all-time flogger.'

A casual visitor gave us warning that the Rear-Admiral was a stickler for strict observance of the uniform regulations. The wearing of 'Ties, black silk, officers for the use of,' was imperative and as such articles were relatively inexpensive and the Sub most anxious we should pass muster, I was sent to Gieves on the Hard to purchase 24 of the same on tick in the

---

* Naval battles are customarily named after the nearest point of land. In this case the battle was fought so far out in the Atlantic that it was named by the date, there being no convenient land nearby, and called 'Glorious' because it was such a sweeping victory. Altogether there were five *Orions* and between them they collected the longest list of battle honours in the Navy. The battleship in which I served added Jutland to the roll of honour in 1916 and the cruiser which followed her in 1932 produced an impressive thirteen, ending with South France in 1944. After the Second World War, *Orion* became the name of the Reserve Fleet at Devonport.

† An admiral 'flies' his flag; his ship 'wears' it.

hope that their silken sheen would blind the eagle eye to other less respectable aspects of the Gunroom's personnel.

I entered the establishment with a mixture of embarrassment and bravado. Embarrassment at having to attempt the purchase of two dozen items on credit, particularly since there was another customer apparently examining samples of cloth at the other counter, and bravado at being vouchsafed such sartorial responsibility for the grand occasion.

My request provoked a slightly delayed, 'Yes, Sir,' as the elderly but very upright counter assistant swept me with a gaze as steadfast as the Wolf Rock Light. I felt some sort of explanation was necessary. I elaborated, with a broadening swagger as my story gathered way. 'You see, we've got a funny old Admiral coming and he's a stickler for dress and that sort of thing,' I boasted. 'Yes, Sir. Yes, Sir,' came the unnaturally quiet response from the gaunt Wolf Rock, flashing me now almost in desperation. 'And I've been detailed off to get these things to keep the old...' 'QUITE, Sir,' hissed the counter assistant, firmly cutting me off. Something told me to pipe down. The shop door clanged in a sudden puff of chilly outside air as the other customer took his leave. 'That WAS your Admiral, Sir, standing right behind you.' On the appointed day I was incapable of tying my own tie. The ship's company, in No. 1 dress, was fallen in on the upper deck a full hour before the event, a good practice to safeguard against last-minute crises. I spent this eternity in a rising tide of panic lest the Admiral should recognize his insubordinate Midshipman — one out of 900, whose face, in any case, he had never seen!

I cannot say that I enjoyed my initial weeks aboard the *Orion*. They were full of perplexity in an environment that was so complicated that at times I despaired that I would ever get the hang of the Navy's way of life. All my training had been in the pully-hauly school of seamanship in a ship handled by the muscle power of her scant crew. Here, as I delved into the ship's anatomy, I was lost in a mechanical maze.

It was a world of drills, inspections and a host of, seemingly, useless formalities. I had been used to practical and economical seamanship and in this new setting I felt frustrated and rebellious in the face of open fatuity. The Navy's way of life struck me as being riddled with petty restrictions and taboos and I missed the easy-going, flesh and blood relationships that had warmed our dog-watch sessions on the fore-hatch aboard the *PJ*.

Gradually, as I burrowed about, I began to glimpse reason in the ceaseless activity. When at last I realized that the size of a ship's company in a man of war is determined by her function in battle I began to see that, in times of peace, a superfluity of men have to be kept fit and alert by drills and exercises, some inherited from the Navy of bygone days.

At the end of the first full month, full of acquired knowledge, I reported to my nurse who, to my relief, was sufficiently impressed to put me on to the normal Snotty's duties. I took my turn as Midshipman of the Watch on the quarterdeck, a duty which taught me the details of the ship's daily routines. I also served as 'doggie' to the First Lieutenant. 'Jimmy the One' was the Senior Lieutenant Commander and, as the Commander's right-hand man, he carried delegated responsibility for the cleanliness and good order of all living spaces. Delivering his many messages brought me in touch with the ship's company and their way of life.

As I grew to know and like my messmates life became increasingly enjoyable. We were a boisterous party and, being of roughly university age, we had much in common with the undergraduate's customary idealism and urge to create a bright new world. In this we were rather inhibited by the Navy's monolithic traditionalism, but this in no way curbed our ebullient ideas on what we would do to shake things up if we were given half the chance.

The Gunroom as an institution had deep historical roots and, though it had greatly changed from the odorous squalor of Smollett's day, it still played an essential part in moulding 'young gentlemen' into an acceptable professional pattern. Within its walls a strict caste system was tacitly observed. At the bottom of the table languished the junior snotties, those 'warts on the face of humanity' who from time immemorial had been distinguished by their uselessness. Next in rank came the senior midshipmen, veterans of a year's service at sea, who were confident in their own vast experience and exercised a lordly superiority over their juniors. In pride of place were the sub-lieutenants, commissioned officers who were the privileged and oligarchic masters of the Mess.

The Wardroom – home of nineteen commissioned officers – was a formidable sanctum whose portals we rarely crossed except when on duty and even then with apprehensive embarrassment. It came as a great surprise to me to learn that these gods who made us poor snotties dance to the Bo's'un's tune had been the very last of a ship's company to earn their own mess. At first they had taken their meals in their sleeping quarters or their own cabins. In large warships there was a storeroom immediately below the 'great cabin.' It contained any valuables which needed to be specially stowed for reasons of security. It was called the 'Ward Robe.' Round about the middle of the nineteenth century this space was designated the official Lieutenants' Mess by the Admiralty and became known as the Wardroom. Redolent of starchy authority, it was presided over by the Bloke.

At the conclusion of a 'working up' exercise to calibrate our guns after refitting during the spring of 1914, our Admiral reappeared over the horizon from a cruise in Spanish waters to rejoin his Flagship. I was bidden to an audience. We lay in a crowded Portland harbour, glinting under early morning sunshine.

My head was reeling from several months of intensive gunnery training and long hours of drilling in the barrack square under the gloating zeal of Gunnery Instructors while our ship had her boilers de-coked. In due course I was introduced to the joys of 'General Drill' which normally commenced with such stereotypes as 'Furl awnings' and 'Out nets' but after that individual Flag Officers exercised their sense of humour, or malice, by introducing more exotic happenings. One, I remember, was particularly gifted and 'Chief cooks proceed to Hospital ship with fried egg,' 'Marine bands pull round the ship playing the Siamese anthem,' and 'Chaplains repair on board Flagship with harmoniums' were three gems in his repertoire.

Evolutions were highly competitive and ships' companies looked upon them as sporting events to be won by hook or by crook. Many involved the use of ships' boats and the Snotties were invariably in the thick of the fray. I recall agonizing moments when my crew was reduced to fumbling impotence by blasts of megaphoned vituperation. Those sweaty forenoons of General Drill, though harrassing, did not lack excitement and it certainly gave us a kick to see the 'Evolution completed' signal hoisted a split second ahead of the rest of the Squadron.

Ships' boats loomed large in the training of midshipmen and *Orion* carried fifteen, ranging from two 50-foot steam picquets down to a brace of diminutive skiffs. After refitting we moved down from the dockyard to Plymouth Sound to shake down and wash away layers of grime which fouled the ship. Befitting my immature state, I was given charge of a modest craft. My duties, which consisted in sailing in to the Hamoaze several times a day with the postman, stewards and sundry passengers, caused me as much concern as if I had been given command of the Flagship herself!

Under pressure of this mass of new information I was expected to absorb by some osmotic process the responsibility of my first boat (however small!) and persistent flickerings of my 'black tie' gaffe at Gieves, the spring of anxiety coiled tight in my bosom. It threatened to snap altogether on receipt of a summons to The Presence. Tension was released almost at once when Sir Robert opened the dreaded conversational exchange with, 'I am told you served in a sailing ship. So did I when I was your age. Tell me about it.'

For a quarter of an hour, with unexpected geniality, he drew me into esoteric discussion on reefing and clawing off a lee shore. I warmed to my subject and to my host.

'Did you hand the sails personally or did the fo'c'sle hands do the work aloft?' he asked, and on being assured that in *Port Jackson* the cadets formed the major part of the crew, he slapped me on the back and added, 'And

22

hard work, what about that? Did you get down on your knees and pray with holystones – eh?' When I told him I was no stranger to such devotions, the Admiral, with a glint in his eye, snorted, 'Excellent – that's what the Midshipmen in the Fleet should be doing every morning instead of sitting on their arses in the Gunroom.' With that he thrust back his chair and, leading me to an open scuttle, pointed at the great concourse of ships about us. 'There,' he said, 'is the most powerful fleet in the world, built by Admiral Fisher. I don't agree with all his ideas but the fact that we are now serving in modern ships equipped with up-to-date armaments is due, in large part, to his genius and,' he added, prodding me in the chest, 'don't you forget it.'

This brief encounter added a new dimension to my experience. Admirals were, by custom, august and aloof. Their art was exclusive and they operated a closed shop. This exclusiveness was carried to such extremes that even Rear-Admirals were not always made privy to the thoughts, plans and objectives of their Commanders-in-Chief. When the history of that time came to be written it was revealed that even at the top of the pinnacle the Navy's war plans were locked in the mind of the First Sea Lord who held his cards close to his chest and kept his counsel.

Thirty years later when we were, once again, engaged in warfare on an epic scale, the importance of clear and immediate lines of communication at all levels within the Service became apparent. By the end of the war I was at the Admiralty, doing my small bit in this respect to aid the distant COs of our polymorphic fleet strung out in protective clusters across the oceans of the world.

Aboard the *Orion* my education continued apace and the gathering momentum of events in Europe caused a change to our normal routine. In summer the Fleet would normally have been in the North Sea on manoeuvres but, in 1914, the Admiralty decided that a 'Test Mobilization' would be an effective way of showing the Navy's readiness for war. In consequence the Home Fleet had a stand easy while awaiting a culminating demonstration of sea power at a Review of the entire Fleet by the King.

The Spithead Review of 1914 was the greatest demonstration of British Naval might ever to have been assembled. More than two hundred ships in ten lines stretched from Southsea to Southampton Water and this visible evidence of Britannia's power to rule the waves aroused national enthusiasm. We were all conscious of the sense of historical occasion and felt pride in playing a part, however insignificant, in wielding Britain's sure shield.

Befitting our modern status, the ships of the 2nd Battle Squadron were stationed in proximity to the *Iron Duke*, the newly commissioned Fleet Flagship. To the north of the Fleet a small flotilla of submarines lay unobtrusively at anchor giving, despite their somewhat sinister appearance, little suggestion of menace to the overwhelming strength of the assembled Armada.

The Submarine Service was barely ten years old and few outside a closed circle of specialists knew anything about its capabilities. It is true that submarines had taken part in recent Fleet manoeuvres but their exercises had been so circumscribed by restrictions to ensure their safety that their real potency was not appreciated and was, therefore, discounted. Though forced to recognize the presence of submarines in their midst, the main body of Naval opinion in the Fleet relegated this rather obnoxious new weapon to the role of harbour defence.

I was on watch on the Sunday evening when the sound of a twenty-one-gun salute heralded the arrival of the King at the South railway jetty and in the distance I saw a Union flag break out at the masthead of the Royal yacht *Victoria and Albert* as an indication that the Admiral of the Fleet had assumed command.

As each ship approached the saluting point the entire side was manned by the ship's company. Being sixth in line we had not long to wait for our turn. With carefully rehearsed synchrony the whole company uncovered to give three cheers to His Majesty whose slight figure could be seen returning our salute from a monkey's island above the bridge of the *Victoria and Albert*. In a matter of minutes it was all over and we increased speed and hurried out into the murky Channel for tactical exercises. Two days later the ships of the Reserve Fleet, flushed with valedictory signals of congratulation on their demeanour, parted company and set course for their Home Ports while the Home Fleet in its entirety returned to Portland.

Before the month was out we found ourselves under secret orders to make ready for sea and prepare for war. Returning on board in the lazy peacefulness of a perfect summer's evening on 28 July we discovered that contact with the sweet-scented shore had been abruptly severed. It was to be half a year before we should set foot on land again.

We sailed north to Scapa Flow. The domestic pattern of our lives changed as we adjusted to war service. Endeavours were made to maintain our accustomed peacetime routine and standards, but the pressures of constant sea-going, coaling, self-refitting and novel extraneous duties absorbed so much of our available manpower that ceremonial spit and polish had to go by the board. I began to feel very much at home in this business-like atmosphere where practical decisions had to be taken and acted on as varying conditions dictated. Now we had a real job to do.

Ceremonial was not completely abandoned. The hoisting of colours in the morning was still a 'guard and band' affair and, as the numbers of our allies grew, the playing of anthems became a musical marathon. Our Flag Officer's General Drill 'Siamese anthem' signal began not to look so silly after all!

Morning prayers survived, though the congregation dwindled under the pressure of secular demands and these brief periods of spiritual reflection touched even the conscript worshippers. The words of the familiar prayer, 'Preserve us from the dangers of the sea and from the violence of the enemy that we may return in safety to enjoy the blessings of the land with the fruits of our labours,' took on a new significance.

My career developed. I was elevated to command of the 2nd picquet boat in which we were frequently away for long periods at a stretch. The stokey boy displayed unexpected culinary gifts as well as remarkable dexterity with his shovel. There is nothing to beat the savour of an improvised meal of bacon and bangers sizzling away on a clean shovel as a chill sea fog gropes inexorably towards you.

More gunnery training followed. Having become a Senior Midshipman I was temporarily attached to the Engineer Commander for a month's training in engineering. They were a hard-worked lot down below and it was fascinating to be in that vital centre of power which, to all intents and purposes, was taken for granted.

I stood watch with the Engineers and was impressed by their absorbed concentration on the sweet running of the machinery in their charge. I tried my clumsy hand at firing a boiler and learned, the hard way, to respect the stoker's skilled economy of effort and developed a lasting admiration for the black squad who, out of sight and unsung, sweated their guts out to provide steam for the ever-hungry turbines.

I next spent a month under the Torpedo Officer working in the submerged torpedo flat. Here the tempo was quieter and I was lucky enough to hitch myself to a Torpedo Gunner's Mate who had the gift of practical instruction. Under his enthusiastic eye I stripped a complete 21" torpedo down to the last screw until the steel deck was strewn with a miscellany of curious and unfamiliar bits and pieces. The subsequent assembly and testing of the torpedo, in which my mentor offered minimal guidance, gave me an intimate understanding of the anatomy of a 'tin fish' which stood me in good stead in later years. Then followed a month's signal instruction and I found life on the signal bridge among the 'bunting tossers' utterly absorbing. Communications were limited to signals by flag, semaphore and flashing morse code by a hand-worked lattice shutter in front of an arc-lamp. Wireless telegraphy, though fitted in all ships, was comparatively new and uncertain in behaviour and it was seldom used for transmission of manoeuvring signals.

I was promoted to an action station as assistant 'Officer of Quarters' in 'B' turret under a lieutenant-commander of amiable and chatty disposition. The interior of the gun-house was dominated by the breeches of the two massive 13.5" guns projecting over wells to allow for their elevation to a degree of 20 degrees above the horizontal.

Shut off by the thick armour we spent many hours in cramped seclusion, blind to the outside world but acutely on the *qui vive* for orders relayed by jerking pointers on our receiving instruments. We tested equipment, practised breakdown drills and burnished steel and brass to gleaming perfection. The guns' crews tended to grow bored by the daily repetition of dry exercises and we welcomed opportunities to fire guns in a practice shoot.

It was not long before practice became reality. I was offered a permanent commission in the Royal Navy and an appointment as Acting Sub-Lieutenant aboard the *Glen Isla* followed my promotion. She was one of the first 'Q' ships on 'special service' during the First War. Her job was to act as a decoy to lure preying U-boats into her sights. The grubby little merchant ship was deceptively innocuous. Her armaments rendered her quite capable of putting the German on the bottom. This she was obliged to do since any escaping U-Boat would have blown the gaff and prejudiced the whole scheme.

Nervous pride in my new status gradually gave way to a glimmer of confidence as I found that by employing what I had been taught, I could get the results required of me on orders from Above.

Our maiden patrol was peaceful in the extreme. In calm weather we trailed our coat along the coast towards Aberdeen and sighted nothing except a floating mine which, in pretence that it was a submarine, we attacked with bravado and sent to the bottom.

I was just getting the hang of my new responsibilities as Officer of Quarters aboard the *Glen Isla* when an urgent signal called us back to the *Orion*. No sooner had I reported, in fairly buoyant mood, to the Bloke than he cut me right back down to size telling me to 'Scrape that disgusting yellow fungus from your chin' and informing me that I would be leaving the ship on our return to harbour.

My next appointment presented me with my first real challenge of man management. I was well and truly thrown in at the deep end. It is a lesson I have never forgotten and one for which I am eternally grateful. A few short weeks in the destroyer *Earnest* taught me more about handling a crew than any amount of theory from lectures or books could possibly have done. My new 'owner' was a Lieutenant, Royal Naval Reserve, who had been serving until recently as Second Officer in a P and O liner. Although an excellent seaman with an Extra Master's Certificate, his experience of the Royal Navy was limited to two periods of a month's training in battleships. If he felt slightly out of his depth as Captain of a ship of war, I certainly did as Acting Sub-Lieutenant of an unkempt and disorderly vessel manned by a mixed bunch of reservists and H.Os (Hostilities Only). They were good enough men in themselves but the former tended to swing their weight about and bully the latter who, rather naturally, dragged their feet in resentment.

The contrast between conditions aboard the *Earnest* and the discliplined, clean and efficient battleship from which I had come could hardly have been greater. I was faced with the difficult job of pulling the ship's company together. I had been brought up on the notion that 'a strict ship is a happy ship' but, at first, I was not very apt in applying this maxim. With memories of the disciplinary effects of the parade ground I started by copying the techniques of the Gunnery Instructors. This method, though effective in a gunnery environment, was sadly inappropriate in handling a small destroyer's company unacquainted with, or strongly antagonistic to, strict command. I had to learn that discipline in a small ship is based more on willing observance of an accepted code of behaviour than upon meticulous drill, shouted orders and enforced obedience. Mine was a maturing job and though I suffered growing pains I learned that a position of privilege has to be paid for and that carrying the can is hard work.

We worked out of Immingham, patrolling the coast. Our work was certainly tedious. Unprofitable days were spent flogging the ocean in all weathers. This thankless routine alternated with occasional boiler-cleaning which enabled us to sample the delights of Grimsby which lay at the end of a long cold pilgrimage in a tram-railway. The Grimsby area gained the dubious distinction of being the first place in England to suffer an air raid in 1915.

Since very little occurred to leaven our days of dull patrolling I began to fear that I was in a backwater and became restive. I missed the sense of urgent purpose to which I had become accustomed in the Grand Fleet and felt growing anxiety that I was in danger of missing the tide.

Taking advantage of a week in dry dock I went to London and braved the Admiralty. This, my first visit to that aloof establishment, was something of an adventure and as I zig-zagged through the dingy corridors of power it was borne upon me that I was sticking my neck out on a foolhardy mission. A Dickensian clerk ushered me into the office of a languid Commander who, stifling a yawn, asked my bidding. 'Humph!' he said. 'The importance of being in *Earnest* is not enough – is that it? What's wrong with your glamorous 30-knotter?' Assuring him that all was well with the fine but ancient vessel (fifteen years was rather long in the tooth for a destroyer) I ventured a timid desire for an appointment to something a bit more modern. Closing his eyes, the oracle ruminated. Awakening some time later, astonished that he still had my company, he brought our conversation to a close. 'All right, Sub. I'll see what I can do.'

He did, in fact, do me proud. A few weeks later I was electrified to receive notice of my official appointment as Sub-Lieutenant to HMS *Obdurate*, one of a brand new flotilla of destroyers attached to the 13th Destroyer Flotilla. I travelled north to Edinburgh in January, 1916, and caught my first glimpse of her lying at a buoy in the shadow of the Forth Bridge. A few cables away

HMS *Lion* and her battle-cruiser consorts lay quietly at their moorings. The anchorage, which is comparatively shallow at that point, was crammed with the ships of Admiral Beatty's command.

There was little time for me to settle in. Within hours of my arrival on board we had orders to raise steam and by midnight I was taking over as Officer of the Watch in solitary charge on the bridge of a ship twice the size of little *Earnest* and steaming out into the North Sea in pitch darkness at 25 knots. Once again youthful confidence dipped and fluttered. Feelings of apprehension threatened to engulf me as I struggled to maintain position amid an unseen concourse of darkened ships hastening silently on their way to war. I had gained useful, if rather happy-go lucky watchkeeping experience in the *Earnest* but I was not accustomed to working with a flotilla.

I temporarily lost sight of my next ahead and, in a panic, increased speed. As I strained my anxious eyes and thankfully picked up her faint blue stern light I was conscious of a shadowy profile silhouetted against the dim light of the compass binnacle. The ominously protruding lower lip was unmistakable. The presence of the Captain, though slightly unnerving, was remarkably consoling and, in the weeks to come, the way in which he always seemed to materialize in moments of crisis was quite uncanny. He normally left me to find my own salvation and seldom uttered, but when he did he took over with crisp decisiveness and, calamity averted, immediately put the ship back in my charge. This was practical training at its best and I quickly gained confidence.

I was blooded in the *Obdurate* in more senses than one. In June, 1916, the Grand Fleet under Jellicoe succeeded in crossing Admiral Scheer's T. Taking up station at the fo'c'sle gun with my crew for what became know as the Battle of Jutland I felt peculiarly exposed. We were in the direct line of fire during the opening salvoes of the engagement but any instincts of self-preservation were quickly submerged by waves of intense excitement set up by the sheer magnitude of passing events. Then came the horror. We watched helplessly as the *Indefatigable*, the last ship in the British line, took a direct hit and then another. Shattered by a violent explosion the great ship rolled over and sank in two minutes, taking with her all but two of her complement of 1017 officers and men.

It lasted a day and a night. It is well-documented elsewhere. The boom and thunder of the night action has never left me. It was an obscenely exhilarating introduction to battle for a newly qualified young Naval Officer. Great warships exploded and were split asunder, baring their entrails of twisted metal in grim salute as they heaved in final agony before slipping beneath the boiling waves. The full impact of the tragedy of it all did not really hit us until we were homeward bound the next day, totally disorientated and groping about for bearings. Virtually no record of course changes and speeds had been kept during the battle. There had been other, more pressing concerns. Things had changed from minute to minute. The pages of the Navigator's notebook which I had hopefully left on the chart table remained blank. At one point during the action I had drawn an optimistic circle on the chart and, marking it '2030 (approx)' I had asked the Captain what we were doing. 'Following Father' was the terse reply. Consequently we were now lost.

The ship was cocooned in a monastic silence. When we had ceased fire earlier in the day a nose-fused lyddite shell had been in the gun and, as it was a somewhat cumbrous matter to eject such a projectile, the First Lieutenant decided that the easiest way of emptying the gun was to fire it. Having warned the Captain, I piped the gun's crew to muster and a few minutes later Petty Officer Tait, the Gunlayer, hailed from the fo'c'sle and was told the object of the exercise. He had an Able Seaman with him and between them they had trained the gun out on the bow and, without waiting for the remainder of the gun's crew, he reported he was ready. The First Lieutenant, satisfied that the range was clear, gave the order to 'Fire!' and together we leant over the bridge rail as the Gunlayer closed up to his position at the left of the gun. As he pulled the trigger there was an explosion and, to our horror, we saw the gun burst just abaft its trunnion. The severed part of the gun was blown back by the force of the explosion and the breech block flying in our direction hit and all but penetrated the protective mattress surrounding the bridge. We hurried to the fo'c'sle to find the Gunlayer dead and the Able Seaman lacerated and unconscious.

Our return to harbour was a sober affair. After the tragic irony of Jutland's aftermath, we spent a clammy couple of months on routine patrol. Then came the welcome news of a refit in Leith. I took the opportunity to make a sortie down to London and found the atmosphere ashore after two years of war feverish. With returning casualties, maimed in body and mind, came tales of inconceivable hardship and courage and this gave rise to growing fears that the deadlock would not be broken until the nation had been bled white.

I returned to Leith much chastened by what I had heard and seen of men returning from the trenches. I thanked my stars that it was my destiny to be embraced by the cleanliness of the sea rather than the mud of Flanders. I reflected that though life in a destroyer had its tribulations and perils we had, at least, reasonable comfort and could recoup in a warm bunk each night. There were thousands of poor devils across the Channel taking their last sleep in rat-infested hell-holes where one could only hope and pray that God would take mercy on them.

The ship's company, too, returned in a contemplative frame of mind, not perhaps relishing the idea of taking up the common task but resigned to the inevitable and indulging in the sailors' prerogative to stave off the prospect of boredom with a good grouse. We rejoined the Flotilla just in time to screen the battle cruisers in a sweep to the Dogger Bank and, after a battle with a nor-wester which washed away the dockyard cobwebs, we returned, salt-laden, to our familiar buoy at South Queensferry. Within the Flotilla we formed a sort of Subs' caucus which met, when occasion offered, to discuss affairs of state over a gentle gin in a friendly mess, or in greater seclusion, in the saloon bar of the Hawes Inn, that unfortunately named hotel hard by the pier at South Queensferry, which lodged our Captains' wives.

With the wisdom of adolescence we held advanced views on everything, but in the main we 'cagged' about which line of specialization would most quickly lead us to appointments offering proper scope for our undoubted talents. The majority of us opted for destroyers and we drank a toast to the immortal memory of seamen coupled with our own salty aspirations. It was, therefore, with a mind full of possible alternatives that I went ashore in Blyth and by one of those chance encounters which curiously shape our lives I altered course to an entirely unsuspected point of the compass.

I encountered our much respected Sub of the Gunroom in the *Orion* who by this time had been elevated to the the exciting position of First Lieutenant of a submarine. He invited me to see over his new domain. Intrigued by this novel experience and fascinated by his eulogy on life in this new branch of the Service, I recapitulated the arguments about specialization and asked his advice. 'Why don't you volunteer to become a submariner?' he said. 'It's a damned good life, you have an interesting box of tricks to look after, you get early command and you work with the best men in the Navy.'

I found this entirely convincing and hastened back on board to write an official letter begging to submit that my name might be forwarded as an applicant for the Submarine Course. Mixing this fateful missive with a pile of incoming correspondence, I placed the sheaf of papers on my Captain's desk and stood back with the feelings of an *enfant terrible* who had dropped a fire cracker under the table at a bishop's tea party.

In due course I saw him read my letter and, in silence, lay it aside. Picking up the discarded papers from the out-tray I was beating a retreat when he cleared his throat — 'Hurrumph! So you want to hide yourself under water eh? I hope you know what you're doing.' I didn't but stammered an affirmative when he replied, 'Very good Sub, if this is what you really want I won't block your ambitions.'

In a state of confusion I returned to my cabin, doubtful if I had made the right decision. But, for better or worse, the die was cast and I tried to figure out how my life would be affected by my somewhat hasty impulse.

4

Submarine Training

FORT BLOCKHOUSE STANDS on a spit of land forming the western shore of the narrow entrance to Portsmouth Harbour. From the 16th century onwards this area has been the site of defensive fortifications. As early as 1522 there is a record of a 'mightie chain of iron' for drawing across the mouth of the harbour. It is said that when Parliamentary troops captured Southsea Castle in the Civil War they were bombarded by loyalists manning the guns of Fort Blockhouse.

The present Fort had its beginnings early in the eighteenth century and the fortifications were strengthened during the Napoleonic era. Blockhouse had been the main depot of the Submarine Service since 1905 in which year it was decided to set up a shore base for a newly formed flotilla of 'submarine boats.' In the following year an accommodation ship, HMS *Dolphin*, arrived in Haslar Creek, a narrow inlet bounding the northern perimeter of the Fort, and in the creek jetties were built to provide berthing for the submarines.

At the end of 1916 I took passage from Portsmouth in an ancient dockyard launch and set foot for the first time in an establishment which was destined to become the entire centre of my career for many years to come.

That evening the six members of my 'Submarine training class' huddled in the corner of the Wardroom trying to be inconspicuous in a patently esoteric and sophisticated society. Bright and early the next morning we were shepherded into a wooden hut to begin three months' instruction into what the Navy scornfully regarded as 'the trade.' The service was regarded with great suspicion and submariners were referred to as 'pirates.'

Training for service in submarines has always been based on practice rather than theory. The one certain piece of relevant collective knowledge our nervous but eager group could muster was that an object which is heavier than water sinks and one which is lighter floats. Our teacher, a senior Lieutenant who had recently returned from command of a submarine in which he had successfully penetrated into the Sea of Marmora, was a quiet unflappable man with an authoritative air of command.

Our formal lectures were set against an historical background so that we could appreciate the evolution of the submarine.

In 1877 John P. Holland, an inventive Irish-American, began the development of a series of submarine boats. For twenty years he persisted and, despite disheartening frustration and disasters, eventually built his Holland VIII which, in 1899, at long last, convinced the American Navy Department that he had 'produced an engine of warfare of terrible potency which the Government must necessarily adopt for the Naval Service.' Holland had not been alone in his experiments. By the turn of the century France and Italy had submarines in operation. The performance of all these early submarines was affected by the fundamental difficulty of maintaining a steady depth when diving, a problem which was eventually solved by fitting horizontal rudders (hydroplanes) at bow and stern. They were also greatly hampered by lack of efficient power units for propulsion on the surface, and when submerged, until the internal combustion engine and the electrical storage battery had been developed to a pitch that could be trusted to give reliable service.

The British authorities took scant notice of these experiments and trials abroad and the Admiralty were resolute in refusing to be submerged in the rising tide of foreign enthusiasm for underwater warfare. It was argued that the submarine was a defensive weapon which might be developed by inferior maritime powers, but that there was no requirement for such cranky, ineffective vessels in the British Navy and that underwater attack was brutish and uncivilized. But, in 1900, public opinion expressed in Parliament brought pressure to bear and the Admiralty ordered five Holland-type submarines from the Electric Boat Company in USA, saving face by stating that the reason for this change in policy was to test the value of the submarine boat as a weapon in the hands of our possible enemies. Accordingly the Naval Estimates for 1901-1902 included, for the first time, an appropriation of money for submarine construction.

By 1904 the five Hollands had completed their trials and were assembled at Portsmouth. These original submarines were, in truth, unseaworthy, unreliable and dangerous to handle. Furthermore, they were manned by officers and men who, though filled with adventurous spirit, had little to guide them in mastering the complexities of their new profession and had, perforce, to gain experience by trial and error.

The Hollands were diminutive vessels, packed with machinery and even when in full surface buoyancy they had very little freeboard. Navigation was difficult and when submerged their periscopes were of such poor optical quality that they were virtually blind. The petrol fumes and storage battery exposed the crew of nine to toxic fumes and hydrogen gas, both of which, in concentration, could be dangerously explosive. Despite the difficulties and hazards which they faced, those first submariners not only demonstrated that they could operate under water but showed that, given improvements, the submarine had definite potential.

The Hollands led the way to the constructions of the A and B classes which, being larger and with slightly greater surface buoyancy, had better sea-keeping qualities. By 1906 the C boats were coming into service. This new class, though bearing evolutionary similarity to their predecessors, were larger boats of 280 tons displacement and, with more than 30 tons of buoyancy on the surface and better machinery, they proved their seaworthiness.

We were instructed in one of this class and, within a few days, embarked on *C34* for our first dive. Our knowledge was elementary and we were bemused by the mass of machinery crammed into restricted space and by the plethora of pipelines spreading everywhere.

On our way out to the diving area in Stokes Bay we toured the compartments trying to hoist in our instructor's complicated explanatory comments on the functions of valves and switches which hemmed us in on all sides. At first sight it all seemed uncomfortably cramped and, in the engine room, distressingly noisy. The whole interior of the submarine was saturated with an overpowering stench of petrol. When the crew closed up at 'Diving Stations' we assembled in the Control Room and sat on the deck out of harm's way. I do not know what my classmates anticipated at that moment but I braced myself for some sort of violent sensation. The engines were still, the crew impassive and we waited in silence. The Captain's legs appeared down the conning tower ladder and, stepping to the periscope, he casually ordered, 'Shut lower lid. Half ahead. Open main vents,' and finally, to the Coxswain and Second Coxswain at their hydroplane wheels, 'Take her down to twenty feet.'

There was a snort of venting air, a gurgle of water flooding into the ballast tanks, a faint hum from the motor driving the propeller and an almost imperceptible inclination down by the bow. The Coxswain, in sepulchral tones, reported, 'Twenty feet, Sir.' This was it, and I found difficulty in realizing that we were actually diving until, in my turn, I was invited to take a look and saw water splashing over the top of the periscope. It was all rather an anti-climax; no sensations, no claustrophobia.

For our instructional benefit the submarine's crew were put through a series of simple evolutions. I tried my hand at the fore hydroplanes, gripping the operating wheel fiercely and gazing fixedly at the trembling depth gauge needle, and at the after hydroplanes with my eyes glued to the inclination bubble.

Finally, with a loud hiss of compressed air blowing water from the main ballast tanks, we surfaced from the quiet depths to begin our noisy passage back to Blockhouse. With some relief I climbed up on to the jetty gulping in the fresh sea breeze to drive away the splitting headache induced by breathing in petrol-laden air. After an eventful day we foregathered in the Wardroom for a gin before dinner and aired our slender wisdom in a mood of pleasant sophistication.

The next day in the lecture room the instructional diagrams hanging on the walls took on a new and purposeful significance. The C class, like their predecessors, were of a type known as 'single hull' which meant that water taken in to cancel out buoyancy was admitted to ballast tanks within the strong, circular-section pressure hull of the submarine. Pretty well the whole of the lower half of the area within the pressure hull was taken up with space for ballast water, fuel and a number of trimming tanks used for adjusting the weight to meet varying circumstances, so that when the ballast tanks were filled the submarine was in a properly balanced state of neutral buoyancy and readily susceptible to easy control by angling the hydroplanes even at slow speed. The theory of neutral buoyancy was straightforward enough but in practice the achievement of this placid state of underwater bliss was something of a hit and miss affair. Relatively little was known about the behaviour of submerged vessels in those early days and they were apt to buck and dive with alarming unpredictability for no apparent reason.

We were instructed that all the ballast and trimming tanks were connected to a pipe system which was the main water service line employed in diving and surfacing the vessel. All tanks were fitted with air connections for bottled compressed air. These 'blows' could drive water from one tank to another or push it overboard. Alternatively, water in the tanks could be sucked out and discharged overboard by an electrically driven pump. The awesome confusion of hardware which had overwhelmed us on our first dive was more comprehensibly rendered as a simple straight pipe running through the submarine — the 'main line.' We perceived that, on issuing the right order, the Captain could move water about at will through the main line, taking his boat up or down and maintaining her submerged at a given depth. In later years when I returned to Blockhouse as Instructional Officer myself, I tried to develop simple diagrammatic representations of the extensive and complex internal plumbing with its valves and blows. It was my endeavour to introduce the young submariners in my charge to the basic principles as concisely and simply as possible. The refinements could come in due course.

We had two days to crawl around *C34* and in a surprisingly short space of time the multitudinous members of the whole box of tricks became old familiars. We then studied the main engines, auxiliary machinery and electrics which were rather more complicated.

All submarines, with few exceptions, have the same layout of propulsion machinery. On each propeller shaft (after the C class virtually all submarines were twin-screwed) a sequence runs from the engine room aft comprising main engine, engine clutch, main motor, tail clutch and, finally, propeller. On the surface with both clutches engaged the main engine is directly connected to the propeller with the main motor turning idly as a sort of flywheel. When diving the engine clutch is disengaged and the main motor, drawing electrical energy from the storage battery, drives the propeller. When re-charging the battery in harbour, or at sea, the tail clutch disengages the propeller from the shaft and the main engine revolves the main motor which, as a dynamo, generates electricity to replenish the storage battery with energy.

Our training class quickly grew into close companionship, bonded together by rising enthusiasm and by our need to preserve an identity in a privileged society which, at first, took scant notice of our existence. We had all been afloat for two years and took full advantage of our freedom to catch the seven bell boat and push off to Pompey to look for innocent gaiety for which, as often as not, we hunted in a pack.

Blockhouse, for us, was not exactly the height of luxury. We slept in barrel-vaulted caverns burrowed into the base of the ancient fortification wall. These dank dormitories lacked windows and were far removed from what were euphemistically called 'ablutionary amenities.' This did not worry us over-much as we were usually flat out at night. In compensation, the wardroom was comfortable and, as submariners were spared the rigours of rationing, food was plentiful. As far as we were concerned it was all a rollicking interlude in the war and, apart from occasional nagging doubts about the passing out examinations, we had not a care in the world.

Fort Blockhouse has a distinctive character. When taken over from the Army in 1905 the old fortification structures were converted into quarters and so, paradoxically, the youngest branch of the Navy lived in surroundings redolent of the past in odd-shaped rooms with domed ceilings.

The Commanding Officer lived in splendid isolation in Ivy Cottage, a tiny, two-roomed bungalow overlooking the submarines lying in Haslar Creek. Years later when this minuscule official residence had to make way for the Admiral's office the workmen demolishing Ivy Cottage unearthed a female skeleton, but, as far as we knew, she was not deposited in our time.

Half-way through our course we progressed to the study of submarines of later construction than the C class in which we had been instructed. The year 1909 had marked a definite step forward when the first of a new D class came into service.

The older, single hull submarine suffered the disadvantage that its ballast water was carried internally within the pressure hull and this not only took up too much space but also subjected the flat tops of the ballast tanks to full pressure of the sea when diving and this was recognized as a weakness. To overcome these disadvantages *D1* was designed to carry ballast water externally in tanks arranged longitudinally outside the pressure hull on either side.

These 'saddle tanks' were made of comparatively light plating, a revolutionary feature which sprang from the realization that, since ballast tanks are full of water when diving, the pressure within and without the saddle tank plating would be equalized at whatever depth the submarine was operating. *D1* proved the practicability of this innovation and, thereafter, with few exceptions, all submarines were designed to carry ballast water externally, allowing greater buoyancy in surface trim and a welcome increase of space within the pressure hull. The D class were also the first submarines to be propelled by diesel engines running on a heavier fuel and thus avoiding the volatile and dangerous petrol which caused so many headaches in the earlier days.

The D boats were half as big again as the C class and, with 50 tons of positive buoyancy on the surface, much more seaworthy, *D1* herself surpassed even optimistic expectations when, on the 1910 naval manoeuvres, she voyaged alone from Portsmouth to the west coast of Scotland, patrolled off 'enemy' harbours, and attacked two cruisers before returning in triumph to Blockhouse. This and other spectacular proofs of the efficacy of the new submarine weapon, though convincing enough in submarine circles, were unfortunately not generally appreciated by the navy as a whole which still ignored the threat of submarine attack when war came.

Almost alone in high places the redoubtable 'Jackie' Fisher had foreseen that the submarine was destined to become a major factor in warfare and, as First Sea Lord from 1904 to 1910, he ceaselessly demanded that Britain must build submarines in large numbers. With this powerful support the submarine service entered into a period of expansion and, profiting by experience gained in operating D boats under taxing conditions, plans were laid for the construction of an improved model.

The first of this new class, *E1*, left her builder's yard for trials in 1912 and in a short time it was apparent that the years of research and development had come to fruition. The E boats with 80 tons of surface buoyancy were a leap forward in sea-keeping qualities and reliability. Equipped with five 18″ torpedo tubes and a 4″ gun, a surface speed of fifteen knots and an endurance of 3,000 miles, these ships were formidable and far-ranging instruments of war. Progenitors of a long line of ocean-going submarines, the E boats were superior to submarines of any nation.

The submarine service continued to expand at the maximum rate practicable in peacetime until, in 1914, the demands of war and the urgent need to replace the older classes by submarines with more power and radius of action set in train a greatly accelerated programme of construction. New types were designed to meet special requirements, shipyards hitherto unaccustomed to submarine work were dragooned into construction and by the end of 1916 no fewer than 83 submarines were on active service in the North Sea and many more were on the building slips.

Blockhouse was alive with activity as new submarines arrived to work up prior to departure on war service. The Wardroom teemed with birds of passage and veteran sailors whetting our interest with first-hand experience of events in the waters of the Heligoland Bight. Tales of adventure came rolling in to be retold with pride and the exploits of submarine captains such as Holbrook (*B11*), Boyle (*E14*) and Nasmith (*E11*) fired the imagination*.

Nasmith was a very pleasant man with an infinitely kindly manner but, by God, he was determined. When he put his hand to something it was meticulously planned and executed down to the last detail. He was perfectly ready to take a risk if a risk was required and such was his manner of inspirational confidence, spiced with a certain diffident charm, that he never lacked for volunteers. Brushing shoulders with these gilded heroes added a certain cachet, or so we imagined, to our humble status as makeelearn submariners. We were slowly beginning to feel members of the 'club' and to respond to the less starchy and more workmanlike relationship which seemed to bind His Majesty's Pirates together.

It was barely ten years since the Hollands had made their tentative dives and a number of officers and men who had blazed the trail were still in the submarine service. We revered those early pioneers who created the submarine lore which became a tradition for their followers. Handling primitive machinery had demanded skill, ingenuity and improvisation. Exposed to risk by failure of equipment and by lack of experience in their slender crews, they learned that they were all members one of another and from this grew a strengthening sense of mutual dependence and trust. All, officers and men alike, exercised self-discipline in their determination not to be found wanting in moments of crisis. They developed 'submarine sense' a constant awareness that the sea, ceaselessly striving to breach watertightness, is a real contender that must be thwarted.

To overcome such difficulties thorough practical knowledge of equipment, understanding of the duties of shipmates and an instinctive attitude of careful foresight must be the basic essentials of a submariner. 'Contrary to the bad habits you have picked up in the big ships,' our Instructor told us, 'it is hallowed submarine practice for officers to take off their coats and get down to it with their men in the job of keeping everything in the submarine on the top line and ready for immediate service.'

The qualifying examinations at the end of our course of instruction, some

---

* All three were VCs and Nasmith went on to become Admiral and CinC Plymouth by the outbreak of the Second World War when our paths coincided under tragic circumstances.

being severely *viva voce* in *C34*, were an ordeal, but we managed to scrape through.

The day the results were announced we sensed a subtle change in the Wardroom, when, as fledged submariners, we joined the charmed circle of First Lieutenants and parked our bottoms on the club fender round the ante-room fire.

After a short period of leave, my submarine career began with my appointment as First Lieutenant of Submarine *V4*, one of a group of eleven H and V class submarines of the VIIIth Flotilla based at Yarmouth. Reporting to Commander (S), a rotund and genial personality bearing resemblance to a 'laughing buddha', I was told that my Captain, Lieutenant A.N. Lee, was on leave for a further three days and I should make myself at home until his return.

This happy circumstance gave me a bit of breathing space and enabled me to study the ship's drawings and ferret through the boat. *V4* was one of a class of four small submarines designed and built by Vickers. Slightly bigger than the C class, she looked exciting to me as I caught my first glimpse of her berthed outside three sisters alongside a fishing jetty a quarter of a mile downriver.

The V class embodied some of the characteristics of the larger E boats, including diesel propulsion and external ballast tanks. They were lightly armed with 18″ bow torpedo tubes and manned by a crew of three officers and sixteen men. The internal layout was conventional. Right forrard the 'fore end' housed the bow tubes and two spare torpedoes, and this space was separated by a bulkhead from a 'battery compartment' leading on to the control room amidships. Abaft this there was space for the two diesel engines and their associated main motors.

The Vs, having a good margin of buoyancy on the surface, were seaworthy craft but lively in foul weather. They had good, but not outstanding, diving qualities and the pressure hull was strong enough to withstand the water pressure in the region of 150′. That is the equivalent of their own length. On the surface they had a cruising speed of twelve knots and when diving the battery had capacity to give a speed of nine knots for one hour or two knots for twenty hours.

V4 was comparatively new when I joined her and throughout her nine month's life she had been engaged on war operations in the Heligoland Bight. My Captain was a Lieutenant of elfin proportions but what he lacked in inches he amply made up for in alertness of mind. He had joined the submarine service in 1913 and came to *V4* from *J2**, where he had been

---

* *J2*, together with all the J class boats, went to the Royal Australian Navy in 1919. *J2* was finally sold to the Melbourne Salvage Syndicate and her hull was scuttled in June, 1926.

'second hand' on her commissioning. *V4* represented a significant step on the promotional ladder for him but one which offered disconcertingly incommodious accommodation when compared with the 275.5-foot length of the *J2* with her complement of 44.

This rather stunted debut in command may well have been a blessing in disguise since we were both, in our respective spheres, somewhat green — a state of affairs which can make for scratchy relationships — but we dovetailed to each other without aches and pains.

I found that actually shouldering responsibilities was vastly more onerous than I had anticipated. Like all other 'qualifiers' I had passed out from my training class under the illusion that I was a submariner. I soon realized that in practice I knew little. All new 2nd Dickies go through a salutory period during which they rely on the old hands in their crew to keep them out of trouble. Bearing in mind the fact that the submarine service itself was in its infancy, there were relatively few hands of any long-standing experience about. They formed a small but vital pool of intelligence. The war had catapulted the Navy into acknowledging twentieth century technology and immediately putting it to the test on active service. The collective knowledge of these submarine pioneers was therefore all the more important to us new boys and I leaned heavily on my stalwarts who never failed to prompt me until I found my bearings.

Within days we were caught up in one of the periodic flaps which occurred whenever the Admiralty got wind of a possible raid by the enemy on the east coast. Hastily grabbing sacks of meat and bread, we bundled on board and slipped down river. Our orders were to patrol an area outside the Scrobie Sands with the object of attacking enemy ships approaching to bombard Yarmouth. We were to keep submerged during daylight hours and to surface at predetermined intervals to listen in for reports of enemy movements.

On reaching our billet the Captain said he would dive to 'catch a trim.' I had adjusted the amounts of water in the various trimming tanks rather hurriedly on our way out to sea, but, being unfamiliar with *V4*, I was not sanguine about my calculations.

When I knew the Captain had shut the upper lid at the top of the conning tower I ordered 'Open main vents' with what I hoped was an air of assurance, and told the Second Coxswain to 'Take her down.' We dived. The Depth Gauge needle whizzed round, the Coxswain growled, 'She's very heavy, Sir,' and the Captain said, 'Blow main ballast,' adding, as we rose to the surface, 'You'd better start again, Number One.' In a state of agitation I pumped out tons of water, most of which had to be taken in again to get the submarine to dive. At long last we submerged and undulated like a love-sick porpoise for a solid half-hour before I was able to catch a controllable trim. There is nothing more frustrating and humiliating than trying to cope with a recalcitrant submarine under the deepening frown of a Captain whose patience is obviously wearing very thin. *V4* could certainly be a little bitch when she felt obstreperous. It took me weeks to learn to master her trick of compressing herself at twenty-five feet and becoming suddenly heavy and expanding at nineteen feet, to rise buoyantly and unashamedly to the surface.

Our patrol was uneventful. Whatever the Germans had in mind they thought better of it and after a day spent circling round at periscope depth we were recalled to harbour.

At the time when I joined *V4* a total of seventy submarines were operating in the North Sea, of which our VIIIth Flotilla comprised eighteen E boats based at Harwich and a contingent of eleven smaller submarines at Yarmouth. The maintenance of ceaseless watch off the German coast had its hazards. The patrols took their toll and in the years 1916 and 1917 no less than fourteen submarines failed to return to harbour, a figure representing nearly one third of the total of 47 British submarines lost during the four years of war.

We were lucky at Yarmouth and, with the exception of *H8*, who struck a mine but miraculously struggled back to harbour, none of the submarines in our section of the VIIIth Flotilla suffered serious damage in those two fateful years.

Patrol followed patrol with but slight variation through 1917 until, on Christmas Eve, I returned to harbour to find that, after only nine months in *V4*, I was appointed as First Lieutenant of Submarine *K6*, one of the mammoth Fleet submarines in the XIIth Flotilla attached to the Grand Fleet. The Sub of *Orion's* Gun Room had not been bandying idle words. At this cracking pace, command was a tangible reality unless, in my youthful zeal, I tripped myself up and caused serious displeasure. It was a heady prospect which spurred many an ambitious young officer on to greater efforts, a motivation which, it must be admitted, owed not a little to the whole dare-devil cachet bestowed by the sobriquet of 'pirate.' We undoubtedly regarded ourselves as something out of the ordinary and 'submariner' was worth a certain swagger-value ashore!

The Ks were the result of a revolutionary design put forward at the beginning of the War by the Director of Naval Construction, Sir Eustace Tennyson-d'Eyncourt. A Fleet Submarine needed to achieve speeds far greater than the little *V4* had been capable of. Despite considerable opposition which held the view that submarines and steam were totally incompatible, the new design embodied two steam boilers and turbines to achieve 24 knots. Vickers were given the contract to construct *K3* and *K4* while Portsmouth Dockyard began work on *K1* and *K2*. These prototypes were in commission by the end of 1916 and thirteen more of the same design were completed and on active service by May, 1918.

With an overall length of 340 feet, the Ks were over twice the length of the Vs and were manned by a crew of five officers and a ship's company of 52 who lived permanently on board. Despite their behemoth-like proportions, living space was at a premium and their designers had shown great ingenuity in squeezing in living space for so large a complement. Even so, each man had but a twenty-fifth share of a lavatory seat and had to wash himself and his clothes in a bucket.

In January, 1918, I travelled north once again to take up my appointment as First Lieutenant of *K6*, attached to the XIIth Flotilla. It was over a year since I had left the battle-cruiser force and during that time Admiral Beatty had taken over as Commander-in-Chief and was now flying his flag in the *Queen Elizabeth*. It had been decided that the Battle Fleet should be based further south and as a result the waters of the Firth of Forth were tightly packed with Grand Fleet ships.

I found the Fleet Submarines of the XIIth Flotilla berthed on *Royal Arthur*, an ancient cruiser, lying at a mooring on the south side of the Firth, almost within the familiar shadow of the great Forth Bridge. The submarines of the XIIIth Flotilla were accommodated in pens in Rosyth dockyard.

From the deck of *Royal Arthur* I looked down at the submarines secured alongside. I had anticipated that the K boats would be large but I was taken aback by the sight of submarines of such gigantic proportions. Like great whales they lay sleek and quiescent in the winter sunshine and as my unaccustomed eye scanned their length I felt intimidated by their sheer size. When I later made comparisons with other ships in which I had served I discovered that they were nearly two-thirds the length of *Orion* and nearly twice the displacement and eighty feet longer than *Obdurate*.

We were ordered to sea for a series of exercises with the Grand Fleet. My new Captain had not yet assumed command and, to avoid overcrowding, it was decided that I should go as a passenger aboard *K7* for the duration of the exercise. Dick Lindsell, First Lieutenant of *K7*, welcomed me aboard and left me to browse over the operation orders in the Wardroom while he got on with the business of preparing his boat for sea.

We put to sea and made for our rendezvous in the vicinity of May Island, operating with dimmed navigation lights in conditions of misty darkness which clamped down altogether from time to time. At about 8.30 p.m. we felt a slight bump. At the time, although it was unexpected, on-the-spot investigation revealed nothing untoward. It was not until much later that we realized it signalled a catastrophe of major proportions for the XIIth and XIIIth Submarine Flotillas which, through a series of misjudgements and accidents, lost *K4* and *K17* and suffered severe damage to *K14*, *K22* and *K6*. Apart from eight men saved by *K7* there were no survivors and 107 officers and men lost their lives. The bump we had felt had been our keel bumping gently over the bow of the stricken *K4*, already on her way to the bottom.

The details of this horrific series of events were not revealed until a Court Martial some two months later. They have been set out at some length elsewhere. My own boat, the *K6*, had been the one to inflict the fatal wound on *K4*, unavoidably ramming her as she in turn had taken action to avoid Captain(S) in the light cruiser *Fearless*. She had been dragged down by the bow with *K4* in her death agony and then broken free with her own buoyancy. Her stem was crushed and the outer ends of the torpedo tubes were distorted but, beyond this, there was no serious damage and after a few weeks in dockyard hands we were once again ready for sea.

I was in sombre mood as I took over my duties as First Lieutenant. *K6* had been on terms of close relationship with the absent *K4*. She had also played her small part in the preparation of one of England's most dashing figures for his future role in the country's history. Not two months before the fateful 'Battle of May Island' she had provided a berth for a young Midshipman doing his small ships training. His name was Louis Francis Albert Victor Nicholas Mountbatten.

5

Officers and Gentlemen

THE CHANCES OF A conscript becoming Admiral of the Fleet have always
been fairly remote. Volunteers stood a slightly better chance. Even so, a
small boy at the turn of the century could not have harboured any serious
ambition of rising from the lower deck to such starry omnipotence. There
was, of course, the odd historical exception, notably the son of a Norfolk
clergyman who went to sea a twelve-year-old boy in 1770, was promoted
Captain at the early age of 35 and sustained his final heroic wound as Admiral
at the Battle of Trafalgar twelve years later. But even young Horatio's
fortunes were at first determined by the accident of birth. Nelson just about
scraped into the Officer 'class' by virtue of his family background, albeit at
the lower end of the social stratum whose sons were considered 'officer
material'. He also had an uncle who was Comptroller of the Navy which,
no doubt, helped.

This medieval attitude towards the recruitment of Executive Officers was
not finally heaved overboard and consigned to the murky depths where it
belonged, weighted down with other equally out-dated postures, until the
Second World War. Prevailing conditions at that time made greater demands
upon the Royal Navy than the service could meet. Officers were urgently
needed. The traditional source of supply – the 'officer classes' – simply
dried up. Signals were hoisted for other men to come urgently to the aid of
the stricken vessel and come they did, in their thousands, from all levels of
society. The proved themselves in many cases to be the equals of their new
masters, a breed which had hitherto considered itself something of a
maritime and social 'élite'.

It is worth looking into this matter a little further to see how it came
about, for the very reasons which caused the Navy finally to jettison the idea
that a 'social' qualification was necessary for appointment as an Executive
Officer are not dissimilar to those which brought about the anachronism in
the first place.

Until the time of Charles II there was no such thing as the Royal Navy.
There were certainly no warships in medieval England. Those vessels which
plied the oceans from Albion's shores did so for purely commercial reasons
and were run on purely commercial lines. Some of this was legitimate trade,
a great deal of it was piracy.

British pirates, of necessity, developed good seamanship and ship-handling. They passed this skill on through the privateers of the eighteenth century. Their contribution to the national concentration of maritime knowledge played a not inconsiderable part in bringing the country to a position of world naval supremacy in both trading and fighting ships at the time of Queen Victoria's Diamond Jubilee. But it all started with trade.

An owner wanted to be sure his ship would not founder. An owner wanted to be sure his cargo would arrive. An owner, quite frequently, wanted his cargo to arrive ahead of the competition. Therefore, to guarantee his ship's security and his own profit, he needed a Master skilled in navigation and capable of command no matter what condition of wind, weather or sailorman bedevilled him during his voyage. I sailed under the descendant of just such a Master in the *Port Jackson*.

The Master's right-hand man was his Bo's'un, decorated with his badge of office, a small pipe or whistle on a chain upon which he 'piped' orders to the crew. He was an expert seaman charged with the awesome task of maintaining the physical safety of both vessel and ship's company. He saw to it that masts, yards, rigging and sails were never allowed to fall into a state of disrepair. He was responsible for the correct handling of the crew to obtain this result and for ensuring that orders issued by the Master were properly carried out. There were other 'mates' to help him. He was a powerful and intelligent figure, well rewarded for his duties. In recognition of the onerous nature of his work he was appointed ship's executioner!

The Master had two officers on board, but, in the days before the Royal Navy had been invented, these were not officers in the sense the term is understood today. They were, however, equally important, pre-echoing the Napoleonic remark that an army marches on its stomach. The Cook and the Carpenter between them catered for the well-being of the inner man and maintained his corporeal security against the ferocity of the watery element in which he had chosen to pass his days, traversing the oceans between the freshly caulked decks of his wooden waller. These men, too, were skilled in their respective crafts and were personages of some importance. The rest − the ship's company of full-time seamen − were afloat out of choice. This was before the days of the infamous Press Gang. They developed great maritime experience and skill. As often as not they matched their officers in 'class' and quality.

'Navy' referred to all English shipping and seamen − to all intents and purposes a merchant service at that time.

When conflict threatened and battleships were required, merchant ships were converted to battle function, much as merchant cruisers were in the

Second World War. The specifications, though, were somewhat different, two 'castles' being added, one for'ard and one aft. The refitted battleship then went alongside at the Tower of London to be armed from the nation's principal armoury.

The question then arose as to who would use these arms, which were initially small arms – muskets, pikes, dirks and the like, and who would command those wielding them. Clearly some sort of 'sea-infantry' was required. These fighting men were not seamen. More often than not in peacetime they worked ashore for the man who commanded them at sea. He was certainly well-to-do, a landowner, possibly an aristocrat, commissioned by the monarch to fight a battle on his behalf. Accustomed by birth, wealth and feudal privilege to a position of authority, he became the Captain of a motley 'army' of estate workers who had been forced into soldiering by their lowly status. They were pressed into service for the duration of the conflict and were certainly not volunteers.

Just in case the enemy finished him off in the fray, the Captain took with him a Lieutenant.

Upon embarkation, the Captain took command of the ship but had no authority whatsoever in regard to the sailing of it. That was left to the Master who obeyed instructions as to where the Captain wanted to position his infantrymen in relation to the enemy and when, but did so by issuing orders to his own crew. The Captain dared not interfere in this. He had not the faintest notion how to sail a ship. His safe return home depended as much on the skill and judgement of the Master of the ship he commanded as it did upon his own deployment of his artillerymen and the inferior fire-power of the adversary.

By the same token, the Master had not the least idea how to conduct a battle. He left all that to the Captain, who had his work cut out handling a taskforce that was 'green' in more senses than one. Upon engagement with an enemy, the 'sea-infantry' fired from the height of the two 'castles' which, theoretically, offered them the opportunity to dominate the opposition and pick them off without too much trouble. Thus the first 'part-time' men o'war accommodated a ship's company which comprised a force of fighting men who could not sail conveyed by a crew of sailormen who could not fight. Neither understood the other's tactics. Their orders, too, must have been mutually incomprehensible. The proportions seem to have averaged out at about 2:1 in favour of the fighting force.

With the battle fought and won, the Captain and his 'army' were returned to the land of their forefathers where they were disembarked, forswearing the navy and all who sailed in it in no uncertain terms. The sailormen were mighty glad to get rid of the undisciplined 'rabble' infesting their ship like so many rats slithering hither and thither, and doubtless flung a few valedictory oaths astern as the Master once more took command of his ship and, with an audible note of jubilation and relief, gave the order to 'make sail!'

The Elizabethans started to redress the balance somewhat in favour of the sailorman. There had been far too much 'dross' recruited onto the lower deck and Her Majesty did not think much of it. But the principal force for change came with a piece of technology which established the Gunroom as the heart and soul of the Royal Navy, a force of fighting ships laid down in the latter part of the 17th century with the specific task of defending the island nation and waging war against her enemies.

This remarkable innovation was the 'big gun' or cannon which, although well tried in land battles, had hitherto never been employed at sea. The introduction of this weapon to naval warfare extended the range of combat, thus reducing the need for boarding an enemy ship and rendering the 'sea-infantry' largely redundant. Hand to hand combat became the last rather than the first stage of engagement. Operation of the 'big gun' demanded new skills co-ordinated with a degree of nautical understanding. Specially trained hands were needed to deal with ropes, gunports and the like as well as to prime and fire the weapon itself. The Gunner emerged, rather in the breech position, blinking his way into a new world of furiously explosive chaos while all about him was turmoil.

The birth pangs of what we now call the Royal Navy were painful and the labour somewhat protracted. Although the ordinary fighting men began to disappear from the decks of merchant ships re-commissioned into war service, their officers did not. They developed a taste for the life. Command came naturally to them. They were accustomed to obedience from those who served them on land and they enforced their authority through their social position. An exchange of tactical information ensued. The lordly landlubbers began to learn seamanship while the Master and his mates — later the 'warrant officers' — developed a feel for military strategy and armament. They were in danger, though, of having their maritime authority usurped.

There were all manner of teething problems. The dissolute and arrogant behaviour of the landed gentry on board ship began to knock this potentially productive compromise off course, but then the Civil War intervened to produce a rank of 'tarpaulins' — officers who rose through the ranks. This came about when half-starved and appallingly badly treated sailors under the 'Cavalry' régime were forced to choose between King and Parliament. They, quite naturally, came down on the side of Parliament and got the Cavalry officers kicked out. 'Tarpaulins' replaced them, inspiring great trust and loyalty from their crews who knew them to be proven seamen, free from fancy ideas about 'society' or need to exert their authority for any other reason than to run a good ship. The Navy broke free of the doldrums, picked up a following wind and got back on course.

The Restoration very nearly broached the whole enterprise. Back came the dual command and the bad old ways and days. It was not until Samuel Pepys' great series of reforms that the Royal Navy came into being. There were 'post ships' and there were 'non-post ships', the former and more important being under the command of a Post Captain with a Master as an assistant and the latter sailing under a Captain who had to qualify as a Master and navigate for himself. For this came the rank of 'Commander' in 1794.

The notion that 'Officers are Officers and men are men' certainly still held in my time. It was a two-tier system which operated strict social as well as professional segregation. Officers were still expected to maintain a certain style of life ashore as well as afloat. It required a great deal more money than could be found in an officer's monthly pay. A private income was essential.

Boys who, for one reason or another, were considered to be 'officer material' would be enrolled as Naval Cadets at Osborne and then go on to Dartmouth for two years. These two establishments, still smelling of wet paint when I first went to the *Worcester*, were built by Jackie Fisher who perceived, before anyone else was fully aware of it, that a technologically improved Fleet would be of little use to the nation unless those in command of it had undergone appropriate and systematic training.

Officer cadets had, until 1902, received their initial two years' instruction aboard the *Britannia* and the *Hindustan*, two hulks permanently moored at Dartmouth. Fisher pensioned them off and built the colleges of Osborne and Dartmouth. Osborne spread itself around Queen Victoria's country residence on the Isle of Wight while Dartmouth's impressive facade kept watch over the site of the old training ship moorings just up river from Dartmouth Castle.

Provided the 'young gentlemen' residents did not seriously misbehave themselves and scraped their examinations with a whisker or two to spare they could, in due course, expect to progress from the lowly position of midshipman to the more exalted rank of sub-lieutenant.

More training followed, both actively while on service at sea and at shore-based training centres. The potential Executive Officer, who had to be familiar with every aspect of the operation of his future command, was trained in gunnery at Whale Island, chartwork at navigation school and so on. The bulk of the theory was taken on board at Greenwich, a berth steeped in the history of England and embellished with maritime anecdote. It is said that Nell Gwynne took passage from Greenwich aboard a yacht bound for the Continental ports thanks to the timely intervention of Samuel Pepys, at that time Secretary for the Affairs of the Navy. By all accounts, quite some affaire!

Charles II decided to build himself a new Palace at Greenwich after the Restoration but, running short of funds after constructing only one wing of his new home, he abandoned the scheme. The building still exists today as part of the Royal Naval College and is known as King Charles' Building. It was Queen Mary who decided, in 1692, that the buildings begun by Charles II should be completed and they eventually became the Royal Naval Hospital for disabled seamen. Its conversion to an educational establishment was effected by an Act of Parliament in 1869 which closed the Hospital and led to the re-opening of its impressive doors as the Royal Naval College in 1873. An infirmary was retained as a 'Free Hospital for Seamen of all Nations.'

Graduation from the Royal Naval College was the thing which designated the budding Naval hero a competent officer. However, there was one other vital requirement for him to be confirmed as an Executive Officer and that was to be qualified Officer of the Watch, that is to say to be left on the bridge by himself. This momentous step was approached cautiously and with some trepidation, under supervision, until the aspirant's Captain felt able to vouchsafe his craft into the strenuously alert care of an eager but nervous young officer. The bestowal of a Watchkeeping Certificate allowed him to wear, with pride and a certain amount of awestruck disbelief, a single stripe emblazoned on his cuff. Subsequent promotion depended on time and academic performance on the battery of courses. Time gained at this early stage, through good marks, could shorten the period spent 'Acting' and hasten the seniority which would then last a Naval officer the rest of his career.

Once he had attained the rank of sub-lieutenant he could more or less predict his career and time it through a series of promotions which would lead him, if his performance satisfied his masters, to Captain. Outstanding skill and knowledge in a particular specialization could take him from there to Rear-Admiral, Vice Admiral and then Admiral of the Fleet. It was a totally predictable course, set by the Admiralty and utterly undeviating − except in times of National Emergency.

The other course to the Wardroom was from the lower deck. In theory any boy with brains, determination and a streak of ambition, ballasted with a good dollop of common sense could improve himself from Ordinary Seaman to Able Seaman to Leading Seaman and thence to the Petty Officers' Mess. If he demonstrated the requisite skills and was deemed capable of leadership, it was then possible for him to gain a Commission. To find senior officers who had come up from the lower deck was rare, even during my time in the Service, but it did happen and I noted with some amusement in later years that it was just such a man who was, in the initial stages, the only one to back a scheme I wanted to put in place while at the Admiralty for improving the training and quality of COs during the Second War. There was well-camouflaged but undeniable prejudice against officers who had risen from the lower deck. Though I never felt it myself, I witnessed it on many occasions. It saddened and perplexed me. It was totally unnecessary and sometimes led, in my view, to the Navy cutting off its nose to spite its face. If a man shows proven ability, that should be enough for his ideas, opinions and desire for responsibility to be taken seriously.

My own passage through to Executive rank had been different again. I had gone straight into the Navy from a sailing ship. Then war had broken out and, despite my status as a junior sailorman of small experience, I had been identified by the Powers That Were as someone who might be useful and was offered a Commission. I was put to work immediately. Consequently I had not done any courses other than my Midshipman's training. On arrival at Fort Blockhouse I became painfully aware of the gaps in my knowledge.

Electricity was a weak point and the First Lieutenant of a submarine has to know something about it. Surreptitiously I sallied forth to purchase books on this and other subjects which, in the dizzying pace of events between 1913 and 1916, had been somewhat neglected. Navigation I had been taught theoretically in the *Worcester*. But that seemed a lifetime ago. Of engineering I knew nothing at all save that which had come from the horse's mouth aboard the *Orion*. The same was true of signals. My Midshipman's training had taught me a lot but I had never actually qualified in anything. I had stood OOW with not an A or an E to my name.

What I did know about, though, was submarines. While *K6* had been undergoing a refit after the War, I busied myself with the finer points of attack on what must have been one of the very earliest Periscope Courses at Portland. This was 'learning in luxury' and great fun it was too.

Submarines had been kept pretty busy during the War and it had not been feasible to formalize the training of new COs. The only way that a lieutenant of a submarine in those days could get any practice was to watch his Captain attacking, which did not represent a particularly substantial teaching method and fell far short of the ideal, largely due to the inexperience of the COs themselves. The problem with 'learning on the job' in submarines as opposed to surface vessels was that, in submarines, everything depended on the Captain's eye. Nobody else saw anything or heard anything. The only order came through the Captain.

There was precious little time to let submarines off to have dummy attacks until after the Armistice. At that point it was decided that submarine lieutenants ought to be given more opportunity to develop this skill and so a course was devised based on the *Vulcan* at Portland.

Off I set in the summer of 1919 to join a small flotilla of submarines which put to sea from time to time and allowed me to attack them under the watchful eye of the Submarine Captain. At that stage there was no particular course of instruction. One simply tried one's hand at it and learned by trial and error under guidance from the Captain whose experience was slightly greater than one's own. Looking back on it now, it seems an alarmingly ad hoc way to have gone about things but submarines were still experimental and, like many weapons throughout history, had suddenly and unexpectedly been brought into action before people really knew much about their operation or behaviour. Every dummy attack added to the collective experience and so a pool of expertise started to accumulate.

Sometime later an attack teacher was built at Fort Blockhouse. It was a lovely little thing, operated by simple mechanical means. It consisted of a length of track, not unlike a railway track, a very simple mock-up of a submarine control room with periscope and an 'enemy ship'. The lieutenant under instruction climbed aboard his little conning tower and peered through the periscope. He had a clear view down the railway line, at the far end of which was a model of a surface vessel mounted on a small cart. On orders from the Instructor, some poor rating cranked away at a wheel and the ship started to come over the land-locked Lieutenant's horizon. As it came within range it was angled for the benefit of accuracy and the Lieutenant under instruction had to give the necessary orders to attack. It was an ingenious device and, although primitive, served its purpose well for a number of years. I came to know it intimately since it was part of my equipment when I later became Captain of Blockhouse.

That early mechanical teaching aid has been superceded by a computer-controlled attack teacher which simulates conditions so accurately that present-day COs under instruction find it hard to believe they are still on terra firma in the 'control room' where realism extends even to the type and level of noise and lighting around them. But the little cart on the railway did its job and helped to rehearse many a Lieutenant in the art of attack before he went to sea and, with the enemy in his sights, gave his first order on war service to 'Fire one!'

After my periscope course I got my first command which was K Boats in Reserve up at Rosyth. In retrospect, the advice so ardently proffered by my erstwhile mentor from *Orion's* gunroom to take the plunge below the surface might well have resulted in me becoming surplus to Naval requirements almost as soon as peace was declared. It was a shock to learn that a number of my friends did, indeed, find themselves in that situation.

During hostilities the Submarine Service had come into its own. It had been part of our job to starve the enemy into submission, which is precisely what we strove to do by preventing merchant shipping access to the Fatherland via the Channel, the Straits of Dover and the Shetland Islands.

To sink merchant ships without warning was against international law, which also stated that a ship's company had to be put in a 'safe place' if it refused to comply with instructions from an enemy vessel, which was then at liberty to open fire. A ship's boats were considered 'safe' under such conditions. Submarines could not meet these requirements, firstly by virtue of their very modus operandum which was by stealth below the surface. The minute a submarine surfaced it became vulnerable. Secondly, of course, it had no boats. The advent of submarines brought with it the necessity to re-think the lines of engagement.

We didn't believe in breaking international law and torpedoing ships without warning. The Germans, too, hesitated for a long time over this question. The feeling that there was something distasteful, almost morally wrong, about submarines was not confined to British Admiralty departments alone. When the unspoken taboo was inevitably broken and unrestricted submarine warfare finally began on February 1st, 1917, the Germans sank so much so quickly that we, as a nation, came within three weeks of collapse.

The stunning efficiency of submarines as weapons of war shook everybody and, in the wide-ranging analysis of events following the Versailles Peace, there was a prevalent opinion that the sooner international agreement could be reached to do away with submarines altogether, the better. In a sense this pre-echoed the nuclear debate which rages on today, and its proponents faced the same fundamental problems. It is quite impossible to un-invent a weapon. Once you've got it, you've got it for good and it is generally only discarded when it becomes superceded by something more efficient.

There is little point in arguing the case of a *fait accompli*. The idea of abandoning submarines never reached a serious stage of consideration but it was talked about and that in itself was enough to halt any grand plans for developing this new branch of the Navy. We serving submariners were all too aware that our future hung in the balance and that this uncertainty was far from conducive to Treasury investment in research and new construction during the 'twenties.

After the war, the discussion had to be moved on to address the particulars of how such a potentially devastating innovation could best be managed for the benefit of humanity rather than its wholesale destruction. Before the war we had been by far the biggest navy in the world, keeping the sea lanes open. When America came in with us her navy was nothing like as big, but naturally she started to build as part of her war programme. The Japanese were also expanding, to the consternation of Britain and America, so a series of arms limitations conferences was held, the Washington Conferences, resulting in the regulation of the size of the navies by ratio. For battleships it was 3:3:2: America and Britain were allowed to build three to Japan's two.

Submarines were argued on a completely different basis, whose starting point was whether or not we should have them at all. In point of fact we had no reason for keeping them since they had no peace-time function. Their role in time of war had been defined through *force majeur* and in those pre-nuclear days before the arms race had gathered momentum there was no thought of a deterrent. The Japanese wanted some, and this was worrying, but our principal aim was to stop the Germans building any more because they had so nearly beaten us. An embargo on German construction was therefore put in place and it was not broken until they started building again, in secret, just before the outbreak of the Second World War. Meanwhile, we were left with our own apparently redundant submarine fleet plus a mass of German submarines which we had taken over.

The cutbacks didn't affect me personally other than in the sense that it altered the way submarine flotillas were organized. I was responsible for Group B which consisted of *K14* and *K16*.* That job lasted just over a year and then I got my first submarine, *H31*, attached to the 5th Submarine Flotilla based at Gosport. I was back at Blockhouse again, this time to command my own boat. I also got married. It is not easy to say which command I was better qualified for!

H31** was a dear little submarine which was very effective and pleasant to serve in and there were plenty of L class submarines about so unless I got chucked out of submarines altogether for some personal reason I could reasonably be assured that I would get command of an L boat and then possibly something bigger. What we all wanted in those days, people of my age, was to be Captain of a new submarine and take her through from the final stages of building to trials and commissioning. The chances of that happening anywhere in the foreseeable future were pretty poor, bearing in mind prevailing political and economic conditions, and my turn did not come until the end of the decade when construction was revived.

The 'twenties was a very unsettling period for everyone, within and without the Services. It is difficult to convey to today's generation the intensity of the feverish gaiety which gripped the country. It was not a

---

* 'Groups': at the end of the War the submarine service suffered a drastic reduction in manpower. Numbers of men had lost their lives, their contribution to the nation's security marked by a stark DD (Discharged Dead) in red across their service cards. HOs recruited for war service were discharged, as were RNVRs. Other officers and men had reached the end of their period of service. The Geddes Axe fell, forcing economies throughout the Navy and only the best men were kept. Consequently there were more submarines than men to take them out so they were put in 'groups' where one crew was responsible for four submarines. Domestic economies threatened from one quarter while the international implications of the Washington Conference put us under a double threat.

** *H31*, launched five days after the Armistice, gave 20 years service and was finally sunk on Christmas Eve, 1941, in the Bay of Biscay.

genuine gaiety born of joy, more a frenzied tarantella beaten out to assuage the grief, relief and terrible reality of starving soldiers home from war. There was a wild desire somehow to create out of the ruins a home fit for heroes, but most of the heroes would never return. There were dances and parties and outbursts of unimaginable extravagance. All inhibitions were thrown to the winds. The nation apparently went mad. It was all very stupid and served only as a brief distraction from the awful truth that all the best men had been killed.

In the 'twenties there were many Lieutenants who, like me, had missed the opportunity of doing their courses during the war, so, when it was over, the Admiralty, in its great wisdom, pronounced that all people who had been Sub-Lieutenants in the war and subsequently missed their courses should proceed to rectify the matter forthwith.

How the mighty are fallen! I had a new wife. I had survived the lonely and somewhat nerve-wracking experience of giving my first order to 'Shut lower lid' and 'Take her down to periscope depth,' as CO of my first submarine. I was a big noise down at Blockhouse. The responsibilities of life began to weigh on my not altogether humble shoulders. It was highly undignified for one of such exalted rank to be packed off to Greenwich to do a Sub-Lieutenants course. It was an awful slur. After all, I'd fought the bloody war. What the hell else did they want me to do?

In fact it did me the world of good because I learned in greater depth about a multitude of things of which I had had only fleeting, if concentrated, experience. It would have been highly irresponsible of the Navy to allow me to get any further on in my career without doing my courses. In the end I was thankful for it but I found it very tiresome and only managed to get through by gritting my teeth and slogging away. I eased off from this turgid approach from time to time by trying to look at the proceedings as an 'educational challenge' in general terms and myself as a 'problem' set for some poor syllabus-maker to solve. This diversion had the effect of distancing me from my immediate frustrations of learning and of enabling me to come up with a few tricks to help myself and others of similar disability to achieve comprehension in the face of overwhelming complexity. I had never been a great one for the classroom and determined that, should I ever find myself in the position of instructor, I would endeavour to cast my pearls of wisdom in as practical and palatable way as possible to the swine before me!

6

China

THE ADMIRALTY, QUICKLY recognizing that submarines were very much a closed shop, was astute enough to realize that EOs who chose to spend their time below the surface might very well become addicted to the life and stay submerged too long, thus depriving the rest of the Navy of their valuable skills. Indeed, on joining the submarine service one tended to drop out and to become rather isolated from what was going on elsewhere by virtue of being kept fully occupied with one's own affairs. A number of potential dangers lurked in these shadowy depths, among them the very camaraderie and closeness of the submarine service which, although a major unifying and motivating force, might develop into too much of a good thing.

There was also the matter of the submarine as a weapon of war. It was, after all, merely a weapon, like any other, whose effective deployment and use in any engagement depended on overall Naval strategy. Captains of surface vessels needed to understand the precise nature of the difficulties and limitations of submarine operations. Submarine COs could usefully learn a thing or two from big ships and, what was more, it wouldn't do them any harm to be plucked from their piratical lair and subjected to a bit of surface discipline from time to time! The Admiralty therefore wisely decreed that after a couple of years or so, Captains of submarines should surface and serve in a big ship to reacquaint themselves with the outside world. My turn came in 1923 and I waited with some apprehension to hear where I should be sent. The summons, when it finally arrived, surpassed my wildest expectations. I was appointed to China as Lieutenant aboard the *Hawkins*, flagship of the C-in-C, China Station. It was a plum job and I could hardly believe my good fortune as I boarded the *Nyanza* for the voyage east that October.

China in the 'twenties was in a state of turbulence. She was moving gradually away from medieval totalitarianism towards the acceptance of elected government representatives. Increasing contact with western nations, through the granting of concessions and the opening up of trade, bred a certain political curiosity. It was not especially vehement at first and much of the population remained indifferent to the elections of 1909, despite the fact that government officials were sent out to all provinces to register people who were eligible to vote. This development was part of a series of modern reforms which ultimately led to the downfall of the Ch'ing dynasty after the

6. *K6* picks up one of her own torpedoes fired in practice. The rating nearest the camera is fending off the stern of the 'tin fish' to avoid possible damage to its tail assembly and propellers bouncing off the ballast tanks.

7. The small submarine *H31*, Lt. Oram's first command., leaving Portsmouth harbour in the summer of 1921. Twenty years later, on Christmas Eve, 1941, she was lost with all hands in the Bay of Biscay, cause unknown. The ancient aircraft is an attraction added by the photographer. Many naval photographs of the period had aircraft superimposed for effect.

4. HM Submarine *K6*, Lt. Oram's second submarine appointment, arriving in harbour. The steam-driven K class submarines were very unpopular with their crews, accidents being frequent. In the background can be seen one of the unusual M class boats, armed with a 12″ gun.

5. *K6* alongside her depot ship, the *Royal Arthur*. Her captain, Commander Crowther and First Lieutenant Stevenson (with the ship's dog) are pictured here with Lt. Oram (left).

2. Bullying in the gunrooms of ships of the Royal Navy was endemic and junior members of the gunroom mess often became the victims of beatings and other unpleasant practices. Sub. Lt. Jefferson, the senior Sub of *Orion's* gunroom, was impressed by Midshipman Oram's experience at sea in a wool clipper and protected him. Here, Sub. Lt. Jefferson oversees the gunroom teams in a sailing regatta in Weymouth Bay, 1914.

3. Destroyer life meant little time spent in harbour and left few occasions for lighthearted pursuits, but here, Sub. Lt. Oram (left) joins in a banjo duet on the quarter deck of the *Obdurate* with Sub. Lt. R.W. James from the destroyer *Lizard*.

1. On board the wool clipper *Port Jackson*, 1913. The young Oram, by now a 'senior', is standing third from left, back row. The crew is in tropical whites with the 'voyagers', boys on their first passage, seated in the front row.

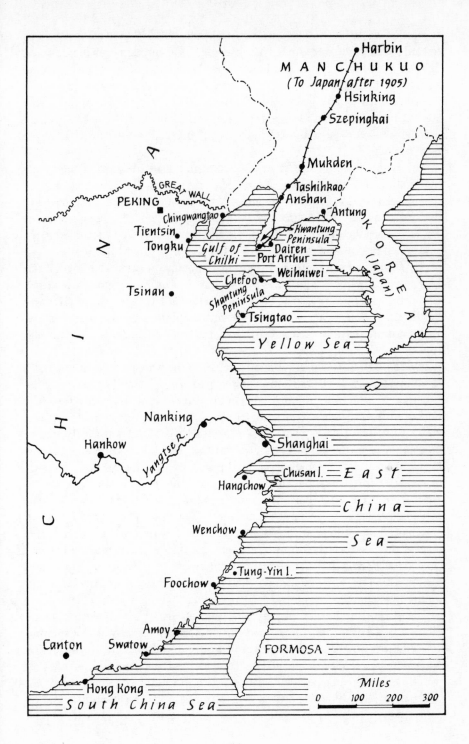

revolution of 1911. As in many other instances, these first teetering steps towards democracy were somewhat insecure. 'War-lordism' was the accepted method of exerting political influence and the vast majority of the electorate was encountering western ideas of self-government for the first time with no clear idea of its wider implications. Bribery and corruption were commonplace and there was a great deal of infighting at local level among merchants, landowners and bureaucrats, all engaged in their own particular power struggles.

The port which springs most readily to mind on mention of the China Station is, of course, Hong Kong, and rightly so. Its sheer volume of commercial traffic, both local and international, together with its busy dockyard and naval base made it the hub of operations. Singapore was also a thriving seaport but had far less Naval work to do. We called there once a season but that was about all. As it happened, I caught my first glimpse of the *Hawkins* from neither of these exotic points of oriental embarkation. It was from the roof of an hotel in Shanghai, an infinitely more mysterious city at the mouth of the great Yangtze River, that I first set eyes on my new berth. And what a pretty picture she made, glinting on her mooring that clear autumn morning, her graceful, long line perfectly balanced by two slim funnels coquettishly aslant.

In a sense, the *Hawkins* was a left-over from the war. Built to an improved Birmingham class specification, she had two sisters, both begun under the Emergency War Programme. Although *Hawkins* was the first of the improved Birminghams to be completed – she actually came out of Chatham on 25 July, 1919, the construction of one of her siblings was accelerated to be completed as the aircraft carrier *Vindictive*. Her function became surplus to requirements with the declaration of peace, occasioning her re-conversion to a cruiser just about the time I was casting an appreciative eye over her sister from the rooftop balcony. A light cruiser of 9,750 tons, *Hawkins* was powered by Parsons turbines generating 60,000 h.p. These gave her a top speed of thirty knots, with her four screws churning at full power. Her normal fuel load was 600 tons of coal and 1500 tons of oil which fed her 12 small-tube Yarrow boilers. Her armaments were 7 7.5" guns, 6 3" guns and 4 3" anti-aircraft guns. I gazed down at her with a mixture of pride, awe and bubbling excitement.

The reason for my joining my new ship at Shanghai rather than Hong Kong was the fact that she was putting in there after spending the summer at Weihaiwei on her way back down to winter in the British Crown Colony. *Nyanza*'s arrival date happened to coincide and the opportunity of what would be for me a 'shakedown' cruise in almost ideal weather conditions for that part of the China Sea after a stretch of five years in submarines and on courses was something of a bonus. I also had the arrival of my wife to look forward to in Hong Kong. She had very shrewdly secured for herself a position as travelling companion to a woman-friend of hers about to set out from England who felt the need for a chaperone on a journey of such length and potential incident. She therefore offered to sponsor my wife's voyage, which enabled us to spend Christmas together.

The outbreak of the First World War put a fairly severe brake on the economic growth of much of Asia. The number of steamers plying the trade routes dropped off sharply and the price of foreign commodities rocketed. Certain overseas markets for Chinese goods completely evaporated. The British Fleet vanished from Liukung Island at Weihaiwei leaving in its wake a suddenly impoverished business community and a number of near-destitute labourers who were encouraged to seek employment on the mainland.

Strangely enough, Weihaiwei benefited from two unexpected side-effects of the war. Firstly, in 1914 the Japanese took over Tsingtao, which induced a considerable number of ground-nut dealers to transfer their export produce to Weihaiwei for shipment. Secondly, Weihaiwei was the designated depot and embarkation point for the Chinese Labour Corps. Enrolled for labour service in Europe, volunteers were recruited to work a 10-hour day on railways and roads, in factories, mines and dockyards. Initial contracts were for three years and wages were set according to the level of skill offered. Recruits were given a return passage, food, clothing, housing, fuel and an embarkation bonus. Their families, who remained in China, also received a regular payment while they were away. This injection of money into the Shantung peninsula enabled very poor families to raise their standard of living and esteem by purchasing small tracts of land. A whole host of support industries grew up around the depot and Weihaiwei put on a busy air of self-importance with its new-found prosperity. Sadly this boom period was short-lived. Land communications had always been a problem and the depot was eventually lost to Tsingtao in 1918 as a direct result. The domestic economy took quite a plunge and the subsequent drought and famine of 1920 which decimated parts of north-east China and brought with it large numbers of refugees did nothing to improve a volatile political situation. The whole thing had been stirred up by the announcement at the Versailles Peace Conference that, with the end of the European War, control of the German concessions in Shantung would be transferred to Japan. This triggered demonstrations and riots and an economic boycott against Japan which lasted into the early 'twenties. Ironically the effects of the latter were worse for Weihaiwei than they were for Japan.

The Chinese felt aggrieved that members of their central government had colluded with Japan and therefore regarded them as traitors. This all helped to fuel the country's growing sense of nationalism and wariness of the motives of foreign powers. Britain's alliance with Japan was a source of deep suspicion which formally manifested itself through the question of the rendition of the Weihaiwei leasehold to China.

I did not set eyes upon Liukung Island until the summer of 1924 when the *Hawkins* sailed in for the season after a long cruise south to Singapore and Java. In contrast to the lush vegetation and vibrant tropical colour of Indonesia, the coast of north-eastern China presented a barren aspect. The rocky island's hillsides were largely devoid of trees while across the bay we looked onto ranges of low, rugged hills. A few were topped with the ruins of ancient fire-towers, used to signal alarms along the coast in times gone by. There was little else of topographical interest on the mainland save some natural sulphur springs which had been developed by the Japanese prior to the British occupation of the territory, and which had become something of a summer tourist attraction. One could understand why. If the landscape had little to offer, the climate was certainly exceptional, and provided welcome relief from the enervating humidity further south. It was wonderfully refreshing and had an immediate psychological effect on tetchy crews who were starting to suffer under damp tropical conditions. I could feel my own spirits perking up as we slid gently onto our mooring. On subsequent visits I would secretly offer up a word or two of thanks that the Admiralty had been tenacious enough to hang on to the island as a sanatorium and recreation area for the Fleet. There was also a passable nine-hole golf course and a dextrous tailor who rejoiced in the name of Jelly Belly.

The British had actually taken over the territory from the Japanese who occupied it after the Sino-Japanese war of 1894-5. The final and decisive battle in that dispute over Korea was won by the Japanese at Weihaiwei in February, 1895, where the Chinese Admiral and five of his officers committed suicide as their own guns were turned and used against them. Under the terms of the ensuing treaty, the Japanese were allowed to occupy the place until China had cleared certain indemnity payments, an obligation which was not fulfilled until three years later and only then with the help of loans from Russia, France and Germany who were all too eager to obtain concessions in the region.

Britain had not joined with the other imperialist powers against Japan and as a result was finding herself increasingly isolated in East Asia. A successful bid for Weihaiwei offered undeniable diplomatic and practical benefits to both sides. Port Arthur and Dairen were just short of ninety miles across the Gulf of Chihli, forming an effective gateway to Tiensin and thence Peking, the Imperial Capital. It was not hard to see the strategic importance of Weihaiwei. Indeed it had been established as a fortified garrison by the Chinese almost exactly five hundred years before the British took over the lease. The very name 'Wei' described the garrison's function as a 'guard station' to protect the Shantung promontory's pitted coastline against attack from both Chinese and Japanese pirates — a defence which was necessary well into the twentieth century as I was to learn at close quarters.

Added to its superb position was the commodious natural harbour approximately six miles long by three to four miles wide, containing the island of Liukung. A notable Chinese Admiral established a naval school there shortly before Jackie Fisher's educational innovations at Osborne and Dartmouth. China indicated at that time that she would not be averse to the British Navy taking a hand in the development of her own fleet. At the beginning the naval school only offered refresher courses — a kind of 'in-service' training — but later it trained cadets and added courses in torpedoes and gunnery using armaments manufactured on the mainland. Two other islands lay across the entrance to Weihaiwei in such a way as to protect the anchorage from seasonal tropical storms which tore in from the Pacific with devastating effect. Entry was restricted to a single western channel by virtue of the arrangement of these islands which meant that all shipping had to pass right under Liukung and the western shore. With these natural advantages Weihaiwei was all set to develop into a thriving military, industrial and commercial seaport with great potential for entrepot trade. A largish herring fleet fished out of the harbour in the season and the Ch'ing Imperial Navy wintered there.

The territory's evident potential was never fully realized, largely due to a combination of the internally disruptive birth pangs of Chinese Nationalism and the failure of Britain to invest in infrastructure and exploit natural mineral resources. Our diplomatic reserve was calculated to exert the least possible pressure on the complex array of interlocking treaties and alliances between all the interested foreign powers.

Weihaiwei was one of two territories which Britain leased from China in 1898, the other being the New Territories of Hong Kong. They were similar in respect of land area and population and were each acquired for military reasons. Russia had recently occupied Port Arthur and Dairen on the Manchurian peninsula and Germany had Tsingtao on the south coast of the Shantung peninsula. A British presence was needed to balance things in the north and Weihaiwei presented an ideal location for a naval base. Further south on the mainland, the New Territories formed a buffer zone which could be garrisoned if necessary to defend the existing Crown Colony of Hong Kong Island and Kowloon.

The handover of Weihaiwei to the British was formally completed on Queen Victoria's birthday in 1898 after somewhat protracted and strained negotiations. China was in the tricky situation of leaving herself open to counter-demands by other foreign powers with interests in the region if she acquiesced to the British leasehold. On the other hand she was ever mindful of the threat posed by continental Russia and was anxious to forge alliances which could strengthen her position. As early as the 1850s Chinese emigration to Manchuria was being encouraged to offset Russian expansionism in the region. The route was via Chefoo, a key port, and the consequent increase in volume of traffic had quite an effect on the economy of eastern Shantung which was already establishing itself internationally through the silk trade. As Manchuria opened up, so the Gulf of Chihli assumed a new significance. Instead of a barrier, it was fast burgeoning into an important commercial thoroughfare, a development which did not go unremarked by western maritime powers.

On 24 May, 1898, HMS *Alacrity* and HMS *Narcissus* anchored in Liukung harbour and fired a Royal Salute. The Chinese flag, which had been allowed to flutter aloft for the three days between the evacuation of the Japanese and the arrival of the British, was replaced by the Union flag and on the mainland, across the water to the west, the bay was renamed 'Narcissus.' The small port of Ma t'ou on its northern side became the British territorial capital of Port Edward. The ceremony marked the start of a curiously anticlimactic period in the territory's history occasioned by a series of political compromises which resulted in the British carrying out a diplomatic holding operation rather than investing in the long-term economic potential of the place. The local inhabitants no doubt regarded the change of flag with some scepticism, believing that the new tenants would merely take what they could salvage from the previous incumbents and then steam away. They almost certainly did not expect us to stay for thirty-two years.

For the first year of the lease the British administration was a Naval one which was then turned over to the military. Neither seemed keen to discharge the responsibility for longer than they could get away with and it was finally handed to the Colonial Office. Unlike Hong Kong, Weihaiwei was not a colony but was leased from the Chinese government. Its inhabitants did not therefore become British citizens but they did come under British jurisdiction and for some nineteen years enjoyed the sympathetic and skilful administration of James Stewart Lockhart, a Commissioner whose thorough knowledge of the language and familiarity with Chinese custom steered them relatively peacefully through very turbulent times.

The leasehold included Liukung Island and all other islands in the bay as well as a strip of land ten miles wide along the coast and all the adjacent waters – a total land area of nearly 300 square miles. We were also granted a sphere of influence of some fifteen hundred square miles which extended from about halfway to Chefoo in the west to the Shantung promontory in the east. Although we never took advantage of it, we had permission to put up fortifications and station troops within this larger area but our administrative jurisdiction was confined to the leasehold proper. A Chinese Regiment did exist briefly but was finally disbanded in 1906 because so many men deserted and new army recruits in any case preferred to emigrate to Korea, Manchuria or South Africa for higher pay. The idea was mooted at a fairly high level in the British military establishment that Chinese troops recruited and trained at Weihaiwei could be used elsewhere when needed in the same way that Indian recruits were employed. Understandably, this somewhat tactless suggestion was less than favourably received by the Chinese government and the activities of the Regiment were kept within the boundaries of the leased territory itself. The one exception was the Boxer Uprising when troops were despatched to Peking and Tientsin and found themselves in the anomalous situation of having to fight against their fellow countrymen. The majority of desertions occurred as a result of this incident.

The Walled City within the leasehold was not under our control. Our lease was to run for as long as the Russians stayed in Port Arthur — an ambiguous diplomatic loophole which may well have had some strategic value but which ultimately stunted the territory's economic growth in comparison with what happened in the New Territories. The choices of Lockhart and, later, his assistant, Reginald Johnston, were inspired. British policy was to preserve the myth of Chinese territorial integrity, thereby avoiding any precedent which might be followed by the other powers. Lockhart handled the thing with kid gloves, even at one point acting as an unofficial peace-broker between the Chinese central government and the governor of Shantung when he became dangerously embroiled in the rebel cause during the revolution of 1911.

There was no British military presence at Weihaiwei in the years immediately preceding the revolution. The original idea of making it into a fortified garrison entailed vast capital expenditure and the maintenance of yet another far-flung garrison did not appeal to the Treasury. Even the financial burden of the China Regiment ultimately proved too great to sustain. Between the signing of the Leasehold and the decision in 1902 to maintain Weihaiwei merely as a 'flying naval base' almost the entire Board of the Admiralty as well as the Secretary for War had changed. Current opinion on the status of Weihaiwei underwent close revision. Nearer home, Britain was becoming anxious about the size of the German navy and the Franco-Russian Dual Alliance was giving some cause for concern. The First Lord of the Admiralty was of the opinion that all expenditure should be directed towards the Navy and ship construction. His thoughts were prophetic.

The turn of the century saw the start of major changes in the international balance of power, particularly with regard to Russian activities in East Asia. The British response was to become allied with Japan in 1902, an arrangement which was renewed in 1905 and which put strain on the relationship with China. However, since China was also looking nervously over her shoulder at the Russians she needed to hedge her bets and attempted, for a while, to play one foreign power off against the other. The military occupation of Manchuria by the Russians following the Boxer Rebellion led to the Russo-Japanese War of 1904-5 and a resounding victory for Japan. The Russians were kicked out of Port Arthur, thus leaving Weihaiwei in a very vulnerable state according to the terms of the leasing agreement. The situation was further complicated in that, if the British wished seriously to consider rendition, they could only do so after consultation with their Japanese allies. Britain needed to extricate herself from this mire with some care and preferably without losing diplomatic face to either side. It was not easy since the Chinese were pressing for rendition and the Japanese, concerned that the German presence at Tsingtao should be balanced, were against it. A compromise was eventually reached in the 'flying naval base' idea and the Chinese were informed that they should regard Britain's continued occupation of the leasehold as a protection against the other powers. It was also intimated that rendition might be possible at some later date.

Japan's decision to enter the First World War on the side of the Allies caused a major reappraisal of all foreign rights in China. Japan forced the Germans out of Tsingtao and then secured a number of international agreements as counter-claims to other foreign demands in Shantung at the Paris Peace Conference of 1919. The Chinese reaction of a boycott against Japan, coming as it did at a time when nationalistic feelings were in any case running high, unsettled British and American entrepreneurs in Weihaiwei who undoubtedly feared that this wave of anti-imperialism might eventually be directed against them and perhaps even force them to leave altogether. Economically Weihaiwei was rapidly becoming a dead duck as far as the British were concerned and it was Reginald Johnston, acting for Lockhart in his absence, who made the suggestion that Weihaiwei should be returned to China if the Admiralty could retain Liukung Island. There had been very little real investment in the place when one compared it with other foreign leaseholds. Despite the fact that the British administration had been a stabilizing influence which managed to maintain unusually cordial relations with the local population, the Chinese were becoming contemptuous of the poor deal they were getting as they looked at the steadily growing prosperity of other foreign leaseholds. Britain had not pressed for mineral mining rights as Germany had, neither had external road and rail links been developed. Rendition would certainly be seen as a gesture of goodwill. Johnston's ideas were amalgamated into a major revision of British policy in China which ruffled a few feathers at the Foreign Office.

China, meanwhile, was becoming more and more keen to get back all her leased territories and to eject Japan altogether from Shantung. She did not get what she wanted at Paris, refused to sign the treaty and lost a certain amount of international sympathy. However, between 1919 and 1921 when world powers were once more exercising themselves upon the question of disarmament, this time at Washington, China's position was reconsidered. There was a general feeling that her demands had been somewhat peremptorily dismissed the first time round and that they had not received just consideration. Both France and Britain offered to surrender their leased territories if the other foreign powers would do the same. Japan would not countenance any discussion of territories gained before 1920 but after the exertion of strong Anglo-American diplomatic pressure and in the face of growing international disapproval at her obduracy, she finally capitulated and Tsingtao was returned to China in December, 1922, although the Japanese were canny enough to keep a firm hold on certain important economic interests in Shantung.

The terms and conditions of Weihaiwei's return were surprisingly difficult to finalize. A draft agreement was ready for signature in November, 1924, but before it could be passed the Peking government was overthrown and the British then felt that withdrawal from the territory was impossible. In the ensuing turmoil there was no constitutionally mandated administration with which they could deal at an official level. Political in-fighting, bureaucratic wrangling at local level and the not inconsiderable external threat posed by Japan, all played their part. When Weihaiwei was eventually handed back to China in 1930, the British Government, mindful of the naval advantages of maintaining some sort of base there, had articles attached to the Convention allowing them to lease back certain areas for consular and Naval use.

While we were very happy to hand over a large quantity of stores to the Chinese authorities, including the island and mainland telegraph and telephone cables, police uniforms, sanitary carts, mules and equipment, cycles and the Fire Engine, we were extremely keen to hang on to our two cemeteries, one in Port Edward and the other on Liukung Island. To keep watch over the quick as well as the dead, we proposed to instal a consul whose residence would be the accommodation formerly occupied by the senior district commissioner. The NCO's mess and surrounding grounds were to be re-vamped as consular offices. Part of the barracks were converted to a British Club and the old parade ground, hardly more than a piece of waste land really, became the golf course.

The National Government took over responsibility for maintaining all municipal services on the island, for dredging the channels already opened up by ourselves and for maintaining moorings, buoys, wharves and so on. In return, we handed over all the moorings and buoys we had laid and were permitted to use them, after the Chinese Fleet, during the summer months. We were not allowed to operate brothels but we were allowed to tow targets out to sea for exercises provided that we took 'reasonable care' to avoid damaging fishing nets. Finally, we were obliged to relinquish all rights if either China or ourselves became involved in a war. This last stipulation occasioned the British withdrawal just one year short of the initial agreed period of ten years. The rendition of Weihaiwei was finally ratified at Nanking on 18 April, 1930.

The general demise of Weihaiwei as a British leasehold was already under way as I took up my duties of Lieutenant aboard the *Hawkins*. The Shantung peninsula was badly afflicted by lingering war-lord disputes at the time. During the summer months when we went north, we tended to confine our shore-based activities to Liukung Island. There was precious little of interest or amusement on the mainland when one compared it with Hong Kong or even Penang. In any event I was in for a busy and slightly unnerving time to begin with. My last period of service aboard a surface vessel had been as a Sub-Lieutenant in the *Obdurate* under vastly different circumstances. I spent the first few weeks earnestly straining to do my best and to fit back in to the pomp, ceremony and formality of the Navy 'showing the flag.' Although the regime was quite different from that which I had recently experienced in submarines, it was, under the benign leadership of Admiral Leveson, not an onerous one and as I began to relax into the job it developed into the best commission of my whole career. I had a glorious time.

7

L12 and *H47*

TWO YEARS IN THE *Hawkins* on the China Station gave me a great deal of confidence. It also had precisely the effect upon me that the Admiralty wished a surface commission to exert upon seditious submariners of maverick character! Politically and geographically it broadened my horizons well beyond their somewhat sketchy limits, hitherto defined largely in terms of schoolroom history. Seeing is believing of a quite different magnitude.

Between them, my wife and the Navy managed to shape me into some sort of socially acceptable animal, although it took some years of assiduous polishing on my wife's part to get me to the point where I was not only seen to be doing the right thing in the right place at the right time, but more, to be genuinely enjoying it. By the time my promotion to Lieutenant-Commander came through, just before we left for England and a spell back at Portland, I suppose I was more or less groomed to handle whatever lay ahead, although there were times when, as I looked at my seniors swanning through professional crises (which more often than not boiled down to a straightforward muddle-headed cock-up on somebody's part) and the obligatory social whirl with equal aplomb, I had my doubts.

Grasping the promotional ladder with both hands I mounted the next rung to find, much to my delight − and relief − that I was appointed back to submarines. Although I had enjoyed my surface stint in China, to my surprise I missed the particular camaraderie of boats more than I had expected. After a short spell in command of M Group which consisted of L boats in reserve, I was given *L16* which was undergoing a refit at Chatham. After our 'cobweb' exercise we sailed away to join the 1st Submarine Flotilla based at Malta. There followed two years of routine patrolling in the Mediterranean from Beirut to Gibraltar putting in at the usual places − Alexandria, Athens, the Greek Islands and Philippeville.

Apart from my brief appointment to K boats in reserve at the end of the war, this was really my first peacetime experience of submarining of any duration. It offered me a golden opportunity to consolidate the knowledge and experience I had gained thus far, partly, it must be admitted, by historical accident, and at last to feel able to contribute in a useful way to the general store of submarine lore.

There were other benefits too. The Mediterranean was an unknown quantity as far as I was concerned, my only experience of it being vicarious, through my own early teachers when I had been at Fort Blockhouse as a young Sub-Lieutenant. A certain amount of glamour attached to their exploits in the war and the prospect of being able to cruise about unhindered by enemy fire in waters where the course of history had so recently been replotted was very appealing. My wife was able to join me in Malta and I even managed to hitch a ride for my car which was somewhat unceremoniously hoisted aboard the transport ship in a large hairnet.

The submarine sailor is a particularly valuable type of man. Obliged to live and work in a very confined space, far below the ocean's surface, he inhabits a domain not dissimilar to his shore-based brother, the miner, whose subterranean profession also involves long cramped hours pushing oil and water about the place.

On board a submarine officers and crew are in close proximity twenty-four hours a day. They learn a great deal about each other from this enforced intimacy. There is no room for prejudice or discrimination. The atmosphere has always been less starchy and formal than that of a surface ship. This may be one reason why submariners have been and still are regarded with a degree of suspicion by the rest of the Navy. The chain of command is still absolute of course but the relationship between submarine officers and men is somehow more humanly based. Respect really is respect and not some resentful hybrid born half out of fear.

This special relationship evolved from prevailing conditions in the first Holland class boats. How to go about selecting these pioneering ships' companies presented the Navy with something of a dilemma since there was no pool of submariners upon which to call.

In 1902 it was a question of appointing a certain number of lieutenants, a certain number of petty officers and a certain number of men. These brave, some would say foolhardy, men had to start their own tradition, totally isolated and sealed off in a hostile element about which little was known. It was not until the 1940s, for example, that life-giving oxygen was discovered to be poisonous at a depth of more than 33 feet.

Various scientific experiments had been carried out since before the turn of the century concerning the effects of breathing oxygen at moderately high pressure over prolonged periods of time. The tests had all been done on animals, the first having used larks. To me this seemed a particularly poignant way of demonstrating the ill-effects of oxygen. Contrary to the notion of purity and beauty associated with 'The lark in the pure air' these joyous little birds were found to convulse and die when exposed to pure oxygen between 15 and 20 atmospheres.

The first recorded case of oxygen poisoning was logged in 1912. In the 1930s more experiments were done using human volunteers. It was widely assumed from the published results that men at rest were safe for at least 30 minutes at a depth of 99 feet and for at least three hours at 66 feet. It was not until 1942 and the innovation of the 'human torpedoes' that further research demonstrated markedly different effects depending on whether the diver was breathing pure oxygen in a compression chamber, surrounded by compressed air and without his suit, or completely kitted up under water.

Divers under training for the 'human torpedo' programme became unconscious while breathing pure oxygen at depths which had previously been considered safe. The area of investigation was widened. Other variables were found to have unexpected influence on a diver's tolerance. Hard work when submerged considerably increased the danger of oxygen poisoning as did repeated dives on successive days. A diver who had suffered no ill effects at all the first time down and had managed to work quite comfortably for an hour at a certain depth could, the very next day, suffer acute oxygen poisoning after only ten minutes at the same depth. The water temperature was also found to have an effect. Lip-twitching, nausea, dizziness and general disorientation are the most common symptoms of oxygen poisoning with convulsions occurring in more serious cases. These were described, in the early days, as resembling epileptic fits.

This crucial knowledge could have saved many lives and may radically have altered the outcome of a submarine disaster in which I found myself taking a principal role much later in my career, just before the outbreak of the Second World War. Primitive escape devices utilizing pure oxygen were actually lethal under certain conditions.

The Navy itself was something of a hostile element too. Submarines were regarded by many as dishonourable weapons because they operated unseen and by stealth. This was not playing the game. Those who manned them were therefore renegades – indeed they were termed 'pirates' by the rest of the Service. They were certainly not officers and gentlemen. This attitude persisted until the First World War when the importance of an operational submarine fleet became abundantly clear. It quite naturally helped to reinforce the submariner's loyalty to his fellow 'pirate' and nurtured something of a club atmosphere. This special bond was symbolically cemented by the characteristic smell of the interior of a submarine which soaked into every item of one's uniform. Redolent with that particular perfume – a blend of dank fustiness, diesel and a persistent grey metallic odour – I would arrive home from a patrol, eager to greet my wife, only to be informed that I smelt. I would then be banished to the garage where my outer gear and uniform jacket and trousers were left to hang, ponging in bleak isolation!

Submarines were dangerous, tricky to handle, and intriguing. Nobody else knew anything about them at all. What was clear was that survival depended on mutual trust and co-operation. Officers and men alike were all too aware that the sea was their great enemy trying to get in and that they must never do anything to help it. This led the early submariners to develop a code of behaviour which would at all times ensure their mutual safety, in as much as this was possible, and enable them cheerfully to operate under the physical and psychological constraints imposed by a very confined space. Officers had to be able to do the work of their men, to be willing to lend a hand, and everyone had to work as a team. It is a particular type of working relationship, unique in the Navy, and one which I thoroughly enjoyed right from that first day, sitting awe-struck on the control-room deck of *C34* while the Captain and his crew brought us beneath the Channel by some mysterious sleight of hand.

This submarine code of behaviour developed over the years as submarines themselves became more sophisticated. It still exists today, even in the age of the nuclear monsters whose technological wizardry is so complex that no one man can carry all the information required inside his head. The present day Captain, surrounded by computer-controlled equipment, needs a team of experts to filter information and advise him. The degree of complexity is a hundred times what I needed to master, even by the time I had command of my own boat. The officers of my day had artificers, of course, to deal with specialist technical detail, but even so they were expected to know how things worked and to be able to lend a hand. It was all part of the team spirit and that is something which has persisted.

The chance meeting in Blyth in 1916 which had set me on a submarine course not only led me into a fascinating career at the 'leading edge' of a revolutionary new type of weapon, it developed in me a latent interest in humanity and the way that human beings learn things.

I have never been an academic. If at any stage my forbears had exhibited great intellectual prowess, it did not filter down to me. I could never lay claim to erudition in any field whatsoever and enlightenment, when it came, was something I beat my way towards, up channel, against a persistent north-easterly. I like to think a certain degree of common sense and a well-developed spirit of self-reliance helped me along. I was often appalled by my own inadequacies and frequently felt totally dimmed by the burning intellects around me!

Throughout my periods of training I habitually found theoretical courses far less digestible than practical 'hands on' learning. This led me to devise various strategies by which I and those like me might advance our knowledge and understanding of certain subjects, which were presented in such well-insulated theoretical complexity that they threatened to remain hermetically sealed for life.

We were all thirsty for knowledge and none of us was stupid, but there were instances when it seemed that the last thing the Navy wanted to do was to let us into the secret!

As I came to know men better through sharing the submarine life with them I discovered that most people are far more intelligent than circumstances allow them to demonstrate. Much talent is wasted. This comes about for a number of reasons, notable among which are deficient systems of tuition and failure to recognize a man's true potential. There follows a tendency to write him off as useless.

Selection and training of personnel began to feature in my life. I found, as a Lieutenant-Commander with more than average experience of submarines and an obvious interest in developing personnel for this section of the Service, that my advice was being sought.

In 1928 the Submarine Service was still only 27 years old. I had already been associated with it for roughly half its operational lifetime, part of which had been spent serving aboard the very earliest classes to be commissioned. One way and another I had picked up quite a bit of knowledge about it. I was certainly full of enthusiasm for it and, at the risk of boring my listeners into insensibility, was only too eager to share this enjoyment of my work.

In the autumn of that year, much to my delight, I was given a plum job that satisfied all my demands and allowed me to assist in the transmission of this ever-growing pool of knowledge and experience. I was appointed Instructional Officer to the Submarine Service.

Based at Fort Blockhouse, I had my own submarine, *L12*, which I used for the practical sea-going part of the courses. There were other, additional submarines available to me if I needed them. I had returned to my alma mater and, with some trepidation, recognized that I was following in the wake of celebrated submariners of First World War fame. They had been inspirational teachers and I had little hope of matching their performance but I was determined to do the best that I possibly could.

As Instructional Officer I had to teach the elements of submarining to the new entry officers who were sub-lieutenants or junior lieutenants, all with sea-time under their belts. Most of them had a Watchkeeping Certificate. Some would only have been to sea as midshipmen, others as sub-lieutenants. They came to me for a three-month course, starting from scratch. They were put in classes of about ten or fifteen each. They knew nothing at all about submarining but by the time we had finished with them they were capable of taking a job as what we used to call in those days 'third hand'.*

They spent three pretty concentrated months getting to grips with the

---

* In the early days it was the custom to refer to a submarine Captain's principal assistant as his 'second hand' and to additional officers as 'third hand and fourth hands'. The 'second hand' (i.e. First Lieutenant) was commonly called the '2nd Dickie' by his crew.

general operation of submarines, diving, electrics and administrative work. Most of that fell on my shoulders. Then came initiation into the operational complexities of submarine engines. There was a final examination and it was rarely that we failed anyone. There is little point in requiring a man to go through three months' intensive work learning about an area entirely new to him if, at the end of it, he has been unable to grasp the basic principles.

It became apparent that certain parts of the course were less attractive to its participants than others and caused much headscratching, inward groaning and general difficulty. This was baffling. The instructors were all men of great knowledge in their various fields. Their pupils were certainly not stupid. It was not until I found myself engaged in amiable conversation with a bright but disheartened young Sub-Lieutenant at teatime one Friday afternoon that I hit upon the reason. I happened to enquire how he was getting on with his engineering course to which he admitted, rather shame-facedly, 'Well, Sir, I'm afraid I'm making rather heavy weather of it.' None of his compatriots was within earshot and, on realizing he had a sympathetic listener, he vouchsafed his worries. Having just come out of the classroom he had all his books and papers with him and it only took a little gentle encouragement on my part for him to illustrate what he meant by turning to some of his most recent work.

No wonder the poor chap was in extremis. I felt deep sympathy with him. His notebook contained page after page of elaborate drawings of the innards of a diesel engine. They were meticulous in their accuracy and wonderfully neat and tidy in their execution. It was all highly professional stuff but did not advance this poor Sub-Lieutenant's general understanding of the operation of the diesel engine one iota. He clearly recognized this shortcoming and was somewhat confused as to what was expected of him. His recapitulation of this highly specialized information in visual form was of an impressive standard and earned him praise from his instructor but left him very far from being able to diagnose simple malfunctions or predict the likely consequences of a fault, should it arise, at sea.

I pondered on this problem over the weekend and decided that first thing on Monday morning I ought to get the instructors responsible for this part of the course together to have chat and try and sort things out. I inevitably trod on a few corns and there was a rather heated fifteen minutes during which educational theories were fired, broadside, across the table! Once I felt the air had cleared a bit I called a ceasefire and we agreed that since time was so short on these courses it was completely useless teaching people something they would never be called upon to do. There was only time to cram in the vital stuff and with this in the forefront of our minds we came up with three options.

We could teach our pupils to become engine drivers. This would involve going below and taking charge of the engine and running it. We could teach them to be engine maintainers which meant that they would be able to perform simple refits and repairs on the job. Finally we could teach them to be engine designers. This last, of course, was the direction in which my poor confused Sub-Lieutenant was being pushed with his meticulous diagrams, and he, not surprisingly, couldn't see the point of it.

Well, the engineering instructors immediately and quite predictably rejected the last choice. With some satisfaction (and a carefully concealed smirk!) I crossed it off the list which lay on the table in front of us. They all agreed that a knowledge of how to stop, start and run the engines was essential, so we kept that in, and then compromised on the maintenance part. Engine Room Artificers were there to carry out the skilled work but our budding young COs had to know enough about it to have a sympathetic understanding of what the ERAs were doing. The consensus was that we should be teaching people to be engine drivers who had a sympathetic understanding of maintenance. This was to be achieved in one of the three months of the course.

Once the aims and objectives were clear the course contents followed on quite logically. I suggested we compare them with what was actually being taught. The discrepancies were abundantly clear. So, the instructors went away and radically re-designed their curriculum which produced immediate and noticeably improved results. The root of the problem of course was that the instructors themselves were theoreticians, not practical engineers.

With one month of the course marked out for engineering, I was left with two to cover everything else including the instructional exercises at sea. It was clear that if I wanted to do my best for the trainees then I should have to practise what I had preached to the other instructors and limit the scope by simplifying things down to basic principles. I relied heavily on the work done by my predecessors in the job and was extremely grateful for the security this gave me. Bearing in mind my own intellectual frailties, I determined to find some sympathetic way of organizing the vast store of information the trainees were expected to take on board.

I went back over the lessons which had caused me such anguish at Greenwich when I had been press-ganged onto the Sub-Lieutenants' course. I tried to analyse what had worked and what hadn't and why. It was a useful exercise despite the fact that it recalled some blushfully uncomfortable moments!

The next task was to marry this up with the operational functions our new officers needed to fulfil aboard their first submarines once they had gone through our hands. Having devised the curriculum, the final hurdle was how, most effectively, to present it.

A vision of our old sailmaker in the *Port Jackson* sprang into my mind.

71

Years of lonely stitching with palm and needle had made him something of a solitary and he had a reputation as a recluse with a caustic tongue. In fact, this crabbed shellback had a soft centre and, in his mellow old age, was disposed to be helpful to first-voyagers like myself, totally bemused by the size and intricacy of the rigging singing aloft. Sensing my utter confusion and despondency at the prospect of ever understanding how our eighteen square sails were rigged with their almost three hundred individual ropes, he hauled his yard-stick and a small rectangle of canvas out of his bag one evening. We sat together on the fore-hatch cover, warmed by the setting sun, and with infinite patience the old man taught me to name the parts of a sail and then 'rigged' his little bit of cloth with lengths of twine. He made me push the sail about as if the wind were veering or backing and showed me how a yard was braced and a sail furled. It was a lesson I never forgot.

With this valuable experience very much in mind, I set about devising my own teaching method for the electrical course, which must have appeared somewhat unorthodox when put alongside more conventional approaches. Instead of presenting my eager but somewhat apprehensive audience with pages of circuit diagrams rendered almost indecipherable by vast spiders' webs of minute detail, I invited them to gather round a largish board which I had had made. Attached to it were lengths of wire representing, for example, a simplified version of the main motor circuits as used when diving a submarine. The system was decorated with simple switching devices and small light bulbs. Correct switching produced light: incorrect switching did not. Simulated faults could be diagnosed at a glance.

I wondered, rather nervously, how the electrically ignorant young Officers under Instruction would take to this teaching aid. It might short-circuit them altogether! To my relief it scored an immediate hit. A few sessions of fiddling about with the illuminated circuit board were far more productive then hours spent poring over abstruse electricity manuals. The odd diffident giggler quickly forgot his embarrassment as he became absorbed by the task in hand and discovered, somewhat to his astonishment, that by the end of the allotted time he had actually added to the vast sum of his knowledge!

My plan was to etch into each man's memory a simplified picture of an electrical circuit or pipeline so that he had a clear idea of its general function and understood how certain effects were caused. Once on board his submarine he could then apply this knowledge with confidence to the mass of piping and circuitry around him, and not become swamped in a maze of complex detail.

It seemed to work. We got results. Other people expressed interest. We had visits from officers running the RAF and Army staff courses. From a position of knowing nothing at all about electricity when I had first taken up my duties as a Junior Submarine Lieutenant, I now found myself rather enjoying it and, most surprisingly, able to teach it quite successfully!

The highlight of the course, usually about two or three weeks before the final exam, was a cruise planned with the specific objective of giving these young officers on the Long Course, as it was known, experience of a submarine operating on routine patrol. We usually took passage up to Scotland. They came aboard L12 and took the parts of actual members of my crew, although we, naturally, had the normal complement of fully qualified Officers and POs.

A General Programme and Instructions were issued for such cruises where attention was drawn in particular to the objective of giving the candidates as much practical training in OOW duties as possible. This was done under the general supervision of more experienced officers and was entirely in keeping with the official watchkeeping instructions laid down for heavy draft vessels. Everything was done absolutely 'by the book', despite the fact that it was a training exercise. In fact on these cruises precautions in excess of the official regulations were taken for precisely this reason.

You cannot train someone for OOW duties if he knows there is someone else doing the watching for him. What you can do is to train him up to the point where he has enough confidence to deal with normal situations by himself and enough common sense to shout for help when he feels he needs it. Nothing is ever lost by asking for help.

We had spent May and June ashore, cooped up in the classroom. We were all ready for a change of scene and looking forward to going on patrol. To give my trainees a taste of what I had felt that first, moonless night out of Rosyth, and to rehearse them in the normal routines of submarine watchkeeping, it was not my habit to place a Supervising Officer with a Sub-Lieutenant under instruction on the bridge unless some unusual situation warranted it. Experience had demonstrated that any form of dual control was liable to cause confusion and was therefore unsafe. I always made sure, however, that experienced back-up was instantly available. I briefed the crew to this effect before we slipped our moorings in Haslar Creek at the start of the exercise. 'Whenever a training class ship officer is on watch,' I told them, 'one of the qualified Watchkeepers of L12 is to be on the bridge or handy in the vicinity to advise, instruct, and if necessary take over from the Officer of the Watch in case of an emergency.' This was perfectly safe and acceptable procedure. Officers of the seniority and experience of sub-lieutenants doing the Long Course were frequently employed on Watchkeeping duties in the Service and had always been distributed throughout Submarine Flotillas for such duties during periodic exercises and manoeuvres. They had for years past performed the duties of OOW in sole charge, without the support which was afforded during a training cruise. This is an important point to remember in the light of what followed on the morning of 9 July, 1929.

The first Long Cruise of the summer had attracted a largish intake so *L14* accompanied us on the cruise to accommodate everybody comfortably and allow the officers under Instruction to gain maximum OOW experience. They were divided between *L12* and *L14* and we were on passage homeward bound in convoy from Lamlash on the east coast of Arran to St Ives Bay. This marked the conclusion of a most satisfactory series of training exercises which had been held during the previous week with other forces. All the Officers under Instruction had done well and gained confidence as a result. I was pleased with their progress and had confidence in them as a team.

At 0600 I emerged from the warmth of my cabin to take over as Officer of the Watch. The morning air struck very chilly on the bridge. It was a grey, cold start to the day for the time of year. We were steaming down the Irish Sea off Pembroke at 12 knots, approximately 40 miles north of St David's Head with *L14* astern like a dutiful chick, following in mother's wake. The sea state was calm with a light sou'sou'-westerly gently ruffling our feathers. Visibility was moderate to good and just about an hour later we sighted the Welsh coast. I estimated we should make St David's Head about 0830. *L14* had dropped back to approximately half a mile astern but was coming up into station. Our course was 200 degrees.

Just before half past seven an H class submarine appeared on the starboard bow. She was bearing approximately 40 degrees. Pennants were exchanged and she was found to be the *H47*, belonging to the Portsmouth Submarine Flotilla. She had been on completely separate business and was now returning to base, so we were now a flock of three, all heading south, on slightly converging courses. I took bearings on her over the next twenty minutes. They remained constant and confirmed this but there was nothing unusual or alarming in the situation. By the instructions laid down in the Signal Manual, and by the custom of the Service, *H47*, as a Junior approaching a Senior Officer, had to ask permission before passing through the line. *H47* did not express any such intention, neither did she request permission. The course and speed of *L12* and *L14* were therefore not altered.

At ten to eight I turned over the watch to one of my Sub-Lieutenants under instruction. He came up on to the bridge to warm the bell with his fellow who had just taken on duties as Navigator for the day. I pointed out the position of *H47* to him which was, by now, two miles distant on our starboard bow steering 252. We discussed the situation. *H47* was drawing slightly aft but there was no immediate problem and my Sub-Lieutenant was quite capable of taking charge. It was a clear, calm morning, there was no other shipping in the vicinity and we were still some distance from the coast. *L14* had caught up with us and was now on station 3 cables astern.

I went below to the wardroom to examine the large-scale chart of the Small's Light and vicinity. We would shortly be making a navigational alteration of course to put us on our home run and I discussed this for a couple of minutes with my Navigator, Lieutenant Keen, who then departed for the bridge, should his assistance be required, leaving me to my breakfast. Not many minutes after this a signal was reported from *L14* to the effect that she had a warm bearing and had eased down speed. This information was relayed to me with a request for permission for *L12* to ease down to accommodate her. 'Yes, certainly,' I replied, turning my attention regretfully from a large plate of· bacon and eggs which had just appeared in the wardroom and heading back to the bridge.

My breakfast must have finished up on the deck somewhere. All hell suddenly broke loose and the next ten minutes telescoped into a maelstrom of feverish activity. My alarm bell sounded and even before I had got through the crew space I heard two whistle blasts. I was up through the hatch and into the conning tower almost in one leap. What the hell could have happened? Was *L14* in trouble, and, if so, why didn't I know about it? Why, as stand-off boat, were we altering to port? The engines suddenly stopped and before I was out onto the bridge I felt them running astern and heard the reply gongs.

The sight which greeted me as I burst out onto the bridge was a great solid slab of submarine dead ahead. The *H47* was well and truly athwart our hawse only twenty yards or so away. We were about to ram her more or less at right angles. Collision was inevitable. I ordered, 'Collision stations, shut watertight doors!' and looked to see if the telegraphs were at 'full astern'. They were. We could not possibly get on any more stern way. Ten seconds later *L12* struck *H47* on her port side at a point just forward of the foremast periscope. *H47* listed heavily to starboard, settled, and went down rapidly.

From a perfectly normal morning at the end of a rather pleasant cruise, the situation had changed in minutes to one of appalling catastrophe. There was no time to try and analyse why we now found ourselves in this horrific mess. My two immediate concerns were to ensure the safety of my own crew and submarine and to pick up survivors from the water. I sent down to the control room the order to pass up everything floatable and then a brisk, 'Jump forward everyone!' to those on the bridge, my intention being to pick up men from *H47*.

To my horror I then saw the bows of *L12* submerging. The collision had been no glancing blow. Impaled somehow in *H47's* side, *L12* was being dragged under. I struggled to shut the upper conning tower hatch and managed to put the telegraphs to 'Stop'. The bridge then submerged and the seven of us who had been standing by on the upper deck to pick up survivors were swept overboard.

The pleasantly calm sea of an early summer morning was suddenly transformed into a boiling cauldron. I was sucked completely under for some seconds and when I finally did pop up found some difficulty in orientating myself. I trod water energetically, anxiously scanning the sea surface for the members of my crew who had been swept off the casing but there was quite a chop going and heads were impossible to spot from my position in the water.

What happened next was really quite remarkable. There was I and part of my crew swimming in the water, not really knowing what had happened at all except that two submarines had been lost, when *L12* suddenly broke clear of *H47* and surfaced. She was at an angle of about 50 to 60 degrees down by the bow and I could just see her propellers and after hydroplanes. She hung in this position for about 10 seconds and then rapidly surfaced with about a half knot of sternway. Except that the mast was bent she appeared quite normal. I instinctively struck out towards her but she moved away. Then I saw something very bizarre.

Submarines were fitted at that time with a heavy wire running fore and aft from the mast. Its function was to prevent tangling in nets and it was known as the 'jumping wire'. As *L12* moved slowly away from me I saw, clinging to the jumping wire in the bows, a dripping figure which slowly unwrapped itself and proceeded aft to climb laboriously up to the bridge. I imagined this to be one of my crew since I had sent someone to the fo'c'sle immediately prior to the impact.

It was not until I had been picked up by *L14* more than half an hour later, dried out with a change of clothing and rowed back across to *L12* in a Berthon boat that I discovered the true identity of this sodden scarecrow. It was the second Stoker Petty Officer from the *H47* who had been on the bridge at the time of the collision and had stepped across from one boat to the other, grasping the jumping wire very firmly and praying for salvation. Somebody must have been listening! With grim tenacity he had clung on as *L12* took him down at least sixty feet and then brought him miraculously to the surface. But imagine the poor man's confusion when he clambered up onto *L12's* bridge, found the conning tower hatch open, the tower itself flooded and the submarine apparently deserted. Apart from the *L14*, drifting down from windward, he believed himself to be the only survivor.

L14 picked up all those belonging to *L12* with the exception of Leading Signalman Charles Bull and Petty Officer Wheeler. One of these men was seen by *L14* a hundred and fifty yards to windward but he sank before anyone could get to him. The other was not seen after we had all been swept overboard.

The loss of any man is a matter of deep sadness but Leading Signalman Bull's death was all the more tragic for two reasons which should have been cause for domestic rejoicing. During the First World War Bull had signed on for twelve years in the Navy and eventually joined submarines in 1925. He would have been released from service in five short months, just in time to see his new baby. He had brought the proud news of his imminent fatherhood to his messmates at Blockhouse only days before setting sail for Scotland and good naturedly stood drinks all round. He was a particular friend of mine. I later became godfather to the child. A peculiarly poignant duty.

Able Seaman Sampson, one of the *L12* deck party swept overboard, was waterlogged and half-conscious by the time *L14* reached him. He was picked up and brought inboard but, sadly, attempts to resuscitate him failed and he died an hour later. The same age as the century, he had volunteered for the Navy in 1923 and spent less than a year in submarines.

Sub-Lieutenant Fisher, one of my Officers under Instruction, kept himself afloat with a lifebelt thrown from *L14* and was eventually brought out of the water alive. The only survivors from *H47's* complement of 22 were her CO, Lieutenant Gardner, Stoker PO Hicks and a Petty Officer telegraphist.

By the time I was reunited with *L12*, most of the crew was up on the bridge breathing lungfuls of fresh air. Sea water had contaminated the batteries when she had been sucked under. This had flooded down the conning tower before the lower hatch could be shut. The chlorine was strong enough for First Lieutenant Lipscomb to order gas masks to be worn in the crew space and control room. Attempts were then made to disperse the gas by drawing number 5 battery fuses, since this was the principal source, and running the turbo fans. The atmosphere was still pretty thick so an air blast from the 50lb service was used and then the blowers were run through the external vents to try and clear the fumes.

None of this was of much avail and Lipscomb had just ordered the battery ventilation to be opened up when, much to his surprise, I reappeared on board. He had done a splendid job in my waterlogged absence and I was mightily relieved to learn that, with the exception of the three men drowned, we had a full complement.

I took over control and ordered the engines to be prepared and run. This, with the battery fans, effactually cleared away most of the residual gas. All the men had been gassed but two suffered particularly badly – CPO Jolley and ERA Hoggett. When HMS *Alecto*, the submarine depot ship, arrived at about 1130, Commander Aylmer DSC RN and Surgeon Lieutenant Panckridge came on board. After examining all the men and finding no other serious injuries, the Surgeon took Jolley, Hoggett and Stoker PO Hicks of the *H47* across to the *Alecto*. Poor Jolley. He had been lent to *L12* specifically for the training exercise and finished up in Bethel Hospital at Milford Haven for his pains.

Temporary repairs were effected in the more essential circuits and with No 1 battery on the board, *L12* proceeded in company with *Alecto* and *L14* into Milford Haven.

Once the flurry of activity aboard *L12* had subsided into a more or less normal steaming routine, we all had time to reflect upon what had befallen us during the last few hours. *L12* came alongside at the docks in a state of shock. However, there was work to be done. The submarine had to be squared up after her ordeal and prepared for sea.

Everyone lent a hand. Salt water was removed from the batteries and all the cells were topped up three times with distilled water. The batteries were then charged separately. We managed to get the battery tanks practically dried out and shipwrights came aboard to wedge up numbers 1 and 2 batteries which had moved forward by about one inch as *L12* had lurched down by the bow. All the essential electrical circuits were repaired. The bilges were dried out, the tanks examined and finally the deckcloths were scrubbed. All the crew were medically examined and by 0700 on Friday, 12 July, thanks to a concerted effort by the officers and men of *L14*, HMS *Alecto*, *L12* and Milford Haven Port Authority, we were ready to slip our mooring.

During the subsequent voyage to Portsmouth everything in the submarine was in use except the telemotor starters, the reducer set and the hot plates. We limped, subdued, into our home port with a bent W/T mast and a defect list which included the removal and repair of one of our batteries and a buckled stem where we had hit the *H47*. As a result our bow buoyancy was damaged. The bow caps and torpedo tubes needed looking at and all our tanks needed testing.

ERA Hoggett had acted with great initiative in quickly releasing the drop keel as *L12* dipped at an acute angle. His automatic and quite proper response to the emergency had been to increase *L12's* buoyancy by any means available. He had reached for the padlocked leather strap securing the brass wheel which operated the drop keel and in a matter of seconds freed it off. Ten tons of steel had fallen away from *L12's* hull, immediately improving her buoyancy.*

This drop keel, a feature of older submarines which was abandoned in more modern designs, was at one stage operated by means of a telemotor

---

* ERA Hoggett had joined the Navy in 1917 aged 15. He transferred to submarines in 1926. His experience in *L12* apparently failed to shake his nerve and he steadfastly remained in boats until the Second War when he went down in the brand new *Tarpon* which was sunk in the North Sea with all hands in May, 1940.

clip but, on the advice of Rear-Admiral Submarines, the telemotor control was removed in 1927 after doubts had arisen as to whether it was foolproof or not. Drop keels reverted to manual operation when extra buoyancy was needed in an emergency situation until the Second World War when they were welded in place. This was done to avoid accidental release and subsequent uncontrolled surfacing if a boat was badly enough depth-charged to dislodge the thing.

Depth-charging had other unforeseen consequences for submarines during the war. The intense pressure change resulting from such an attack was liable to cause the upper hatches of escape chambers to pop open. They were therefore clipped shut from the outside — something which had hitherto been unnecessary since water pressure alone would secure the hatch on its seating with the submarine dived under normal conditions.

L12's drop keel required replacement. Various circuits needed rewiring and a number of motors and starters had to be repaired. The refit would take some time. Meanwhile, I was for the high jump.

8

A One Gun Salute

THE COLLISION WAS a grave matter. A lot of lives had been lost. One submarine lay disabled on the seabed and a second had been damaged. I was court-martialled, together with the Captain of the *H47* and my Navigator, Lieutenant Keen.

On Tuesday, 8 August, 1929 I received notice that my trial would be held ashore at 16, South Terrace, HM Dockyard Portsmouth the following Friday. Together with this document I received a copy of the charge sheet and a list of the witnesses for the prosecution. There was also a copy of the Circumstantial Letter reporting the facts on which the charge was founded and showing the real nature and extent of the offence with which I was charged, namely that I had suffered *L12* to be hazarded.

This Circumstantial Letter was a most important document. It had to state, in the clearest possible terms, the details of the facts upon which the charge was based. There were two reasons for this: firstly, to enable the convening authority to decide whether or not a court-martial should be ordered and secondly, to inform the accused of the precise nature of the allegations against him in order that he should be able to prepare his defence. The charge against me was broken down into two parts. Broadly speaking it said that I should never have left the bridge in the first place, with *H47* on the starboard hand on a converging course, and that I had omitted to make a proper turn over to Lieutenant Keen who was required to take over as OOW from the officer under Instruction in case of emergency.

I was informed that if I pleaded 'guilty' I would be considered to have admitted the accuracy of all the material statements contained in the Circumstantial Letter. I also received a copy of the summary of evidence in support of the prosecution but was warned that it did not profess to contain all the details which witnesses might give on cross examination. I was entitled, but not obliged, to give evidence on my own behalf and told that I would be liable to cross-examination by the Prosecutor and examination by the Court.

I was allowed to summon witnesses on my behalf, including character witnesses, and was allowed to have a 'prisoner's friend' to assist me at the trial. I was remarkably fortunate to have Guy D'Oyly Hughes.* He had been Nasmith's First Lieutenant aboard the *E11* during the First World War when Nasmith had got his VC. On one remarkable operation in the Sea of Marmara, Guy had swum ashore, pushing a small raft supporting demolition charges in front of him, and with astonishing bravery attempted to destroy a railway viaduct. He was something of an adventurer with a most acute mind, if a slightly macabre sense of humour with which he would attempt to divert me from the gravity of the matter in hand during our preliminary consultations. I could never quite work out why he told me this particular tale at the precise moment he did. Whether he intended it as a parable or a bit of light relief never became apparent. I like to think it was the latter.

The salt content of the world's oceans is prone to a wide variation for a number of reasons, not least of which are local effects caused by currents bringing streams of a lower salt content and therefore lower density into contact with 'thicker' water of a higher density. A certain position in the Sea of Marmara offered just such conditions which suited Nasmith's purposes very well. The success of the operations on which he was engaged depended on stealth and stealth depended on remaining undetected, in other words invisible to both the eye and the ear of the enemy.

Nasmith located a conveniently 'light' freshwater layer streaming down through the Bosphorus and by getting on an accurate trim he was able to lie silently cushioned by the denser salty layer below with no need at all to run motors. Each night, after a brief surfacing exercise to charge her batteries, down went the sub and silently to bed. There was always one man on watch whose job it was to keep an eye on the depth gauge in case the boat, through some unforeseen circumstance, became suddenly lighter and started to rise towards the surface.

One night Nasmith, subconsciously alerted by that sixth sense all COs seem to develop about the behaviour of their vessels, woke up in the small hours to find his telegraphist, who should have been on watch, dozing in his chair. The submarine was slowly rising to the surface.

Nasmith fired off orders on the instant to rectify the situation and then called for D'Oyly Hughes. 'I want this man brought before me tomorrow morning as a defaulter in neglect of duty.' 'Very good, Sir!' replied Guy and thought no more about it.

Next morning the cox'n arraigned the unfortunate telegraphist before his CO who administered the expected dressing down. 'You realize of course,' he rapped out, 'that your neglect of duty in falling asleep placed not only your life but the lives of the entire crew and indeed this whole operation in

---

* Guy D'Oyly Hughes was lost in 1940 whilst in command of the aircraft carrier *Glorious* after distinguished service in the Norweigan Campaign.

jeopardy. You have put your ship and therefore your country at risk.' The telegraphist's upright form, snapped tight to attention, threatened to shatter under the strain. 'IF we had gone to the surface,' Nasmith went on, 'and IF we had been seen and fired at, you would have been responsible for the loss of everything we have worked for through your negligence.'

These were remarks of the greatest severity. Nasmith the man was the kindest person one could wish to meet, possessed of infinite courtesy and gentleness. But this was a most serious matter and Nasmith the Captain was only too well aware how close his operation had sailed to disaster. A terrifying sort of cold rage seemed to have overcome him. The contrite telegraphist could only stammer out, 'Yes, Sir. I'm sorry, Sir,' and wait for his punishment to be pronounced.

There was a pause.

Then Nasmith said, 'I sentence you to death.'

Well, everybody staggered back a couple of paces and Guy said, 'Yes, Sir,' and the Cox'n said, 'Dismiss!' Not very much dismissing could be done because it was quite a small submarine. The stunned players in this maritime drama simply turned around and went about their business in an atmosphere of disbelief.

Once the First Lieutenant found himself alone with his CO he stopped acting the part and enquired,'This business, Sir, what will you do? Have him court-martialled when we get back to the depot?' 'No,' Nasmith said looking faintly surprised, 'I will shoot him.' Realizing with some horror now that his Captain really meant to carry out the punishment and feeling that this was completely of character, Guy decided he had to speak his mind so he said, 'You can't sir, that would be too cruel.' Nasmith was adamant. 'That man risked our whole operation. He risked all our lives and we must make an example of him. Personal feelings must not come into this.' Guy could hardly believe his ears but the Captain had spoken, so he asked what arrangements were to be made. 'Just before dawn tomorrow we will surface. You, the Cox'n, and the accused will present yourselves on the bridge. You will hand me the revolver and I will shoot him.'

Poor Guy. He was almost beside himself wondering what the hell would happen. He couldn't let things go on as they were. He couldn't see his Captain acting like this and felt he ought to intervene somehow or another. He wracked his brains thinking through every possible argument to deflect Nasmith from his terrible purpose. Eventually he went to him and said, 'You know Sir, our whole operation is going to be jeopardized because we only have one telegraphist and if you shoot him we lose all our communications with the base.' Nasmith responded to Guy's objection perfectly smoothly. 'I realize that, First Lieutenant. You will take over the wireless!'

There was nothing for it. The order had to be obeyed. Guy retired to the wireless cabinet where he parked himself beside the very green-faced telegraphist who spent his final hours on this earth trying to teach his First Lieutenant how to operate the set. They got as far as they could and eventually turned in with precious little hope of gaining any comfort from the oblivion of sleep. Guy's bunk was below his Captain's. He tossed and turned and lay miserably in the dark and then at some point during the night felt Nasmith tapping him on the shoulder. 'Ssh. Quiet!' came the whispered communication from above. 'Number One, I've been thinking about what you said and I do think it's necessary for us to keep the telegraphist so I'll defer this man for punishment until we get back to harbour, BUT dawn tomorrow morning is to go ahead as I ordered.'

At the appointed hour Guy turned out, climbed up to the bridge and handed the revolver to Nasmith who then addressed the ghost-like figure quivering before him. 'It seems to me that your duties as telegraphist are vital to this boat. Therefore I intend to defer punishment until I get back to harbour.' The tension on the bridge was audibly relieved. Once more the Cox'n said, 'Dismiss!' and Nasmith started giving the orders to dive back down to that safe, hidden layer which had so very nearly yielded up its crucial secret.

'What happened to the telegraphist?' I asked, 'Oh, he was eventually put ashore and went to prison,' said Guy. 'It wasn't a death-deserving offence really. After all, the chap wasn't guilty of cowardice. He simply fell asleep, but the point was he fell asleep on duty. As far as I can make out from all this,' he paused and tapped the report and other documents pertaining to my own court martial which lay on the desk between us, 'there is no question that you were in neglect of your duty. Now, there are just one or two more points I'd like to go over with you.'

As my supporter Guy offered sound advice on the important question of clarifying the exact nature and function of the *L12's* cruise as a training exercise. In examining the witnesses he really did me proud.

The Judge-Advocate of the Fleet also informed me that, under the King's Regulations, I was entitled, if I asked for it, to his opinion on any question of law relating to the charge or trial. I was also to submit any certificates I felt necessary and these would be laid before the court.

In accordance with Post Orders, Article 54(2), the Naval Saluting Battery at Fort Blockhouse was to fire the 'Rogue's Gun' and the Union Flag was to be raised in the *Victory*.

The doubtful honour of a one-gun salute is not a perquisite of the commissioned ranks 'Any poor sod,' my staunch but fatalistic prisoner's friend remarked as we presented ourselves at the appointed hour, 'found guilty in the old days was keel-hauled you know.' I did know. 'And,' he went on with an enthusiasm which I felt was totally misplaced at the time, 'when the poor bugger popped up the other side they fired a gun over his head.' I forbore to put the implied question but got the answer anyway. 'It obviously put the fear of God into him and acted as a dire warning to anybody else contemplating a major crime. But the real reason they did it was to get all hands on deck to witness the execution from the yard arm.'

I cannot deny that the days between *L12's* return to base and my court martial were not anxious ones. My position was extremely awkward because, as CO, I had to furnish various reports and a statement of what had happened immediately prior to, during and after the collision. This was very difficult since, at the point of impact, I was swept overboard and could only look on helplessly as my own submarine first of all sank and then re-surfaced before my very eyes. The only way of finding out what had gone on during my absence was to ask, so this is precisely what I did. My research produced the middle of a story for which I could only supply the beginning and the end.

As soon as my Navigator arrived on the bridge shortly after 0800 on the morning in question, he examined the chart. The Officer of the Watch, Sub-Lieutenant Wise, who was one of my trainees, drew his attention to *H47* and remarked that if present courses were continued, *L12* would have to make an alteration of course by the rule of the road as the bearing had remained constant for nearly eight minutes. Keen decided in his own mind that an alteration of course would eventually become necessary as the boats by now had approached to about 6 cables. He, quite correctly wishing to inform me of the reasons for his decision, ordered, 'Tell the Captain *H47* is trying to cross our bows.' This was completely new to me. I had received no such message. The only thing which had come through to me was the request to ease down to accommodate *L14*. I discovered in the course of my investigations that the message concerning *H47's* progress across our bows was passed to the Able Seaman on duty in the Control Room just before five past eight. This at least solved one mystery which had exercised me considerably during the hours and days since the crash — why I had not known about the close proximity of *H47*.

Lieutenant Keen, surprised at getting no response to his message, therefore decided that he would make the alteration of course early so as to avoid a possibly larger alteration later. He said that he wondered why I had not replied to his message but that he did not have any feeling of alarm, and was quite prepared to take action himself in what seemed to be a safe and very usual alteration of course, that of 'giving way ship porting her helm*

---

* 'porting the helm' comes from the early days in sailing ships. If the tiller (helm) is put to port, the vessel turns to starboard. These helm orders were still in use in the Royal Navy until the Second World War and were the direct cause of the loss of at least one ship.

and passing under the stern of the standing on ship.*' *H47* had closed to a distance of 4 cables and in the opinion of my three officers on the bridge, she was bearing at this time about 60 degrees on the bow.

In accordance with my orders, Lieutenant Keen took over control from Sub-Lieutenant Wise and put on 20° of port helm. When *L12* had swung through about 4 or 5 points to starboard all three officers on the bridge realized that *H47* was getting close, but they still thought *L12* would swing clear of her by virtue not only of the helm alteration, but also the reduction in speed which had been made, on my order, to accommodate *L14's* problem with her warm bearing. They were right. She would have done if *H47* had not at that precise moment decided to observe the Naval rule of precedence which she had hitherto ignored and, realizing the serious breach of etiquette she was about to perpetrate in crossing the bow of a senior Captain, put her engines full astern. Furthermore, she appeared to my officers to be altering course to port, a manoeuvre confirmed by two whistle blasts.

Keen, faced with the inevitable, endeavoured to lessen the impact by reversing his previous order, giving 'Starboard helm,' and only striking *H47* a glancing blow. He responded with two whistle blasts which were what had caused me such alarm in the crew space. Keen then ordered: 'Full speed astern both,' which is what I felt as I made my dash for the bridge. All this had happened in less than five minutes. Both submarines had altered to port and it was this final decision which led to Keen's undoing.

Through questioning the members of my own crew and talking the incident through with the Captain of the *H47* I was able to establish the sequence of events after my order 'Collision stations, shut watertight doors' had been issued from the bridge.

The hands were at breakfast and the forenoon watchmen had taken over. I discovered that my order was received in the Control Room at about 0809, but appeared to have been passed aft only. Thus the engine and motor rooms were immediately isolated from the rest of the submarine but all other spaces were common until First Lieutenant Lipscomb felt the shock of the collision and realized the gravity of the situation. Imagining I was lost and gone he immediately assumed command and very smartly ordered the forward compartments to be evacuated and shut off. Thanks to his prompt and correct action all valves and bulkhead doors, with the one exception of that between the Control Room and the crew space, were shut before *L12* went down. He set a magnificent example to the crew in his cheerfulness, ability and courage in taking complete charge of a very difficult situation.

---

* 'standing on ship': the vessel which maintains course and speed in a situation where two or more vessels are in proximity and precedence must be observed to avoid collision. The vessel obliged to alter course and speed is the 'give way ship'.

Further enquiries confirmed that my last-minute lunge towards the engine room telegraphs had been successful. The order had got through and the motors were indeed stopped by telegraph order. I knew that both conning tower hatches had been open because I had shot up through them when my alarm bell had sounded. Also the Sperry repeater compass was led up through the conning tower so that they could not be properly clipped. I suspected that my wrestling match with the top hatch had been lost as I had been swept overboard.

What I didn't realize until I started talking to people was that they all thought they were diving at great speed as water flooded down the tower. The *L12* took up an alarming angle of approximately 50 degrees down by the bow and the crew were left hanging from overhead valves or thrown to the foremost ends of the compartments. All moveable gear broke away. In the engine room a big end brass fell the length of the compartment. This accounted for ERA Hoggett's speedy attention to the drop keel. The gun tower starboard hatch was properly shut but the port upper hatch was not clipped.

As the story gradually unfolded I became aware of the commendable actions of both regular crew members and Officers under Instruction in the face of dire peril. With gallons of water cascading over their heads, the Coxswain, CPO Betty, and CPO Jolley, one of the instructional staff, struggled to get the lower conning tower hatch shut on to the Sperry lead — an action which undoubtedly saved the submarine. They managed it, but not before a great deal of water had flooded into the Control Room. Water continued to spurt in past the Sperry lead at apparently great pressure, thus reinforcing the crew's belief that they were diving rapidly. CPO Betty was in considerable pain, jammed against the W/T cabinet by the hatch lever pressing on his chest.

In the crew space Leading Seaman Sidney Reynolds ran up the gun tower and endeavoured to clip the upper hatch which had been open for ventilation purposes on a calm, clear morning. A salt water torrent gushed about his ears and the clip defeated him but, recognizing the critical nature of the situation, he actually held the hatch on its seating. A considerable volume of water came through this hatch, but not enough to flood the battery boards whose vulnerability Reynolds was only too aware of.

The angle of the submarine was so steep that the First Lieutenant and four or five others fetched up standing on the shut watertight door at the forward end of the crew space. From this position they saw an avalanche of water hurtling towards them from the Control Room. The lights continued to burn for a few moments but as the water level inevitably reached the switchboards there was one blow-out after another. A series of switchboard fires broke out and attempts to extinguish them with Pyrenes failed.

8. Four candidates for the 'Perisher' course, the Commanding Officers' Qualifying Course, pose for a photograph on board the submarine depot ship *Vulcan*. Lt. Oram is standing, centre. Frock coats and winged collars were quite common in the Royal Navy of 1919, the coats disappearing with the advent of the Second World War, although the occasional collar was still to be seen.

9. HMS *Hawkins*, resplendent in Far East colours with Royal Marine Guard and Band assembled on the quarterdeck and hands fallen in for entering harbour, makes her way up river for a courtesy call to Saigon, 1924.

10. HM Submarine *Regulus*. The newly promoted Commander Oram oversaw her building and commissioning, being appointed to her on 19 May, 1930. As her first Captain he had a great affection for the boat and her crew. He felt her loss, in December, 1940, deeply. From the actions of the rating in the bows it can be deduced that *Regulus* is preparing to enter harbour. The Union flag is being laced with codling to keep it taut against the jackstaff. The signal for hoisting is when the first heaving line hits the jetty.

11. Officers and crew going to join ships in foreign ports preferred the luxury of travelling in passenger ships rather than 'Grey Funnel' line where 'passengers' were expected to keep watches. Here, Commander Oram, en route to China, relaxes in a most unseamanlike manner with his hands in his pockets!

12. HMS *Medway* and her brood of 'P' and 'R' class submarines in China. 'Mother' *Medway*, for some strange reason, was extremely popular with submarine crews. Other depot ships, the *Maidstone* for instance, never acheived this happy status.

13. HM Submarine *Oswald* leaving Weihaiwei for Hong Kong en route for England, Saturday 19 June, 1937. She is seen here being cheered on her way home as she passes HMS *Medway's* stern. Captain C.B. Barry, DSO, (rear view, left) Captain of the Fourth Submarine Flotilla who succeeded Captain C. G. B. Coltart, Cdr. Oram's C.O., leads the cheers. The minelayer *Adventure* is in the background, right.

Eventually Lipscomb brought the situation under control by breaking the selector switch. This put the submarine in complete darkness as the police light resistances had already gone.

So, there they lay, suspended at an acute angle below the surface, unable to orientate themselves and in some trepidation as to the onset of chlorine gas emissions from the batteries. They knew they had collided with somebody but had no idea who, or what her fate was. Their Captain was presumed lost overboard and with him six members of the crew.

Nobody quite knew how long it was before the *L12* gave a slight lurch and, in pitch darkness, quickly settled on an even keel. The obvious assumption was that *L12* had hit bottom; so, believing this to be the case, Lipscomb ordered the engine room to remain shut off. This was quite understandable in the light of persistent spurts of water leaking in around the Sperry lead from the lower conning tower hatch.

The thing to do if you are on the bottom and out of control is to get rid of as much ballast as possible and try to resurface. With the drop keel already away, Lieutenant Lipscomb gave orders to blow the internal Z tank and put the fore hydroplanes 'hard to rise'. His small team of somewhat disorientated crew members consisting of Hoggett, Jolley, Leading Stoker King and Able Seaman Fry slithered to it with flashlights and a certain amount of difficulty. After some moments of groping about in a waterlogged and glimmering twilight they reported their success and Lipscomb was just going to order the motors 'ahead' to try and get off the bottom when CPO Jolley stopped him with the puzzled observation, 'Depth gauge registering 5 feet only, Sir.' Not believing what he heard, the First Lieutenant opened up the deep depth gauge. At almost the same moment, Leading Seaman Reynolds discovered that the gun tower was out of the water and hurriedly passed this extraordinary intelligence to the Control Room.

Meanwhile, the engine room – completely forgotten in the excitement of the moment – took the lights going out as confirmation that they were on the bottom and consequently turned their minds to thoughts of escape.

Lipscomb and the rest had been of the same opinion, taking the water spurting down through the lower hatch round the Sperry lead as an indication that *L12* was submerged. In fact what had happened was that she had broken free from *H47* with a conning tower full of water and as she had surfaced this had leaked in through the imperfectly shut hatch. Lipscomb could hardly believe his luck. He still had no idea how *L12* had surfaced but since there was no longer any doubt that she had, he ordered all hands on deck with the exception of four or five who remained with him in the Control Room. He shouted up to the bridge for news of the Captain and was considerably mystified to be told by Sub-Lieutenant Anthony Miers that he was in *L14*.

It was Miers who, when the hands first went up on the bridge, found Stoker PO Hicks in a state of some shock. Whether this was purely the result of his watery ordeal or whether the sudden appearance of *L12's* crew momentarily convinced him they were all gone together to Davy Jones's locker, he never disclosed. Miers attended to the poor chap and it was from him, eventually, that my First Lieutenant learned that *L12* had sunk *H47*.

Lipscomb and his team, now wearing gas masks against the quite strong fumes issuing from one of the batteries, set about clearing the air below and getting things put to rights. CPO Jolley persisted in this work until he was practically unconscious. He set the highest possible example both in his behaviour and in his dedication to the job in hand.

About a quarter of an hour after the collision, one of the engine room hands, still shut off aft, remarked on the sound of water swishing around the hull. 'Listen 'ere, Sir,' he remarked in tones of some excitement, 'there's gurglin'.' Warrant Engineer Jenkins, whose confident reassurance had preserved an atmosphere of business-like calm in the torchlit engine and motor rooms, called for hush. After some seconds of intense concentration he exclaimed, 'Right you are lad!' A squint through the inspection hatch in the watertight door revealed daylight on the other side and Jenkins gave the order to open up. This done, all hands were ordered on deck to join their incredulous crewmates.

My crew, including the Officers under Instruction, had acted with commendable presence of mind, tenacity and courage to save the boat. Particular members deserved special recognition which they got in my report. The only way I could get this information was by questioning. It was the worst possible course of action I could have taken.

My motive was broadly misinterpreted as an effort to save my own skin. There was nothing whatever I could do about this except weather it out and, trusting in the judicial powers of the members of my Court Martial Board, present the facts in as complete and straightforward a manner as I was able.

At a court-martial the junior one always goes first. Being the Senior Officer, I was third in. This did nothing for my nerves, despite the fact that expert legal opinion reinforced my own belief that the charges upon which I had been arraigned could not be substantiated. Both the Captain of the *H47* and my Navigator came off badly and were reprimanded. I felt sympathy for them. Keen was RNR and, whatever official line was promulgated about objectivity and even-handedness regarding RN and RNR, I knew jolly well that the dice would automatically be loaded against him. Gardner and I had shared the experience of Jutland where he was wounded at the tender age of sixteen. He later flew close to the wind again when he was withdrawn at the last minute from the *L24* which promptly went down off Portland after being rammed by HMS *Resolution*. At the time of the *L12/H47* accident, Gardner had only just been promoted Captain, having completed his Staff Officers' Course six weeks earlier.

The pomp and circumstance surrounding a Naval Court Martial are enough to make the accused feel guilty even if he was in a completely different sea area at the time of the alleged incident. I removed my cocked hat, took a deep breath and prepared myself for the ordeal. It was nerve-wracking.

The well known and oft parodied words, 'I swear by Almighty God that the evidence I shall give on my own behalf shall be the truth, the whole truth and nothing but the truth,' for a split second render a man starkly vulnerable as he grasps the Bible and commits himself to those sitting in judgement upon him. The sight of my own unsheathed sword on the table between us gave me an uncomfortable jolt.* It is one of those accessories of rank which was usually a damned nuisance and many a time I had cursed the thing for threatening to capsize me at the wrong moment. Standing before my judges, I felt absurdly naked without it.

Guy read the statement in my defence to the Court and then the questioning and cross-questioning began. At length, the Court was cleared for the Board to consider its verdict. Guy and I withdrew to an anteroom and, nervously lighting up, discussed the proceedings under a gathering haze of cigarette smoke. He was a damned sight happier about things than I was. Then came the recall. I stood up, straightened my uniform coat with what I hoped was the dignified gesture of a Lieutenant Commander, even though it might be his last, and stuck my chin purposefully forward to receive whatever might come. As I re-entered the courtroom, my apprehensive glance swept the table. There lay my sword – hilt towards me.

---

* 'A traditional custom still in use at the court martial of a naval officer is that of using his sword, which has to be delivered up at the outset to the trial and lie unsheathed on the table before his judges, to indicate to him their verdict. If the point is turned towards him, he has been found guilty; but if the hilt confronts him when he is brought back into the court room, the verdict is acquittal. This delicate hint of the shape of things to come dates from sterner times when a beheading awaited a luckless offender on shore should a court decide against him in a capital trial. On leaving the place of trial he was preceded by the headsman, who carried the edge of the axe towards the prisoner if death was to be his fate, or away from him if imprisonment was the only sentence.' (*Just An Old Navy Custom* by A. Cecil Hampshire, Kimber, 1979.)

9

The Admiralty and Invergordon

AS IS OFTEN THE CASE in accidents, both submarine and surface, there were several contributory factors which resulted in the *H47/L12* crash. No one regretted more than I did the fact that I had not been on the bridge to avert disaster, but the crucial message concerning *H47*'s intentions, which would have had me up there some minutes sooner than I in fact appeared, never got through and the fact that I apparently 'failed' to respond to it was not immediately followed up.

H47's behaviour presented the Court Martial Board with a nice arguable point. The whole thing happened because of a difference between Naval practice and Rule of the Road. Under Rule of the Road I was the overtaking ship and I had to keep clear. My navigator decided to go under *H47*'s stern, which was the right thing for him to do. Just at this moment the Captain of *H47* took the Naval Rule which said never cross the bow of a senior officer. There was nothing legal to back it; it was merely a custom which had grown from the days of sail. So he rather belatedly went full astern and the consequence was that we impaled ourselves in his side.

It was one of those borderline cases where, if one had argued harshly, it could have been said that I should never have left the bridge in the first place. On the other hand, there are others who would support the view that, in calm sea conditions with good visibility, a single vessel in the vicinity is a matter for the Officer of the Watch to deal with, not the Captain. In the event, the Board found that I had fulfilled my duties as Captain of *L12* quite properly and I was acquitted of hazarding my vessel. I should think my name stank for a while though, and I was quite convinced that my promotion would be knocked. I went back to Blockhouse to complete my teaching duties – not an easy thing to do under the circumstances – and then, to my great surprise, instead of being excommunicated, I was given a brand new submarine!

The *Regulus* was building up at Barrow and I was given the job of overseeing the final stages, training the crew and then taking her out on sea trials before commissioning. This is every submarine captain's dream, to take command of a brand spanking new boat. It was a rotten day for the trials, typical November weather, but nothing could dampen the crew's excitement as they busied themselves on board, making ready to leave the yard.

The Captain was pretty excited, too! I ordered, 'Let go for'ard! Let go aft!'

and watched the bow swing gently out as the engines pulsated eagerly into life for their first real seagoing adventure. For sheer job satisfaction, this beat even the experience of taking *H31* out for the first time.

Then, the pride and excitement of my first command had been somewhat clouded by the enormity of my responsibilities as CO, with the result that I was only really able to enjoy my first patrol in command retrospectively. Nine years on, as an experienced submarine captain, I relished the privilege of being the *Regulus'* first CO.

With an overall length of 290 feet and a beam just short of 30, *Regulus* displaced between one and a half and two thousand tons. She was a twin-screw diesel electric capable of attaining seventeen and a half knots surface speed with a submerged rate of 9 knots. Her eight twenty-one-inch torpedo tubes were arranged six for'ard and two aft. She carried a four-inch gun and two machine guns. With a complement of 53, she and her sister ship *Regent* later went to Singapore with the depot ship *Medway* for the opening of the new Naval Base there in 1938. Altogether there were four of her class, the name boat being *Rainbow*.*

We took passage to Cameldon in Scotland, completed the trials successfully and returned to Barrow where a cheery team of charladies bustled my crew out of the way to polish the *Regulus* up for her formal handover. This ceremony marked the official commissioning of a new submarine into the service and I signed a chit worded to the effect, 'received from Vickers – one submarine in good working order with full fuel tanks.' I joined her at Blockhouse around Christmas time and found myself starting a bright New Year not only with an addition to the Flotilla, but also with a bright new ring on my sleeve.** It appeared that my sins, if there had been any over the sinking of the *H47*, had been forgiven and I was promoted Commander.†

Despite my unexpected elevation, Their Lordships evidently had it in

---

* The sole survivor of the Rainbow class boats after the Second World War was the *Rover*. However, she was so badly damaged at Crete that she was eventually scrapped.

** Gold embroidery first appeared on the cuffs of Flag Officers' full dress uniforms towards the end of the 18th century – 3 rows for full admirals, 2 for vice-admirals and 1 for rear-admirals. It was not approved for all officers until 1856 with 3 stripes for captains, 2 for commanders and 1 for lieutenants. When the rank of sub-lieutenant was introduced everyone moved up a ring and EOs got a curl on their top stripe. As a newly promoted commander I therefore became a 'three-ringer.'

† Gardner's career was not unduly affected by the accident either. He went on to become CO of the destroyer *Achates* at the outbreak of the Second World War and then commissioned the aircraft carrier *Premier* which was involved in operations off Norway. He did not, however, get a medal for his part in the action and one can only assume the court martial influenced this decision as in all other respects he showed himself quite worthy.

mind to keep me out of harm's way for a watch or two. When my next appointment came through I found myself buried in the labyrinthine corridors of power at the Admiralty. A long and gloomy passageway led to the Director of Naval Equipment upon whose staff I was appointed to serve. There were two submarine desks to service all the submarines in the British Navy with a Commander apiece to run them. For the next two years my time was consumed with the administration of 'Alterations and Additions' to the submarine fleet.

It was not a particularly scintillating job. Once the decision had been taken to modify a bit of plumbing in a submarine, arrangements had to be made for the refit, dockyard berths had to be booked and then Admiralty records had to be amended to keep up with the changes. After the stimulation of working at sea with enthusiastic fledgling officers, my patience was sometimes sorely tried. At times I was at a loss to understand how the Fleet and the Admiralty could possibly be part of the same body. In fact it was a miracle how the Fleet managed to achieve any kind of buoyancy at all, loaded as it was to the very gunwales with paperwork and bureaucracy! Recognizable patterns did emerge eventually and I was able to build up a picture of how the need for a particular modification was first noted – usually from immediate sea-going experience – how it was then translated into a technical application by design engineers and architects, and finally effected in the dockyard. In fact, seeing the process from the Admiralty point of view was a valuable insight for me. It encouraged me to think anew about the importance of accurate reporting systems inboard and of open lines of communication at all levels, but especially within the Admiralty.

Poor communications and muddled thinking led directly to an enlivening interlude shortly after my installation in the Department of Naval Equipment. In truth the whole episode was of the gravest possible concern, not only to the Navy but to the country as a whole. Times were hard. The Wall Street Crash of '29 led to the most appalling scenes of misery on both sides of the Atlantic. People were committing suicide. No jobs were to be had. Britain went off the Gold Standard and the Government imposed stringent economies on the nation. For the second time since the end of the War, the Navy was forced to tighten its belt. The situation was so serious that pay cuts were ordered.

The Civil Servants got down to it and, in their inimitable fashion, declared that, in the Navy's case, the only fair thing to do would be to divide this sacrificial burden equally among its serving members. This they set about doing on the basis of an appraisal of what had happened to ratings' and other ranks' pay during the previous ten years.

Immediately after the end of the War all three fighting services had received bonuses. A huge gap had opened up between wages paid on shore and naval wages in the years between 1914 and 1918 so that by the time hostilities were drawing to a close there was a serious feeling of unrest throughout the Fleet, strengthened by the so-called 'police strike.' The bonus awarded to all three forces was really a stop-gap measure until something more detailed could be worked out. A committee was established to enquire into the pay and conditions of serving men under Admiral Sir Martyn Jerram. As a result of its findings, ordinary seamen and lower ranks received proportionately larger increases than their seniors, thus bringing them more into line with shore-based jobs.

By the mid-twenties Britain's economic fortunes were on the decline and the idea of a reduced pay scale for new naval recruits was introduced. The deadline date was given as 4 October, 1925, and at first it seemed that all men serving on this date would be paid at the increased rate until their date of discharge from the service. The government evidently got its sums wrong and by the end of the decade the country could not afford to sustain this promise. Eventually the decision was taken to put everyone on the new, reduced, 1925 rates of pay. In the interests of equanimity the civil servants took it upon themselves to reduce the differential in pay rises between ranks by inflicting the largest cuts upon those who had received the largest rises following Admiral Jerram's committee. This unfortunately resulted in the lowest paid ordinary seamen getting much larger cuts than the highest paid Admiral. Just exactly the wrong way round.

This beautifully worked out plan was published by the Admiralty in an Admiralty Fleet Order which went to some lengths to explain the whys and wherefores of the belt-tightening exercise. Moreover, it pointed out just how fairly all this was going to be done.

Meanwhile the Atlantic Fleet was gathering at Invergordon for summer exercises. The Admiralty post-clerk assiduously folded the Fleet Order into its envelope and addressed it to what he thought was the flagship – the *Hood*. As it happened, the *Hood* was in dock refitting, her place having been taken by the *Nelson*. So this most important document whose contents should have been communicated to the men face to face by their COs went south to Portsmouth instead of north to Scotland, where the flagship *Nelson* lay commanded by the Vice Admiral who had stepped in at the last moment to take over from the Admiral and C-in-C who had fallen ill.

The first the men heard about their reduction in pay was from the newspapers and the wireless.

There wasn't a great deal for the men to do at Invergordon by way of recreation. They had a canteen ashore which was their principal meeting place and this formed the hub of their somewhat sparse social lives for the duration of the exercises. It is not difficult to see how easily general discontentment grew, encouraged by boredom and genuine fears for the welfare of their families in the prevailing economic climate.

When news of the pay cuts appeared in the press, the men were stunned. This latest hardship was one too many and at once became the sole topic of conversation in the canteen. With a little revolutionary fanning from one particular communist sympathizer operating within the Fleet, the smouldering embers broke into flame and an Officer of the Guard had to go in to quell the hubbub. Throughout the trouble at Invergordon this was the only instance of violence. The ringleaders themselves stressed that the men's behaviour towards their officers should at all times be correct. They should not display violence or insolence and, if addressed by an officer, should stand to attention and listen. They should not, however, make any reply. Thus the bloodless Mutiny of Invergordon was plotted.

Had the men taken their grievances to their officers at that stage, all might not have been lost but they did not. Instead they planned what we would nowadays call a work-to-rule, to be followed by a sit-in (in fact the men refused to weigh anchor) and if that did not have the desired effect they would desert ship and march to London.

If the Admiralty had been guilty of neglect in the matter of efficient communications, the malcontents certainly were not. Through carefully worked out secret signals they spread the word and encouraged others to join them in their endeavour. The first 'official' meeting in support of the protest was held on Saturday, 12 September. There followed five days of non-cooperation from Ordinary and Able Seamen.

There were disconcerting similarities, or so it seemed to me, between the events leading up to Invergordon and those at Spithead and the Nore a hundred and thirty-four years previously. The intervening years had brought unimaginable changes to the physical appearance of the Navy. Steam had replaced sail, weaponry had been developed to a degree of sophistication and accuracy which transformed battle tactics at sea and, most significantly, there was the submarine which opened up an entirely new dimension of warfare and defence.

The management side of the operation had, regrettably, not kept pace. The ancient systems of Naval command and administration in place at the time of the war with France in 1797 were defective in a number of areas, the critical one being the lack of means for crew or men to express genuine grievance. Thus it was that commanding officers of the Channel fleet manned their quarterdecks ready for battle one bright breezy morning only to find that their crews refused to put to sea. This was mutiny and mutiny was a capital offence. The perpetrators risked their very lives simply because their simple, and quite reasonable requests (including the issue of provisions at sixteen ounces to the pound rather than the fourteen doled out by the purser who purloined the two extra ounces allowed by the Admiralty for 'shrinkage' as his perks) had fallen upon deaf ears.

There were in fact five major grievances expressed in letters to the then C-in-C Channel Fleet, an ailing but sympathetic man of 71 who was taking the spa waters of Bath at the time. He, in good faith, passed the letters to the First Lord of the Admiralty who, expressing disbelief that the writers (a few educated men who were not traditional seamen but who had come into the service from various professions) could possibly be representative of the fleet as a whole, dismissed them.

Receiving no answer the appellants, all the while maintaining strict discipline and endeavouring to use established channels of communication, wrote to the Lords of the Admiralty and to Members of Parliament. Their correspondence was neither answered nor even acknowledged.

The principal cause of dissatisfaction was pay, as at Invergordon. The crews who went to sea at the turn of the eighteenth century did so on rates of pay which had been set a century and a quarter earlier. The army, just to rub the poor matelots' noses in it, had recently had an increase. Eventually things were sorted out at Spithead and reforms were put in train. However, the negotiations dragged on and on and, just at the point when Portsmouth broke out the bunting to celebrate the end of hostilities in a remarkable dinner party hosted by the now recovered C-in-C and his wife for the delegates who had led the action and to which he brought the King's Pardon for the mutineers, five bells were struck in the dog watch in ships at the Nore.

The Spithead action could, I daresay, be compared with a modern-day industrial strike and the subsequent events at the Nore, which made much more of a splash in the history books, secondary action in support of the people at Spithead. The Nore Mutiny was largely irrelevant by the time it happened. It created a deal more unrest than Spithead and ended with deaths, not dinner parties. It also threatened to destroy the recently hard-won respect forged between the lower decks and the brass hats, which caused more than a few over-zealous officers to heave to and reappraise their own performance in the matter of personnel.

My boss at the time of Invergordon, the head of the Naval Equipment Department, was Admiral Sir Percy Noble. He was a very wise and elegant man who set an example of perfect good manners in everything he did. It was his habit to gather half a dozen Commanders together every day at teatime to have an informal chat about work. I suspect that, when trouble broke out at Invergordon, he was asked by members of the Board of the Admiralty to ferret about and find out which way his junior officers were thinking. The Admiralty was concerned to know how far the infection had spread — it was known that one other ship not at Invergordon had problems

– and whether the POs had become involved. Admiral Noble certainly did some tactful but persistent pumping, and very skilfully he managed it too. Since he was not actually in command, he could afford to be disarmingly forthcoming on the subject of the mutiny and this, quite naturally, encouraged us to put in our own two pennyworth.

'Of course,' he said by way of an opening gambit, 'the acting C-in-C was put in a very difficult position because he had only just taken command. I sympathise with him but I'm not altogether sure I would have tackled the thing in quite the same way.'

'No, Sir?' prompted one of my more affable colleagues who was always good for a juicy post-mortem. This interjection had the desired effect and after a long, but elegant, draught of tea Sir Percy amplified. We settled back with brimming cups and sharpened interest to hear what he had to say.

In his opinion decisive action had not been taken soon enough. He felt that 'divide and conquer' should have been the immediate response, rather in the manner of the police who employ such tactics to bring an unruly mob to heel. He would have split the Fleet up at once on any pretext at all – war with Germany, what you like – but the main thing should have been to separate them so that the rot could not get hold and spread among them. As things happened, the men cheered each other on from neighbouring ships and passed intelligence back and forth according to prearranged shouts. 'It is easy enough, I know, to be wise after the event,' he conceded, 'but this is precisely the sort of situation that calls for as much pomp and ceremony as the Navy can muster. It is the uniform which symbolizes the Office, not the man wearing it. He is merely the King's representative. Look how even the ringleaders in this show exhorted the men not to rise against their Officers. Now those are the sort of feelings that have to be played on. A man's loyalty to the Crown is not easily broken.' He had a good point. We were fascinated to hear how he would have gone about dealing with the muddle had he been C-in-C. It was a typically elegant solution.

'I would have gone on board every ship dressed in all the gold glitter I could manage,' he said. 'I would have played my position as C-in-C to the full – bands, gold lace, the lot. As soon as I got wind of the first rumblings I would have addressed every ship's company and told them, "I am your C-in-C and I do not agree with all these cuts and I'm not sure that I know the answers but I'm going to find out for you because I'm your C-in-C. It will take far too long to do all this by letter so I am going to send my Chief of Staff down to London by aeroplane. He will investigate and report back to me here. I am going to do this immediately and if I do not get satisfaction my flag will come down from that mast." By the time I had done that,' he said, 'the whole thing would have been called off.' We believed him.

Of course it didn't happen that way, but the thing was stopped within the week. The Admiralty telegraphed to Invergordon on the Wednesday following the canteen disturbance to the effect that it would consider cases of special hardship among ratings sympathetically. It ordered ships of the Atlantic Fleet to their home ports forthwith and further stated that any refusals of individuals to carry out orders would be dealt with under the Naval Discipline Act. It was a masterly stroke to order ships to their home ports since most of the men were natives and they knew they would be able to get ashore to their families.

Even so the Admiralty had to send a pretty tough Admiral to put the whole thing together. The fact that the last recalcitrants fell to and the mutiny was over by the 17th was due in large part to his sense of humour. On leaving Portsmouth to sort it all out and get the Fleet moving, Admiral Joe Kelly made a signal which went round the Navy faster than anything. 'Ships on leaving harbour will parade guards and bands,' he said. 'Any bandmaster playing *Anyone Here Seen Kelly?* will get the sack.'

On board the *Nelson* one forenoon he came across a sailor on the foredeck, leaning against a stanchion half asleep in the sunshine. Admiral Kelly was not a beautiful man. His bulldog jowls were the outward manifestations of a steely spirit but they belied his humorous manner and lightness of touch. Stepping quietly so as not to rouse the dreaming tar from his reverie, he positioned himself on the other side of the stanchion and casually leaned against it. Suddenly the awful bulldog face growled, 'All right, mate. I've got the strain!' The poor rating nearly went overboard.

The Invergordon Mutiny shook everybody. The Cabinet was recalled urgently to consult on the matter. Parliament debated it and the ensuing enquiry led to a considerable number of reforms within the Navy. These created a much better liaison between officers and men and encouraged greater understanding between them.

I finished my stint at the Admiralty during which time the Labour Government foundered in the treacherous currents of economic decline and finally went aground. Ramsay MacDonald found himself steering a coalition through the choppy waters of British and European politics, while on the far side of the globe, in Manchuria, the Japanese were doggedly toiling away to establish a puppet state which became a major contributor to their own economic collapse. 1933 began with Hindenburg's appointment of Hitler to the office of Chancellor, a move the significance of which had yet to unleash itself on the rest of the world. I was appointed back to Blockhouse as Senior Submarine Officer in command of Submarines in Reserve where I spent a year or so as 'harbour master' organizing movements in and out. Then I got a second chance to take a closer look at the changing world of politics in the Far East.

10

China-bound Again

MY NEXT JOB STARTED to make sense of the many oddly-shaped pieces
in the jigsaw of Naval life which had been shaken out of my own particular
box. The frame was now finished and a certain amount of in-filling had been
done. In some cases pieces had been tried several times in different places
before the appropriate home had been found for them. But the whole had
yet to be completed. There were lonely promontories projecting into the
half-filled rectangle like drying shoals on a falling tide. Before the invention
of submarines, the Navy had only needed to concern itself with what
happened on the surface of the world's oceans. Since the turn of the century
the Admiralty had been forced to peer down through their murky depths to
consider a new dimension whose importance had been made abundantly clear
between 1914 and 1918. What happened below needed to be co-ordinated
with what went on above and officers were needed who were masters of both
environments. Accordingly I found myself appointed by their Lordships to
command a surface ship in charge of submarines and in February, 1934, I
went back to China to be second-in-command of the 4th Submarine Flotilla
there. I was Captain of a ship called the *Bruce*. My job was to deputize for
the Captain of the Flotilla and to take responsibility for training the
submariners. My new command was a destroyer. She had been laid down
in 1917 as part of the Emergency War Programme. I had been a newly
fledged submarine First Lieutenant then, having just completed a fairly basic
course of instruction at Fort Blockhouse. Our instructor had rammed it home
to all of us that as 2nd Dickies we assumed responsibility for training the
crew and for maintaining its morale. This element of training fascinated me
throughout my years in submarines and really became a passion. It was the
training element of the China job which I really looked forward to getting
my teeth into. As it happened, Captain (S) let me have a pretty free hand
during my two years on the China station with the result that I was able to
indulge my special interest by trying out various schemes to improve
performance and, I hope, effect some psychological changes for the better
among the crews. The only clouds on the horizon were the fact that I should
be sailing away from my family and, on the outward journey, into the sad
decline of a senior officer with whom I had once shared rooms in London.

We left Southampton on a chill February day, packed like sardines aboard our troopship. There were about seventy officers of all types, including a couple of Army people and Marines. The rest were men. At least it was a clean tin.

The crowd to see us off lacked both colour and sparkle. The ship was unable to shake off this atmosphere of gloom, being denied the conventional band which is traditionally part of troopship departures all over the world. The tin music of a gramophone made a poor substitute. Long-drawn-out goodbyes are the very devil and not something my family was any good at. As I embarked I caught a glimpse of my wife firmly pulling on her white gloves with a brave little gesture and turning to get into the car.

It was to be an almost non-stop voyage. We should put in for only twenty-one hours out of our 34 days on passage. These brief encounters with terra firma were at Port Said, Colombo and Singapore. Colombo sticks in my mind by virtue of one of the lady guests who joined us ashore for cocktails and dinner at the Colombo Club. She was attired in pale green voile. It floated over her ample bulges with a sort of flaccid insolence, giving me the impression I was addressing a large jellyfish in a tank.

On our first night out from England the doctor's cabin burst into flames – the result of a faulty radiator. The doctor was a genial practitioner of 73 who enjoyed horseracing when not at sea and told extremely funny stories. He emerged from the inferno unscathed but commented that if this was an example of the level of comfort he could expect for the rest of the trip, he would rather get off at the next stop and go home to Chester! The following evening the cinema equipment broke down and caught fire.

To prevent the entire ship's company from falling into a morass of unrelieved boredom during the voyage, the several Commanders among us took it upon themselves to organize lectures, sports and entertainment. The latter fell to my lot. I always knew my juvenile music-hall visits with Peggy would come in handy somewhere along the line. I invited any potential entertainers to a meeting with the idea of setting up a concert party. My invitation got a good response and the meeting turned out to be funnier almost than the show itself when we came to put it on. Unexpected talent blossomed in the smoke-wreathed atmosphere of the mess deck. Ideas buzzed in all directions. Gestures became expansive, indeed declamatory in some cases! In next to no time we had a wealth of material. All that was needed was a bit of rehearsal to knock it all into shape. To my great delight four of my new *Bruce* crew volunteered to take part. They formed the nucleus of a 'funny party' which kept almost all of us amused for the whole voyage.

The first opportunity to go shopping for the props and costumes came eleven days after leaving England, at Port Said. We conveniently put in at half past seven on a Monday morning. One of the group of senior officers on board was a painfully serious character who could quell any merriment in his sea area by simply appearing on the horizon. He, gawd 'elp us, had put himself in charge of lectures. As he had never been caught with a smile on his face since leaving Southampton, we lived in constant dread of the results. Hoping to animate his humourless persona, we took him ashore. The troopship was due to sail again just after lunch.

Port Said was very French even though it reeked of Egypt. We shouldered our way through the 'gully gully' men who started on us with 'You want good time, Sair? Lovely girls! Exhibition French house, Sair! Spanish dance naked!' and gradually worked down the scale to an altogether more furtive and less sanitary sounding 'Dirty book, smutty picture, Sair!' in a sort of rasping whisper. The Serious One steered an undeviating course through this lot, as if stone deaf. One of my lieutenants vanished momentarily into the mêleé and reappeared seconds later with a wicked grin on his face. Meanwhile, the Serious One led us into a large souvenir shop and asked with a completely straight face if they had any view postcards. This reduced us all to such rib-aching hysteria that we had to sit down and draw breath. He proceeded with his purchases, completely oblivious of the effect he was having on the rest of us.

Back on board at dinner that evening, my grinning Lieutenant kept on asking to borrow small items from him. First it was a cigarette lighter. The Serious One reached into his jacket pocket and came out with a delicious smutty postcard. Then it was a pen to note down details of expenses for the concert party. His hand went into his other pocket and produced another naked delight. When asked for a pocket diary to check a date, we couldn't believe he'd fall for it, but he did, and out popped yet another lovely. Waves of amazement washed across his otherwise immobile visage. By the time the port came round, the poor man's place was covered with postcards of 'views.' The entire company was in paroxysms of uncontrollable laughter. I was also full of admiration for the dexterity of my Lieutenant who had planted the things so successfully. He finished up doing a very good sleight of hand act for our show.

The Suez Canal was a most inspiring sight, years ahead of its time when built. What vision must have driven the engineers on to achieve such aesthetic as well as technical splendour. The *Kent*, homeward bound from China, passed us and treated us to *It's a long long road a'winding* and *It's a long way to Tipperary* from her band as we came within range. Men crowded onto the decks of both vessels and cheered wildly as they slid past each other but the feelings of our men were summarized by a stentorian 'Change places you lucky sods!' as the music faded into the distance.

The *Kent* had been the flagship of the C-in-C China Station, Admiral Sir Frederic C. Dreyer. With the *Kent*'s departure for England he transferred his flag to the *Sussex*. Admiral Dreyer had played a brief but historic role in my career and it was interesting to reflect that he was partly responsible for my present situation. He had been Captain of the *Orion* in 1913 and had informed me, about a year after the outbreak of the First World War, that 'Their Lordships' had approved a recommendation made by him that I should be offered a permanent Commission in the Navy. The occasion is tattooed on my memory.

As a full member of a boisterous Gunroom, I could claim my fair share of youthful misdemeanours. Any summons from the Bloke sent a shiver of apprehension round our mess deck and a muted sympathetic groan of, 'Oh, gor' blimey!' On that particular day, I prepared myself for the worst. Captain Dreyer was an imposing figure, well above average height with a pink, heavy-jowled countenance and deep rumbling voice. His manner was ponderous, to say the least. He represented complete Authority to us and was held in awe. We were all terrified of him.

He informed me of Their Lordships decision in tones of dismal foreboding − as though he bitterly regretted ever having mentioned my name in the first place. Casting his lugubrious gaze slowly over me from head to toe his eyes returned to mine and he said, 'Wha-at, Mistah O-rah-m, is your inclination in this mattah?' Taken aback, I wallowed in a welter of emotions. Gathering stern way I was backing out of the cabin stammering my thanks when I was brought up all standing by his deep voice booming, 'Come to anchor boy and join me in a glass of marsalah wine.' As he ceremoniously drank to my future he opened up a benevolent face of his character which, I must confess, I had not suspected.

This benevolence had evidently been all but extinguished by the responsibilities of Dreyer's elevation to Admiral. It is one thing for a bunch of rowdy midshipmen, getting their first taste of the Service and its ways, to be in fear and trepidation of their Captain. It is quite another for senior officers of experience and proven ability to harbour similar feelings about a C-in-C. This, I found as I started my commission, was the prevalent atmosphere. It worried me considerably.

One's feelings towards authority change as one assumes a certain degree of it oneself. 'Discipline' is a most useful and productive concept if handled properly. As I rose through the Service I developed my own definition of discipline. It went something like: 'A spirit of co-operation enabling a group of men to achieve a common aim through willing obedience to a set of rules.' The key words here are 'willing obedience' and 'co-operation.' People have often and probably always will continue to confuse the real meanings of 'obedience' and 'discipline.' The best kind of discipline holds when all those involved in the activity, whatever it is, wish to co-operate with each other to achieve their goal. Results can be got by blind coercion but they are, in my experience, less satisfactory from a number of points of view. I was to ponder this question of discipline on a number of occasions over the coming months and sometimes to wonder whether I held too idealistic a view of the whole thing. My feelings of isolation in this respect were gradually broken down as I came to know my fellow officers on the Station better. We passed many a grey squally evening sitting out the passage of a tropical storm and chewing the matter over.

There was a special rate for Suez Canal dues for troop transports, into which category we fell. It came out to about 8/4d per head for our ship's complement of just over 1500. We were presented with a bill for £650. The senior pilot who took us through only drew a salary of about £1200 a year. This seemed a very small amount to me considering the size and varied nature of his responsibilities.

Once through the Canal we came into much warmer waters and went into whites. It was surprising how much brighter the ship appeared, but I suppose this was purely a matter of association of ideas. In China, where we were heading, white is a symbol of mourning. The appearance of shiploads of white-clad officers and men must have been quite funereal to them. The daytime temperature was rising all the time and with so very many people crammed into such a relatively small space, we were all starting to pant a bit.

On the opening night of the concert party there was very nearly another fire — me! Our 'theatre' took shape on the after deck beneath the stars. The Great Bear hung low in the sky with the Pole Star just above the horizon. Our marker now was the Southern Cross. No pretence was made to fix up such luxuries as a front curtain. What we lacked in sophistication we made up for with ingenuity and enthusiasm. The after hatch draped with a few flags served as a very good stage. The acoustics were poor but this seemed immaterial to the audience jammed noisily into every available space and eager to join in the fun. We were fortunate in being under no obligation to keep the party clean. Coarse it was meant to be and coarse it was. The audience roared. One of *Bruce*'s POs emerged as a very good actor and our new cook was practically an operatic tenor. I was playing opposite him in the role of Yeoman of Signals in Operatic Attacking. It was a rather lively part which culminated in my being fired as a human torpedo following one of my own signals. I got extremely hot. I had been a bit optimistic about the size of the jumper I had borrowed to complete my costume. During the energetic 'Attack' it welded itself to my roundish form and I really did think at one point that I might simultaneously combust. It took three men to haul the thing off me! The sailor always likes to see an officer making a fool of himself and we certainly gave the Boys and the POs plenty to laugh at. Most of it wasn't in the script, either!

The concert party ran for several nights and helped to diffuse that peculiar combination of restlessness and lethargy created on long sea voyages. Not unlike the feeling you get when lying in bed convalescing from a debilitating illness. Irritation and bad temper often set in. We had the added handicap of being far too closely packed, so the concert party was a good chance for everyone to let off steam. Sports were far harder to accommodate because of this lack of space but some ingenious compromises were worked out by the Commander in charge who added an element of theatricality to some of his efforts.

Although there were the inevitable moaners (of all ranks!) on board, the atmosphere settled into one of congenial tolerance and I took the opportunity of interviewing a few members of my new crew each day in the forenoon. They, quite understandably, regarded me with suspicion since I was a submariner, abruptly surfacing from years beneath the waves to take command of a surface ship. Whether my stage performances had reinforced or relieved their fears I am not sure, but one ERA greeted me with a broad grin and claimed me almost as a long-lost brother among a crowd of barbarians. I couldn't remember who the dickens he was but his fellowship was touching!

Discipline had to be maintained on board and it was not easy to strike the right balance between control and relaxation, given the overcrowded conditions. Arriving at one's destination with a lot of disaffected men who have been cooped up in hot and humid conditions for five weeks is not a good way to start a new commission. Commanding Officers were, generally speaking, sympathetic to the problem and handled minor infringements humanely. Sometimes, however, their attempts backfired. One morning a little drummer boy taking passage, who had been attached to the Boys division, was arraigned for flagrantly disobeying a 'no smoking' order. Evidently a lad of character, he attended quarters with a lighted cigarette secreted in his hand. He was brought before the CO shortly after breakfasting (very heartily) at 8.30 on the morning after the offence had been discovered. The CO (who had breakfasted with caution) laid two of the blackest cheroots in Christendom on the table between them and, acting on Admiral Cochrane's principle that an officer should always be capable of carrying out any order he gives, informed the astonished drummer that they would now light up and smoke one each! The Master At Arms, with a solicitude worthy of the head waiter at the Savoy, proferred a match. At the end of this ordeal the boy emerged apparently unmoved. The CO, controlling his early morning digestion with some difficulty, spoke. 'You have deliberately and flagrantly disobeyed an order, thereby endangering the safety of this ship and the life of every man in it. I urge you to take "Obedience" as a motto in future.' The boy, with some spirit, replied that he preferred his regimental motto. 'And what is that?' mouthed the CO, by now feeling very green. 'Firm,' said the drummer who was smartly dismissed before the CO made a most undignified dash to the heads. Relating the outcome of this saga later on he remarked to the rest of us, 'Discipline has been preserved, but the boy wins − it was too soon after my breakfast and I felt damn sick!'

It was a matter of personal sadness to me that within weeks of my arrival in Hong Kong I was called upon to attend a Court Of Enquiry into the behaviour of this same officer. We had not been particularly close friends but had shared a London flat for a while. He was an ebullient sort of character, full of enthusiasms, but rather prone to heavy fuel consumption. I was not the only one surprised to hear that he had been posted to China. My fellow Commanders on the troopship were all of the opinion that, unless he was able to take a very firm grip on himself, he would ruin his career within the year. Actually it happened much sooner than that. His alcohol consumption seemed to rise steadily the further east we got and all vestiges of self-respect were thrown to the four winds as he appeared on mess decks and in PO's cabins in a state of complete inebriation. The final straw was when he claimed to have discovered that his Messenger was completely devoid of any religious knowledge. He ordered the poor chap to present himself at his cabin nightly for 'religious instruction.' Since the boy was a practising Catholic, we saw this as a battle between the Pope and the Devil!

The Admiralty must surely have been aware of this man's dependence on the bottle. If not, his previous Captain must have concealed it. Such misplaced 'kindness' only makes things worse for everyone in the end, including the Service itself. If recommendations are not rigid and truthful the whole system crashes. We did our best for him in the short time available but the unanimous opinion was that he was medically unfit to continue to Hong Kong.

The Serious One showed great zeal in arranging lectures. To save the trouble of refusing him daily after my faltering debut in sail, I agreed to lecture on 'Submarines' when required. This was altogether more recent and therefore much safer territory. What on earth the men thought of this forced intellectual feeding I dare not imagine. Subjects on the Admiralty list (the Navy is often too thorough by half) included 'The Life of the Ant' and 'Worms and their Work.' Luckily we arrived in Hong Kong before anyone was persuaded to speak on the last!

As the end of our journey appeared on the chart so the loom of the C-in-C, Admiral Sir Frederic Charles Dreyer, came over the horizon. Far from lighting our passage into harbour, his spectre had a noticeably dampening effect on the entire ship's company and ever more lectures fell in torrents on our defenceless heads. By the time we docked just abreast of the *Bruce*, our conduct was exemplary! I looked across to my new command − 1,530 tons of destroyer, her slim, level funnels glistening in a chilly rain which had fallen upon us ever since we entered harbour. She had five 4.7-inch guns and six twenty-one-inch torpedo tubes arranged in two triple mountings. Her 40,000 horse power would take me cruising about the China Sea for the next two years, acting as a target for submarines to fire dummy torpedos at and then clearing up behind them afterwards.

11

Command on the China Station

POOR OLD *Bruce* was suffering from a bad bout of indigestion. Her rumbling boilers needed expert attention so we were laid up for three weeks more than I had anticipated while completing the refit. She was a pretty sorry sight when I boarded her to start getting installed. Peeling paintwork being stripped, dust and dirt everywhere and all the usual dockyard flotsam and jetsam lying around. It was a bit like turning into the gate of your new home in the removal van only to find that you had arrived on a building site. It was good to be back in Hong Kong though, and I spent some time renewing my acquaintance with familiar walks, restaurants and watering holes. There was a good cinema too. The New Territories were as remote and peaceful as ever. Heron, barking deer and whole flotillas of wild duck abounded. It was astonishing to be able to find such tranquillity within a few miles of bustling Victoria and the harbour. Nature supplied its own little excitements, however. I had to abandon ship and jump overboard during my first game of golf out at Fanling Golf Club. A very large and fast-moving water buffalo chased me across the eighth green. Fortunately it was muzzled.

The *Bruce* was not alone in suffering poor health. Captain (S) welcomed me heartily aboard the submarine depot ship *Medway* for my first briefing, greeting me with the disturbing statistic that they had a permanent VD list of between 40 and 60 men. He said it really was a serious problem on this station which had got a lot worse since Hong Kong had been 'cleaned up.' Previously there had been a sort of unofficial list of brothels which were more or less 'inspected' on a regular basis. The Administration got wind of this and with typical British hypocrisy announced that Hong Kong sailors would cease their traditional shore-based activities forthwith. To make sure they were no longer able to do what sailors have always done all over the world for hundreds of years, Sir Cecil Clementi, the Governor, had all the 'inspected' brothels closed down.

As far as Captain (S) and I could see, the only way to ensure the desired result from the Administration's point of view would have been to take the same action as the Imperial Court of China in the matter of its household staff. Remove the offending parts. Not even the Admiralty would put up with a parliamentary lobby to transform the British Navy into a bunch of eunuchs in the interests of moral propriety! The sailors carried on as they had always done but were forced into using 'sly brothels.' VD was rampant and the consequences were wholly predictable. It has always been a mystery to me why the British can't, like the French, acknowledge human frailties and stop aping the gods.

After the *Bruce* was recommissioned I decided I would have to speak to my crew on this subject. It was no good being mealy-mouthed. The evidence was sufficient to convince me that the vast majority of men would go with women even at the risk of disease. I needed a healthy and able-bodied crew and the way to achieve the same was through co-operation, not coercion. I endeavoured to appeal to their sense of cleanliness, their esprit de corps and their common sense in urging them to reflect in moments of exaltation and to try and keep enough will-power to take precautions. We promptly got three cases of German measles – a parting gift from our troopship – and spent a nervous couple of days living under threat of possible quarantine. Served me right! I later heard that on inspecting the aircraft carrier *Eagle*'s sick bay, the C-in-C paused beside a cot and enquired of its occupant, 'What is wrong with you?' The patient hastily spluttered out 'Opidermatoid scrofunenlus.' The C-in-C moved not a muscle of his face but turned to the PMO and asked, 'What is this illness?' 'VD, Sir,' came the crisp response. A good try. Almost a pity to spoil initiative like that.

Having addressed my own men, I in turn was called before the All Highest for interview. Ten minutes was my allotted period of sunshine as opposed to twenty for Captains. It was amusing to go on board the flagship and see the Commander playing with guards and bands as we used to in the old *Hawkins*. I secretly wished I were making my way to an audience with Admiral Leveson. That really would have completed the feeling of 'coming home.' This Admiral was a very different kettle of fish. His reputation as C-in-C went before him and it was quite plain from the gathering nervousness in our transport even before we had arrived that he operated on a 'rule by fear' principle. In the course of preliminary discussions with my fellow Commanders on the station I very quickly learned that little tolerance was shown towards independent initiative. Indeed it was roundly condemned unless it happened to be engraved upon one of the tablets of stone presently ballasting his flagship. 'Stop! Do not criticize! You are here to do what I want you to!' as so frequently said to his staff betrayed a policy of such arch-centralization that it could never, in my opinion, lead to anything but disaster in war. His abundant zeal may well have produced abject obedience (at the expense of killing off his staff from frustration) in peacetime because nothing was overlooked. Everything was controlled down to the last detail and it was this deliberate squashing of initiative which worried us. It could so easily lead to inaction in time of war and war was what we were here to prepare against. All these thoughts ran through my mind as I trimmed for my ordeal but, since I had now joined up, I thought I had better jettison them over the side and toe the line like a good boy.

I presented myself at the appointed time and was given a set homily on the virtues of leadership followed by a small dissertation on the events aboard the troopship. The meeting was rounded off with a few jovial reminiscences of the *Orion* and precisely nine and a half minutes later I was courteously dismissed — dazzled! Save for the passage of twenty years, little had changed.

Safely back on board the *Bruce* I made a reluctant start on the mass of Service literature I was expected to plough through. It looked as though it would probably take the whole of the commission to read and digest! Trying to find my bearings amidst the welter of paperwork which habitually surrounded our immediate god, I was appalled to think of the errors and pitfalls into which I might subside. The voluminous 'Most Secret' papers made interesting reading though, and I was forced to temper my criticisms of the C-in-C's style. Preparation for war is a thing which gradually fades over the horizon as one continues in years of peace, as we had done since 1919. The Admiral had to be given his due in making the organization for immediate hostilities his major consideration. This assumed of course that such instantaneous action would be necessary. Would the diplomatic wheels be capable of such quick revolution as to cause a war at a moment's notice? Communications had improved radically since the First World War. It was conceivable for a nation to be swept into aggression at such speed that no one would know anything about it until the first shot had been fired. The C-in-C's brief was to be ready for ignition. I myself doubted that things would happen that fast, if indeed they happened at all. The creaking of the diplomatic wheel would echo round the world a few times before hostilities were declared. But orders were orders and it was my job to make sure the 4th Submarine Flotilla was up to the mark.

There were various opinions current on the development of the political situation *vis-à-vis* Japan, Russia and China. In Hong Kong the feeling seemed to be that the Japanese would be content to consolidate their position in Manchukuo for the time being. They would then operate a penetrative policy, preparing the way in Mongolia, which would be their next move. Overt action in the form of a declaration of war on any of the big powers was not considered to be part of their strategy. Our arming of Hong Kong and Singapore, although prudent, was therefore unlikely to be put to the test. The C-in-C endorsed this belief, and I followed him. I could not help thinking that if Japan struck offensively as far south as Hong Kong, she would be deliberately sacrificing her greatest asset — geographical advantage. It seemed much more logical for her to pursue a policy of penetration and leave it to us or the USA to take the offensive. The Japanese meanwhile were pushing ahead as fast as they could in the Kwantung peninsula. Dairen, originally planned by the Russians and then captured by the Japanese in 1904 during the Russo-Japanese war, had become the premier port in North China.

Since I was to spend my time floating about up and down the China coast fairly detached from the world, it was interesting to hear first-hand accounts of what was going on inland from people who had had recent experience of events. The Chancellor of the Exchequer to the Shanghai Council, a man called Major Ford, had travelled home overland through Russia the previous summer. War had apparently been very close at that time. He said that the Russians were well prepared for conflict and he put the subsequent amelioration of the situation down to this fact. His view was that Japan's own stability was threatened by the internal power struggle going on between the civil administration and the military. She was consequently erring on the side of caution by consolidating her position in Manchukuo and was not, in his opinion, as aggressive as she appeared. He lamented the lack of our cruisers at Shanghai and said that we were losing a lot of face by not showing the flag in China more than we did. This echoed my own feelings as we had steamed into Singapore on the way out. The Cabinet was getting the wind up about Singapore's vulnerability and not before time in my humble opinion. Our weakness there was quite evident. As we went in to the P and O wharf we passed the *Terror* with her two 1.5 inch guns, anchored in the roads. She had only recently arrived as a panic stop-gap until the proper defence scheme was completed. Even if the place were never attacked, the defences would act as a powerful deterrent to discourage the Japanese from attempting occupation. In 1934 it would have been pathetically easy for them to just walk in and take it.

While sheer strength of numbers was an obvious priority in our defence and security arrangements for the Far East, the picture I was beginning to get convinced me that we were neglecting, at our peril, our proper peacetime function which was mainly diplomatic. The 'war tomorrow' threat under which the various captains were being asked to organize the Fleet exercises was really chasing a shadow and probably jeopardizing our overall image in the process. We seemed to be the legatees of a sort of 'Jutland complex' which so imbued our Leader's consciousness that he regarded the China Fleet as a 'Grand Fleet.' This was not Scapa Flow. When all was said and done we were really nothing but a cruiser squadron which would anyway have had to scuttle south in the event of war with Japan.

12

China Sea Exercises

MOVING THE *Bruce* from the dockyard to the buoy was the first manoeuvre of a surface ship I had done for some time. My Navigator, Elwin, who turned out to be a very good squash partner as we settled into the commission, had instructions to enquire my intentions if he thought I was about to err. One of the most important lessons you learn in a submarine is that your crew keeps you alive, and vice versa. It is absolutely no good thinking you are God Almighty and therefore always right. Of course, there is a command system, and orders must be obeyed, but there is also a great feeling of fellowship and mutual support. No 'face' is lost by asking for advice and indeed during certain submarine evolutions it is the job of one submariner to check the work of another, standing by him as he does so.

Moving the *Bruce* was not difficult but it was strange after commanding a submarine. The new helm orders took a bit of getting used to and twice I put the rudder the wrong way. My Navigator handled me with the utmost discretion whilst being extremely quick off the mark when it looked as though I might be heading inland!

The next day we went to sea and I must admit that Hong Kong Harbour looked an absolute nightmare from the bridge. It was crowded with vessels of every conceivable kind. There were conventional cargo boats, ocean liners, clinker-built junks with their high poop-decks and dark red batwing sails trailed by fussy little sampans scuttling everywhere. Criss-crossing the whole circus, the Star Ferry calmly plodded back and forth. The smell was indescribable.

The imminent prospect of piloting the *Bruce* out through that lot had made breakfast alone in my cabin a nervous way to start the day. I felt a lot better once we had actually slipped the mooring. The *Bruce* was far more flexible than any submarine and consequently I had much greater control. Nevertheless I felt insecure and was, once more, supported by my splendid Navigator who heartily endorsed the four siren blasts I directed at one reckless ferry charging straight at us. He abruptly changed his mind and went full astern!

I felt as though I was a very long way up, going abnormally fast and undulating to strange rhythms! In fact it was a perfectly ordinary bit of pilotage with no alarms. For almost the first time since my arrival in the Far

East the sun shone and as Victoria Peak drifted gently abaft our beam I began to feel the old familiar habits taking over. It took about a week for me to 'surface' properly.

I wanted to practise various elementary drills as a prelude to getting my crew shaken down. I also wanted to see what I was inheriting. There were a lot of replacements who had come out with me in the troopship and although I had talked to all of them I obviously had not seen them at work. They had to settle in, just as I did. There were new shipmates to get used to. The 'old' *Bruces* had played the 'new' *Bruces* at football while we were refitting and that had broken the ice a bit. There was the climate to cope with as well as a new ship and a quite different kind of shore life.

Our gentle exercise was quite creditable and we finally anchored in Taitam Bay where it was so warm that I let the hands bathe. Then I thought we'd better have a go at picking up a torpedo since this was, after all, our *raison d'être* in the South China Sea. We dropped a plank over the side to represent a 'fish' and I steamed away so as to approach at the right angle. The result was that we lost sight of it and spent a quarter of an hour circling before we finally found it and picked it up!

At last all our refurbishments were completed. The boilers boiled healthily away. My cabin was very tastefully done out in an attractive shade of pale green which set off the mahogany panelling and 'sackcloth' cushions rather well. My furnishing plans had gone a bit awry since the space was squarer than that I had measured up for, with the bath in a curtained recess off the sleeping cabin. Never mind. As I got my belongings unpacked and put away I felt quite pleased with my new kennel. I had worked out the details of a submarine exercise we were to do on the way north to Weihaiwei with the Captain (S), Alan Poland. He was a charming man and it was a genuine pleasure to serve under him. I was only sorry that, by the time my wife joined me later in the year, he and his family had been posted back to England. They would have enjoyed each other's company immensely.

Poland told me that he wanted me to superintend all submarine operations. This entailed a good deal of paddling between *Medway*, the submarine depot ship and *Bruce*, but I didn't mind this at all because it kept me in touch with the submarines. He made it quite clear that he was ready to leave the operational side very much to me, a responsibility I looked forward to. It would give me a chance to bring something of what I had learned as an active submariner to the organizational side. I would also be able to relieve him somewhat. The job of Captain (S) on the China Station with the *Medway* and twelve submarines to look after was one of the most arduous in the Navy — not to mention the additional burden of His Highness under which we all laboured.

Before we sailed north the *Bruce* received a Visitation from On High. His

Mightiness arrived fifteen minutes early which rather caught us with our pants down, but after inspecting the bridge and a mess deck he addressed the sailors. We were all pleasantly surprised. It was not nearly as bad as we had been led to believe, but still, his style was irritating and peremptory. Later that summer I was sitting in the harbour at Weihaiwei pondering on the movement of a typhoon reported to be in the Tsingtao area, two hundred miles away. Sunset the previous evening had shown a peculiar coppery gleam – a sure sign of impending meteorological fury. The morning brought low cloud, a fine penetrating drizzle and a large swell coming round the north-east promontory. All harbingers of doom.

The mine-layer *Adventure* was in the next berth to us, anxiously awaiting her own typhoon in the shape of the C-in-C who was due to carry out a full ship's inspection. I watched, through a telescope, the gradual building of a spider's web of wires, ropes, spars and what not as evolution followed drill. It was very hot and humid. The air was sodden. Water dripped from every spar and stay. I saw the flustered First Lieutenant come at last to an exhausted halt, remove his cap and mop his brow with an air of fatalism. I did my best telepathically to transmit my heartfelt feelings of deepest sympathy.

The inspection apparently did not go well and a small mistake in *Adventure*'s gunnery led to total damnation. It was just their luck that the C-in-C had become a gunnery specialist early on in his career and established a reputation as a prolific inventor of intricate gun controls and mechanisms. He rose to become the brightest star in the armament constellation. *Adventure*'s poor old Gunnery Officer looked as though nothing would have given him greater pleasure than firing the man smartly into the firmament.

Adventure's experience was not an isolated one and I really couldn't for the life of me see what profit there was in fixing on the one or two negative things while pointedly ignoring the one hundred and one positive aspects. These inspections came to be feared throughout the Fleet, instead of being occasions of slightly nervous pride. Morale suffered accordingly.

What a contrast to our own inspection by Captain (S) at the end of the summer cruise. We were suffering from a shortage of crew for various reasons but the ship looked better than at any time before. Wily Captain (S) wasn't having the wool pulled over his eyes that easily. At general drill he made us point ship with a kedge, land a platoon, rig all hoses for going alongside a burning vessel and rig sheers over the foremast capstan. This last caused a deal of headscratching for one of my officers who had no spars. He eventually used two shores from the fore messdeck. Our shortage of hands became apparent the minute Poland started to probe beneath the surface.

At Action Stations he killed me off almost at once and then proceeded to decimate the majority of the crew in the resulting chaos. He was extremely understanding and instead of taking the customary attitude of judicial severity, went round making affable conversation and cracking jokes. He had got rid of me right at the start of the battle quite deliberately just to see what would happen. Rather than condemn the ensuing mayhem, he was amused by it and my resurrection was a cheerful affair culminating in an assurance that all was very satisfactory and we should get a good report. There is a lot to be learned from that sort of attitude and I hoped that when I reached a similarly exalted position I would be able to impart the same air of friendliness in my official dealings with subordinates.

One of the most difficult and challenging parts of my job as second in command of the Flotilla was motivating the men. Our principal function was to show the flag up and down the China coast from Singapore in the south to the Kwantung peninsula in the north. We were not at war with anybody, although there was a great deal of speculation on the subject and my secret orders told me that readiness for action was the name of the game.

Preparing a lot of sailors and their ships to go to war when there is no war to fight involves putting them through various fairly mechanical evolutions and drills, time after time, so that their reactions speed up, their accuracy is spot on and their responses become automatic. During the First War aboard the *Orion* we used to be sent to Action Stations for an hour every day even when there was no action anywhere over the horizon. We would go through a dummy run of loading and firing the guns so that we could more or less do it in our sleep. In time of war, of course, adrenalin helps all this along. If you don't give it a hundred percent, or even a hundred and fifty at times, you lose the battle. It is a question of survival and the instinct to survive drives men on to outperform anything they could possibly achieve on an ordinary exercise.

There is nothing like an external threat to a community to meld its various dissenting members into a unified whole and concentrate their minds. Without the aid of open hostilities I somehow had to achieve and maintain this state of readiness, not only for my own crew in the *Bruce* but also for the twelve submarines in the Flotilla. It was not so much of a problem for the submarines because submariners tend to be very much a club anyway and they work under the constant threat of the enemy without − the sea. For the *Bruces* it was different. In a sense, they were nobody's children, standing apart from the rest as 'Flotilla Leader'. Leaders often find themselves curiously isolated from those they lead. It goes with the job. There is a 'barrier of respect' which either party crosses at his peril. If a subordinate goes too far he is upbraided or punished according to the seriousness of his breach. Despite this, he still knows where he is. The punishment itself bestows a kind of security. If, on the other hand, a Senior breaches this divide then not even the articles of the Naval Discipline Act can redress his position. He has put himself all at sea and there he is likely to founder.

Bruce and *Keppel* were both Flotilla leaders and, as such, were each communities unto themselves. The *Keppel* had reason to pat herself on the back after a recent satisfactory inspection by Himself which prompted an unusually laudatory report ending with the following gem: 'In the introduction to Admiral Cradock's book *Whispers From the Fleet* are found the words, "They are all alive!" This aptly describes the *Keppels*.' Naturally everyone offered Keatings by signal.*

When it came to the usual sort of Fleet competitions like regattas, which did so much for morale and the sailors' feeling of Fleet identity, Flotilla Leaders were all on their own. There were no other ships in their class. There were no other ships which did the same job. There were quite a few permanent niggles on this station heightened by the very uncomfortable climate, the crew replacements and the stultifyingly authoritarian atmosphere which percolated down from above. I scratched my head long and hard about how to get my own crew the way I wanted them and give them a clear sense of identity. The football match we had played while finishing the refit seemed to have gone down very well and created a certain amount of interest and camaraderie so I hit on the idea of a *Bruce* Trophy.

As we started our passage north via Chusan and Tsingtao I spoke to my crew to bring them up to date on matters of current interest and to outline for them the programme of work ahead of us. As well as nurse-maiding the submarines we had our own house to get in order and gunnery needed some attention. Our first attempt at a full-calibre shoot had distinguished itself by neither speed nor accuracy. Sluggish inertia would have more aptly described our thundering performance. Gun control was all right though, and we managed to straddle the target with our salvo, but spotting corrections didn't come out fast enough. Conditions were ideal for our first demonstration of bellicosity − flat calm, hazy afternoon sun and little wind. The noise of our own guns firing created a curious exhilaration in everyone. The ship's company could almost be seen physically to brace itself in anticipation of the sudden violent explosions which, as they erupted across the millpond of the South China Sea, released an excited and pugnacious joy on all decks. I could not share this exhilaration, having got it out of my system once and for all during the night action at Jutland. A passive distaste at the sound had lodged itself somewhere in my subconscious and refused to budge.

---

* The modern reader will be blessedly unaware of Keating's Powder, a preparation used in large quantities by the Services to discourage body lice and other unwelcome boarders!

The weather closed in for *Bruce*'s first night shoot and we essayed forth in a thick drizzle. Our puny searchlight, far from lighting the path ahead, only served to imprison us in a cloud of reflected droplets. This dampening slowed everything down for some reason. Gunnery seemed to be groping about rather than getting to grips with things. Eventually we fired star shells to illuminate the towing ship. My patience was wearing pretty thin as the minutes dripped on and nothing happened. Eventually my peevish remarks urged the poor Gunnery Officer into action and he got his guns off. In two minutes the agony was over. With a sigh of relief and removing great wads of cotton wool from my ears, I made for harbour only to run into a fog which caused us to anchor at sea for the night. Altogether a damp squib finish to a bad-tempered exercise but it was useful in that it broke the ice and showed the necessity for improvement in the spread of control.

This was the sort of thing I wanted to outline in very general terms to the crew as we started our cruise. It gave them a sense of purpose and hopefully enabled them to accept with greater understanding the reasons for some of the apparently senseless drills we had to perfect. They were just beginning to go off the boil when I told them I proposed to present a *Bruce* Trophy. The ship's company would compete for the prize, a spider on a web surmounted by a Naval crown all worked in Chinese silver. Eyes returned to the front and a small buzz of interest went round the deck. There would be a competition each month and once a quarter the trophy would be decorated with the colours of the winning section.

Having given the men something to enthuse about, I now needed a bit of encouragement myself to face the first exercise with submarines. My prayers were answered and the *Bruce* awoke to a perfect morning – calm sea conditions and a sun which poured a pleasant heat out of a clear blue sky. I was to pick up torpedos fired by submarines at the cruisers and managed to catch my 'fish' without loss or damage. A nice easy day to start off with. *Bruce*'s only casualty was her Captain's face, burnt fiery red in the unaccustomed sun. They could have rigged me on a forestay and used me as a spare port light!

The following days' manoeuvres cut me right back down to size. The submarines attacked *Medway* during the afternoon. *Bruce*'s role on these occasions was to keep well to heel until someone threw a torpedo. Then she had to go panting after it to retrieve. We collected three during the exercise. One hit the *Medway* and after circling round running on the surface, eventually hit me a resounding crack putting a 1″ dent in my delicate side. *Odin* fired her final contribution just at dusk as I was having a go at taking some star sights – a thing I hadn't tried for years. Darkness fell before we could find it. Sod's Law said there was no moon that night so we wandered around 'fishing' by searchlight. An hour passed. It was a glorious night, the intense black of the heavens prickled with stars, but for us demented 'fishermen' no bite!

Something had gone badly wrong with the submarines' navigation – they were miles out of position. Captain (S), with justification, displayed spleen by signal and called for reports on arrival at Chusan. It was a good job we weren't relying on my rusty astral navigation to get us there. When I checked with Elwin, my results differed from his by 4 miles. He checked my workings which seemed to be all right and tactfully suggested my altitudes may not have been very accurate. I resolved to practise. Navigation had always been an interest of mine, ever since the old sailing days when as a boy I had witnessed the mysterious rituals of sun-sights and star-sights. How on earth those magical passes with sextant and compass could possibly be translated onto the great blank space of a South Atlantic chart never ceased to astonish me. The resultant pencil mark indicating our position seemed akin to a miracle. To be only four miles out on my first miracle for some years didn't seem too bad and with a likeable and enthusiastic expert at my elbow I thought I should probably make progress.

13

Navigational and Other Hazards

THE CHINA COAST IS NOT an easy place to navigate. Tides are strong and variable. Fog is prevalent at certain times of the year. I was reminded of the poor little *Petersfield* as we passed the lighthouse on Tung Yin Island. Steering straight for it in thick fog, she counted on seeing the light but failed and met her end in a head-on crash. She was wrecked but there was, fortunately, no loss of life despite the fact that before running aground she had made two attempts to save another vessel, paralysed and in imminent danger of running on to a treacherously jagged shoreline battered by heavy seas.

The plight of this beleaguered junk had been relayed to the *Petersfield*, a 1,000-ton sloop employed as the C-in-C's yacht, from a signal station located on Tripod Island. The C-in-C, Admiral Sir Howard Kelly, Lady Kelly and their daughter Cynthia were aboard on passage from Shanghai to Hong Kong at the time. The C-in-C ordered the *Petersfield* to proceed to the junk's assistance.

Like his brother, Joe, who became C-in-C Home Fleet after Invergordon, Sir Howard was a man of strong personality. Unlike his brother he was not blessed with the gifts of tact or humour. He was an autocrat of formidable presence with an unerring talent for demoralizing all but those with the most robust constitution. Had *Petersfield's* newly-qualified and relatively inexperienced Navigating Officer felt confident enough to follow his quite proper instincts of extreme caution under the prevailing conditions of sea and visibiilty, disaster might have been averted. Had he made a firm alteration out to sea, towards Formosa and away from the hazardous 'inner' passage among the islands, the *Petersfield* might have arrived at her destination safe and sound – if slightly overdue. As it was, he found himself unable to make stronger representation against the C-in-C's insistence on taking a coastal 'short-cut'. The Captain was also under stress. He was undertaking his first voyage as a fully-fledged Commander and, although an experienced officer, was undoubtedly somewhat in awe of and possibly intimidated by his C-in-C whose every utterance had the ring of command. Finally, there was a senior Admiral of forceful personality and wide sea experience who had been a navigation specialist in his youth. Thus the *Petersfield* took the inner passage in adverse conditions and effected a successful rescue before she herself got into difficulties.

The disabled junk to whose assistance *Petersfield's* somewhat stressed Captain was ordered to proceed turned out to be rudderless, without sails, dismasted and suffering damage to her poop. She was at anchor but slowly dragging towards certain disaster when the *Petersfield* managed to get her in tow for the first time. She yawed so badly due to the absence of her rudder that, wherever the towing hawsers were secured, they gave way. A second attempt was made with a grass line. It failed. The two vessels finally parted company, leaving the junk in an even worse state than before, since she had had to cut her anchor away. The crew by this time was moaning in concert with pitiable supplication, a call duly answered by *Petersfield's* courageous whaler which succeeded in getting every man-jack of them off. The Captain of the junk, however, was not amenable to rescue, no matter what peril his saviours risked on his behalf. Enshrined on board were the bones of his ancestors. This priceless cargo was being transported in coffins to its final resting place according to Chinese custom. It took a couple of brawny sailors to moderate his histrionic and almost certainly suicidal devotion to filial duty but in the end Muscle triumphed over Moral and the entire company was safely landed on a nearby island from whence they would be able to return to their junk and salve the coffins once the seas had abated.

After the rescue the C-in-C decided to anchor for the night in a sheltered bay, if such haven could be found. It was, and early the next morning the *Petersfield* weighed and resumed her passage to Foochow. That night the fog clamped down again and in the early hours of the morning *Petersfield* went aground on Tung Yin Island. When it became clear that she could not be got off without sinking in deep water, the C-in-C gave the order to abandon ship. Lady Kelly, Cynthia, the Captain's dog and Lady Kelly's canaries were put ashore first, together with provisions and an armed guard to make sure no harm befell them. Tidal rips and inclement local weather systems were not the only terrors to be unleashed along the gaping jawline of this stretch of coast. Piracy was an ever-present threat and the armed guard was no mere formality. Even so the official reason for its existence was, first, the safe-keeping of the ship's cyphers and the C-in-C's confidential papers. They duly survived the bumpy ride through boiling surf and jagged rocks and were landed, securely, if somewhat damply, preserved from enemy eyes.

In response to an SOS from the *Petersfield* when she grounded, three ships altered course and steamed to her aid. Lady Kelly, Cynthia and the livestock were taken on to Hong Kong aboard the *Empress of Asia* while the *Suffolk* anchored some way off ready to send her boats across once things had calmed down a bit.

Naturally there were courts martial which must surely be unique in Naval history for the astonishing fact that the C-in-C was, in person, the convening authority and also the prosecutor's principal witness, being himself deeply

18. Mr Brock, the Wreckmaster from the *Vigilant*, makes a desperate attempt to enter the submarine through a manhole on the pressure hull with the intention of exposing the Z tank, the aftermost tank, in order for rescuers to cut through its thinner wall with oxyacetylene equipment. As the tail began to swing in the tide, Mr Brock was ordered off and could only watch helplessly as the submarine pivoted and disappeared.

19. Sad and forlorn, *Thetis* lies beached in Moelfre Bay, Anglesey. The damage to her periscope standards, conning tower and gun bear witness to the difficulties of the salvage operation.

17. The After Escape Chamber of HM Submarine *Tribune*, similar to
that of *Thetis*. The lockers contain DSEA sets, the cylinders watertight
torches and the brass plaque on the door is inscribed with operating
instructions. The chamber could be entered from either side of the
bulkhead and operated internally or externally. The escapees could be
monitored through the sighting ports at the top and the upper hatch
operated by rod gearing. This cumbersome system was replaced in later
T class and other submarines by an escape hatch and a simple method
of flooding the whole compartment.

15. HM Submarine *Thetis* takes to the water on 29 June, 1938. Launched by Mrs A. J. Power, *Thetis* was destined for a very short career, 99 people dying in her during diving trials one year later. 62 more sailors perished when she was lost in action having been re-launched under the name *Thunderbolt* after salvage from Liverpool Bay, five months after the accident.

16.   The last known shot of the *Thetis* taken shortly before her fatal dive from the Isle of Man Steam Packet *Fenella*.

14. The proud father encouraging the continuation of the family
tradition. Captain Oram with his son, Cadet John Oram, at HMS
Dolphin, 1938. John served throughout the war in sea-going ships,
preferring the continuous excitement of destroyer life to the occasional
thrills of submarines. He saw considerable action in HMS *Obedient* and
HMS *Zealous*, including several trips escorting the Russian convoys in
the Arctic, jobs regarded by many sailors as nightmare experiences.
John Oram retired from the Navy with the rank of Lieutenant
Commander.

implicated in the disaster. The press had a field-day and a lot of dirty linen was washed in public. The disaster underlined, to my mind, a gross failure of the system which was beginning to worry me more and more as I climbed up the ladder of command. There is no doubt that the *Petersfield* had been in the hands of three very skilled and able men, all of whom were perfectly willing to employ that skill to save the ship, but they were constrained by inhibitions fostered, if not directly imposed upon them, by the system within which they worked. It was a supreme irony, matched only by the healing of the personal feud which had raged between the brothers Kelly for untold years. The *Petersfield* accident brought them together again, but it had the detrimental effect of dividing the China Station between those who came out in support of their C-in-C and those who favoured *Petersfield's* Captain. This, not unnaturally, generated quite an atmosphere on the station and was partly responsible for the state of affairs I found on my arrival there almost three years later. The intervening period had of course seen a quite substantial change of personnel and the C-in-C himself had been succeeded. However, new faces do not always betoken renewed morale and it was particularly unfortunate that Admiral Kelly's autocratic rule gave way to an almost equally impermeable authoritarianism in the shape of Admiral Dreyer. The aftershocks of the *Petersfield* incident could still, on occasions, be clearly felt.

The convening of two courts martial absorbed the entire resources of the China Station in terms of Captains and Commanders in command. The C-in-C's secretary was allotted the unenviable but interesting task of prosecutor. After it was all over, *Petersfield's* Captain had to kick his heels in Hong Kong waiting for passage home in the *Berwick* which was due to pay off in England two months hence. Under normal conditions he would have been sent home by the first P and O but it was 1931 and Naval economies dictated by the deepening financial crisis on the other side of the globe blasted their way clean through any such fine points of Fleet sensitivity.

As I got into my stride in the new job and began to take soundings, all manner of treacherous little undercurrents started rippling their way to the surface, compounded by unavoidable irritants like the enervating climate, the permanent health problem on the Station and The Lord Almighty. There were times when I would have heartily welcomed a declaration of open aggression by Japan. At least it would have melded the somewhat divided company unto a unified whole and made them forget their petty internal politicking. However, the best I could do was muster my Flotilla to be prepared in the event of such action and it turned out that plucking torpedoes out of the vastness of the South China Sea was not the fairground pastime of 'hooking the fish' that it sounded.

The ship-handling part of it was an art in itself — to locate the beast in the first place and then get alongside at the right angle to retrieve it on board presented quite a challenge. There were other, unforeseen difficulties.

Chinese steamers seemed to have a penchant for wandering over to have a look when we were angling anywhere within range. Our frenzied signals and hoots were brazenly disregarded as these arrogant little craft nonchalantly lined themselves up to ram our quarry gently floating on the surface.

I got the dickens of a shock one morning when a spout of water appeared dangerously close on my starboard bow. Thinking it was one of my submarines — *Oswald* — surfacing, I let fly a few choice expletives and prepared to remonstrate with him in no uncertain terms. A whale popped up, had a look at us, and popped back again!

Today, when submariners can 'submerge' on dry land in a computer-controlled simulator which looks and feels exactly like the control room in the real thing, all our exercises pale into insignificance. One can even fire a torpedo ashore now, whereas in my day the only way to learn was by taking the boat down and giving the order to 'Fire One!' They had to be recovered because they were jolly expensive items. There was only a finite quantity of them. We couldn't simply wire home to Mother for replacements if we started to run short. The loss of a torpedo on exercise was a serious enough affair to warrant an enquiry.

Most of the time we were successful retrievers, even under quite difficult conditions, but occasionally we slipped up. One sticky June day of water-laden wind and muggy squalls, I was at sea with the submarines. The exercise had not been a great success. The whale appeared ahead of me again to the severe detriment of my nerves. *Odin* followed this up by finishing an attack 100 yards on my beam. To get as close as that was a bit over the odds and courting disaster. I had no wish to act the role of tin opener and said as much at a post mortem afterwards.

We had sailed at 06.48 and I spent the next twelve and a half hours on the bridge, picking up sixteen torpedoes and giving the submarines twelve dummy attacks. These attacks were a sort of cat and mouse game which involved the submarines creeping up on me and trying to get within a certain pre-determined range without me spotting them. If they managed to get inside the circle then I was 'hit'. If I spotted them before they went deep then the attack had failed. On this particular occasion *Rainbow* missed his attack and *Orpheus* lost a torpedo.

The loss of a 'fish' being a potentially serious matter, we knew we were in for long hours of diving to recover it. We were lucky in managing to mark the position accurately with a buoy and were optimistic when we returned just after dawn the next morning towing a diving boat astern. We started sweeping the bottom with two whalers. The first time the sweep caught, the divers reported a false alarm. The second time we were quite convinced we'd got the damn thing but the divers once more reported nothing to be seen. We were about ready to pack up and go back to harbour with the threat of an official enquiry looming over our horizon when a shout went up and to our joy the divers reported the torpedo buried in mud with only a foot of its tail visible.

How to extricate this fish from its underwater lair was the next dilemma. One of the divers took down a wire which he shackled onto the torpedo's tail. I brought the *Bruce* round and took the wire to the capstan. So heavily was the torpedo embedded that we actually hove the ship up to it and I was just wondering what to do next when to my enormous relief it came up covered in clay. It must have buried itself by its own momentum. We were naturally elated at recovering it and returned to harbour in celebratory mood. The operation had taken the whole day and we were not in our berth until after nine. I sank, exhausted, into my bunk.

That the submarines' performances in attack were improving as the summer wore on was beyond doubt. Nevertheless, I felt we needed some sort of measurable scale, so I started to draft out a system of attack analysis. This enabled both Captain (S) and myself to differentiate individual submarine performances at a glance and so judge comparative efficiency. It took a while to perfect and involved SSOs in some additional record-keeping but in the long run it cut out an awful lot of investigative post mortems. Results of exercises were recorded at the time of action and in such a way that their implications were immediately apparent. I found it a great help.

It was not until somewhat later in the commission when I found myself taking part in a special patrol born of the fertile brain of the C-in-C that I realized how my own 'innovation' had probably been received by those who had to put it into action. The submarine *Phoenix* was singled out for the doubtful honour of testing the effects of a prolonged patrol in hot weather on a submarine crew. A Medical Officer would be present to assess results. For a full fourteen days she stayed dived during daylight hours, only arising from all-enveloping boredom after nightfall to recharge her batteries. Eventually the *Bruce* took her turn with a patrol of darkened destroyers in playing her at a game of nocturnal 'tig'. The idea was to see if the submarine could spot the destroyers before the range got down to 1000 yards. Presumably the assumption was that the longer the submarine personnel had been submerged, the dimmer their eyes and wits would become. They would therefore be less likely to make a successful attack or escape unnoticed.

Bruce steamed off to the rendezvous at 2130. It was a calm, moonless night and forty miles later we dowsed our lights and moved into the 'zone'. On this night the honours were even. Phoenix didn't see me the first time I went in but later on spotted me a mile away. I wondered how *Suffolk's* Surgeon Commander was doing. He was very familiar with psychological and physiological conditions in submarines and had gone aboard earlier in the day to take copious records and samples. These would no doubt be added to the considerable pile of information which already existed on the subject. The fact that a lot of us involved in this patrol had fought a war under conditions considerably less favourable to submarine personnel seemed to be summarily discounted by those who had not been in it. Each investigator is in his own eyes a pioneer. The Surgeon Commander's approach to his work was luckily well-balanced by a healthy sense of the ridiculous. He felt that the effects of long-term submersion on the crew's alertness could be quite adequately measured by issuing a deck of cards and getting the Officers to cut the POs for drinks.

I am quite sure that the objects of my own submarine efficiency scheme regarded that whole business as unnecessary and savouring of pedantry. They undoubtedly groaned with exasperation and immediately classified me as yet another paper merchant. They were probably quite right, except that from where I stood on the bridge, I called it enthusiasm!

Shortly after getting my little scheme operational, I received my come-uppance. Together with three fellow Commanders I was instructed to form a board to examine midshipmen from the *Cumberland* in seamanship. It was so long since I had done any formalised seamanship myself that this intelligence provoked uncomfortable schoolboy twinges round the back of the collar! I was not alone. Emergency signals flashed back and forth. The reluctant quartet rendezvoused to commiserate in my cabin one evening. Anyone walking in would have thought we were plotting the annexation of Northern China, so confidentially were our serious heads drawn together over half-empty whisky glasses. Actually it betokened mild panic. The upshot of our initial war-conference was that the exam was more in the nature of a Commanders' seamanship course and had undoubtedly been planted on us as such! The tension was suddenly relieved by a splash of oars and a hoarse voice cheekily yelling, 'Look out and shut yer lower deck scuttles for the bow wave when we comes back!' It was a racing cutter's crew being towed past to the started point of a practice pull for first *Bruce* Trophy competition.

I was looking forward to the competitions. There was a certain air of purpose about the ship. We started with a two-part test of rifle efficiency. For the first part, teams of a leader and six men had to perform various simple marching movements finishing in line in front of the judges. They were then required to 'Fix Bayonets' and 'Present Arms' before being inspected. To my amusement this caused instant perturbation, so I gave the teams a chance to practise by sending the whole jolly lot off with the Gunner. He was quite impressed and reported back that they were very keen and extremely smart, despite sweating profusely under the hot summer sun! The second part of the test was for teams of five men (who had not been in Part One) to equip themselves quickly and correctly in 'Marching Order'. They looked like over-decorated Christmas trees the first time they tried it, but there was time in hand for improvement. It was up to them to get on with it and, by jove, they did.

The competition was rounded off with a 'regatta day' which was one of the happiest I had spent since leaving England. It went down so well that I thought it would be a good idea to get our summer exercises at Weihaiwei off to a celebratory start. I asked the Lord High Executioner's permission to organize a Fleet Regatta in the harbour soon after we all arrived. Poland was keen on the idea since it would be a good opportunity for socializing between ships who had been off round the place doing different jobs for the last few months. It was also a chance to involve the shore community in our fun. The *Bruce* had her own contests enthusiastically established by now and it was time to get the whole Flotilla together to let off steam a bit. Permission was granted and over by the mainland in serried ranks we lay, waiting for the starting gun of the first race. It was a perfect day, warmer than any so far but with a light breeze which kept things comfortable.

The high spot of the two-day event was provided by the aircraft carrier *Eagle's* wardroom crew. These bronzed he-men pulled their race, coming in a very creditable second. It was so warm they wore no singlets. The mighty voice of Jove, terrible in its intensity, dictated the following masterpiece: 'From C-in-C to *Eagle*. Commander-in-Chief took a party of ladies to witness the Officers' race and was amazed to see *Eagle's* crew pulling without singlets half naked. The C-in-C, who has been 43 years in the Navy, has never seen such a spectacle and is extremely displeased. The Coxwain of the boat is instructed to repair on board the Flagship forthwith in dress number 8B with sword to report to C-in-C.' The unfortunate coxswain duly arrived, this time fully clad, and apprehensively entered the Presence. Since he was not seen again one can only suppose he was blasted to eternity.

The C-in-C himself then vanished over the horizon to Japan in the *Suffolk* to speed the renowned Japanese Admiral Togo on to his eternity. Following the announcement of the great man's death, this message of condolence was despatched: 'And this man died leaving his death for an example of noble courage and a memorial of virtue not only unto young men but to all his nation'. Its solemnity was rather undermined by a cryptic 'Two McBEES' following the quotation. After some difficulty I deciphered this as being the signalman's representation of the Second Book of Maccabees!

The C-in-C, despite being forced to appear in stockinged feet, did the Navy and Great Britain proud by delivering a remarkably fine funeral oration over the unsuspecting Togo's corpse. His impressive demeanour went down extremely well and British shares boomed in appreciation on the Japanese market. One retired Japanese Admiral present at the ceremony approached the Captain of the *Suffolk* afterwards and, with a stiff bow, abruptly remarked, 'Your power is your discipline.' He then made a second bow and withdrew. The *Suffolk's* guard had evidently been called to attention as he passed, whereas American, French and Italian crews had ignored him! A pretty tribute. Greater honour yet was in store. As the *Suffolk* was leaving, two Japanese cruisers and an aircraft carrier were sent out as a mark of respect to the C-in-C. This went totally against the Japanese norm of intense secrecy and reluctance to display. When some miles distant, one of the cruisers was observed by the *Suffolk* to be firing. Up popped the Fleet Gunnery Officer who, stop-watch in hand, reported to the C-in-C that their rate of fire was slow. Only 8 rounds a minute. It was later discovered that the cruisers had in fact been saluting the C-in-C's flag!

Admiral Togo was an astonishing man, ranking in popular estimation second to Nelson I should think. He was educated in the *Worcester* and whilst I was there came and visited the ship. It was 1910. I was fifteen and totally in awe of this diminutive but none the less impressive figure. I was cox of the boat that took him ashore. I wasn't sure whether I would expire from nerves at getting the thing alongside smoothly without pitching the Admiral overboard or pride at being told off to escort him to his car. As we walked together he asked, 'How many have you in the *Worcester*?' I replied, 'One hundred and sixty, Sir.' This caused consternation. Our lines had obviously got fouled somewhere and I began to splutter with embarrassment. The kindly ADC extricated me with a kedge. The Admiral, he gently explained, was interested to know how many years I had been in the ship.

14

Showing the Flag

TOWARDS THE END OF the summer *Bruce*, with four submarines darting playfully about her, cruised north to Chingwangtao, a mere stone's throw from where the Great Wall of China comes down to the sea. Here we met the end of a line as powerful in its imagery as the Equator. More so, since it was in reality a physical barrier. Within its confines lived a large part of the human race. For them, the Wall represented the outer limits of civilization. Beyond was the wilderness. It is a remarkable fact that late twentieth century astronauts viewing their own planet from the wilderness of space have been able to pick out the Great Wall quite distinctly. From our vantage point in the Gulf of Chihli, any stray echoes of the mysterious Middle Kingdom still resonating faintly down the centuries through those gigantic stones were firmly smothered by a pall of black coal dust. Chingwangtao was the only decent natural harbour on the north China coast. Its main business was the export of coal from mines at Kailan. Trade seemed to be brisk. We were aware of considerable traffic in and out of the roads as we splashed about on exercise before setting a south-easterly course which would take us around the tip of the Kwantung Peninsula to Dairen for a series of official calls.

Things did not get off to a very auspicious start. I entered harbour at 1000 and lay like a wilting wallflower for half an hour, completely disregarded and with no idea where to go. Having been invited to the ball, we were left standing in the courtyard with no one to greet us. Eventually what appeared to be a passer-by in a motor boat directed us to a buoy in the harbour where, having secured, we were visited by the Harbour Master and Port Doctor. The Consul sent a message to say he had arranged official calls for the next day. We got ourselves sorted out and scrubbed down after the exercises on passage and then looked out our best bibs and tuckers.

The foul morrow dawned, wet and windy. Just the weather to send us rejoicing into the diplomatic breach where conversation would no doubt proceed in excrutiatingly slow time through an obsequious interpreter. The participants in this obligatory game of International Courtesy Calling would exchange the usual greetings with passable spontaneity before glazing over. With expressions of fixed interest they would then each frantically try to remember what the beginning of the sentence had been about. The longer the 'discussion' went on, the more each would begin to resemble an infant desperate to break wind. The prospect of two or three days of that sort of thing, endured in steamy bathroom conditions stirred up by the odd wet blow from an errant typhoon, did not appeal. However, duty called. *Bruce's* motor boat was out of action so my First Lieutenant and I, in clean white uniforms, had to go ashore in a whaler. We arrived to start on our round of official calls decorated with patches of damp.

Dairen was much bigger than I had expected. We passed extensive wharves dealing with a large volume of trade in and out of Manchukuo. We met the Civil Administrator, the Mayor and the President of the South Manchuria Railway. The first was affable and the second an unpleasant upstart. I was wrong on all counts about the tenor of the visit. Polite conversation was carried on through the Consul, a very friendly and interesting man called Austen. He was doing everything possible to help the British Navy, having lived in Japan for 30 years. In spite of this he had no love for the Japanese and described Japan as being, 'A third class power with a first class nerve'. He said that the great mistake we had made in Europe was in accepting Japan as an equal of the great powers.

We were able to speak directly with the President of the South Manchuria Railway, a quiet, scholarly man whose name was Count Hayashi. His English was good. He held the rank of Cabinet Minister and appeared to be the virtual ruler in this area. His appointment two years earlier had come as quite a surprise locally. There had apparently been a good deal of political skirmishing over the post. The choice of a mild recluse had upset many calculations. Though quiet, he was an approachable man who answered our questions gravely and in as much detail as we could have expected. Austen filled in the rest when we were out of earshot. This combined intelligence, very much from the horse's mouth, confirmed our speculations about the thrust of current Japanese policy.

Consolidation in Manchukuo was a means towards redressing the imbalance of the vast Japanese National Debt. The country's domestic economy had been in a parlous state for some time. Large blocks of bonds had been floated on the open market to fund Japan's expansionist policy in South-East Asia. Nothing had been invested at home. Instead, huge amounts of money and goods were being poured into Manchukuo in the pursuit of an Imperialistic colonial dream.

Now the race was on to see whether the infrastructure which had so quickly been put in place in the Kwantung Peninsula would enable Manchukuo trade to bale out the home budget before the impending financial crash came. The targets were extraordinary. Over the following three years, that is by 1937, the Japanese were planning to treble Dairen's cargo capacity. New wharves were already under construction and arrangements were being made to increase the town's Japanese population to one million. Count Hayashi's supremacy was explained by the fact that the South Manchuria Railway owned pretty well the whole place.

Relations between the USSR and Japan were in equilibrium since the Russians were aping the Japanese in the Vladivostok area by developing it as fast as they possibly could. It looked as though this uneasy balance would continue for some years before either side would be free to turn its attention to the perpetually conflicting interests they each held in China. For the time being it was enough that the Japanese made life as difficult and unpleasant as they could for all foreigners in Dairen and Manchukuo, something I was later to witness at first hand as I travelled back to England overland through China and Russia at the end of my commission.

My concern at what I felt to be the lack of visibility of the British Navy in these waters seemed to be justified by the story which unfolded as we steamed about our business up and down the China coast. Austen had drawn an interesting parallel between the capture of Tsingtao in 1914 and a possible attack on Hong Kong which he felt might well prove to be a campaign of a similar nature. The outstanding points in the broad scheme of operations were the distance at which the Japanese had made their landing (100 miles); the length of time that the landing of a force of 50,000 had taken; the need for close contact in combined operations and finally the great value of an eminent position in directing gunfire. His feeling was that, if it came to the point in Hong Kong, the Japanese would be occupied for at least eight weeks in landing their men and in preliminary fighting before they were faced with our first strong line of defence.

Although not relishing the shore-based exercises which lay ahead, we determined to approach them in a properly seamanlike manner and carry them through, dressed over all in suitable diplomatic apparel. The results of our efforts were somewhat mixed. On completion of our first round of official visits in the forenoon, we were appraised of our social engagements for the evening before braving the whaler again for lunch aboard the *Bruce*. I got back to find a typhoon warning posted and the submarines away at anchor. All junketings ashore were smartly cancelled.

Our economic and political education was completed two days later when, the typhoon having sashayed tantalisingly close and then gone roaring off in a completely different direction, courtesy calls were returned aboard ship. The Civil Administrator and Mayor partnered each other for this duty, accompanied by a pleasant little interpreter called Mori. With unconscious humour the Mayor explained at some length that the Japanese were a people who lived only for peace. He explained that the Sino-Japanese War, the Russo-Japanese War and the so-called 'Manchukuo incident' of 1932 when Manchuria had been set up as a puppet Japanese state had been forced upon them. He assured us that they had gone not a step further than was absolutely necessary, but he understood that some foreigners held the very mistaken attitude that the Japanese were aggressive. This calumny, he rather naively explained, could only have been perpetrated by Japan's poverty as propagandists!

For me, the high spot of the visit to Dairen, conducted almost entirely in the oppressively murky weather surrounding a tropical storm, was making my first voice recording. This technological première was facilitated by Mr Ken Asaoka, late of the Japanese Embassy in London, who captured my attention at a conventionally starchy official reception by describing a machine which he had invented for making gramophone recordings. My First Officer and I were captivated by the retired diplomat's lively enthusiasm and accepted the offer to visit his home and see the contraption with rather more motivation than we had been able to summon up for the obligatory reception.

We were greeted at the door by the inventor and his wife (the fattest Japanese woman I had ever seen) colourfully attired in native dress and wreathed in smiles. There was much bowing and giggling and business with outdoor shoes and slippers. We were led across a peaceful ante-room floored with fragrant tatami matting into the main reception room of the house. The machine sat in solitary splendour on a low lacquered table finished to such a violent sheen that it mirrored our curious and admiring gazes with disconcerting clarity. The invention was quite remarkable. It could record voices, record from a gramophone record, record telephone conversations, in fact almost anything seemed to be possible. The loudspeaker for playing back the sound was a standard gramophone or wireless set and the cost of this innovative piece of apparatus was a mere $323. The visitors were invited to perform. Our shyness of the microphone was somehow intensified by the nakedness of our very large European feet, scantily disguised in dainty 'house slippers'. We eventually succeeded in recording messages to our respective children. The results were astonishingly clear though uninspiringly parental.

The visit to Dairen seemed to be going very well from an official standpoint and that, after all, was why we were there. The only, relatively minor, political problem we had on our hands was an objection to the Flotilla visiting Tsingtao in the autumn on account of Japanese manoeuvres in the area, until, that is, Our Father's secret war plans were very nearly triggered prematurely by three sailors and a taxi-driver.

The whole thing had been precipitated by the seamen getting into a brawl with the driver who locked them into his cab until they agreed to pay up. A policeman was called. On sighting the law, the miscreants exercised uncharacteristic initiative and dived out of the cab's windows. The policeman gave chase and one of these wretched seamen hit him. The three got away and vanished. A perfectly innocent stoker was then arrested and placed in prison where, because he wouldn't confess, he was hit about the head and face with a truncheon at intervals of four hours.

Meanwhile the police had turned very nasty. In Japan, if you hit a policeman you hit the Emperor and there was hell to pay. All might have been settled if two blithering idiots in my crew had not thought fit to try and get away with a souvenir from the Perroquet Club where they had obviously been sampling a good deal of the local brew. They couldn't filch anything so mundane as a beer mug or even one of the smaller prints adorning the walls. Oh no. They had to go for a full-grown potted palm tree which they attempted to bring back on board. They were obviously more than half-seas over when they attempted the theft. The weight and awkwardness of their booty took them the rest of the way before they had even cleared the steps of the club. They fell out into a crowd of angry Japanese wielding baseball bats. One sailor had his arm broken and the other was knocked unconscious. Somehow or other they both managed to get away.

A third man who had peacefully slept through all this commotion with his head on a table inside the club then woke up and decided it was his bedtime. He rather unsteadily rose to his feet and lurched over to the door. He had not gone more than a few steps down the road before he too was set upon, wounded quite badly in the head and then arrested and flung into gaol.

The police took the attitude that the behaviour of our men was beyond all bounds, was inciting the citizens to riot and was tantamount to a diplomatic incident. I groaned inwardly. This was the precise opposite of the intended impression our 'diplomatic' call was supposed to impart to the aggressively colonizing and only too flammable expatriates of the Land of the Rising Sun. With great difficulty we managed to spring the gaol-birds from their unwholesome cage on promising to pay damages at the rate of £6 each. Poor devils – wrongfully arrested, ill-treated then forced to pay. The police threatened that if there were one more case of hooliganism they would not be able to guarantee protection for ordinary British residents against the inflamed passions of the mob. Since it seemed from reports I had received that the flames certainly needed no fanning, I had no alternative but to stop all leave. Apart from the risk of a casual encounter with the police there was the chance that those of my men who had been accidentally caught up in events and who were naturally incensed would organize a party to go ashore and beat the place up. It came to light later on that just such a band had formed up to take revenge, so it was as well that I confined all hands on board. It went against the grain though to limit the amusement of the 99% who behaved extremely well on shore because 1% behaved like fools, but that 1% had let the side down badly. I talked to all the *Bruce* and submarine sailors along these lines and they seemed to take it reasonably philosophically. I could have strangled those two idiots with the palm tree though!

Trying to get to the bottom of the whole débâcle was not so easy. The sailors shut up like clams. It was pretty clear, as far as I was concerned, who had hit the policeman in the first place but whether or not I could raise enough evidence to prove it was another matter. A foolish able seaman appeared to have been the ring leader in both incidents. Instead of taking up his rightful abode in a cosy police cell, he finished up with a broken arm in Dairen hospital. I could cheerfully have broken his neck as well.

Events determined me to take the rather unusual step of talking to all my ABs privately on their mess deck to point out that the acts of one had to be the responsibility of all. This 'heavy father' approach was greeted with a sullen silence. I suppose I could not have expected much else. Thinking I might as well give my head one final bash against the brick wall before departing with all pomp and circumstance I also pointed out that one sixth of the ABs had contracted VD since the start of the commission. This got slightly more reaction than my disciplinary comments on shore behaviour, but only just!

Quite naturally the wrath of the Almighty fell upon my head and I was summoned to explain myself. I was expecting this of course, but assumed that it would not happen until after I had put in my official report on the incidents. This could not be completed until I was in full possession of the facts, so to receive a thorough dressing down in advance of my report left me feeling angry and disheartened.

I stood before the Admiral, quite prepared to take responsibility for my men. 'I wish,' he enunciated in a tone of clipped determination, 'to know precisely what happened.' I told him. I also pointed out that certain matters were still under investigation and a full report was being prepared. He brushed this aside as though removing an offending fly and announced, 'I do not wish to prejudge the issue.' There was a lengthy pause before, in his customary ponderous style he did just that. 'When I go ashore in Japan, not as a full Admiral but as an ordinary man, I find myself surrounded with the greatest courtesy. This business of hitting people and breaking up cafes is most reprehensible and discourteous and your men must be made to realize this fact.'

I had been expecting something along these lines. I pointed out that my men certainly recognized this and that the incidents were the work of just three troublemakers. This could not dislodge the Executioner's expression of frozen distaste. I was then told that a ship's company must be responsible for the deeds of any one man and that it appeared to him that my crew was riotous. He followed this by adding, 'A short time ago when I gave you permission to hold a regatta your men made a tremendous noise in the harbour,' implying that the Dairen rowdyism was only to be expected from such a motley crowd. This infuriated me and I said that I accepted full responsibility for the regatta and had organized it myself. I added that my men were perfectly decorous and that Captain (S) and Mrs Poland had been on board the *Bruce* for the duration. His only answer to that was 'I know. I have seen Captain Poland.' I was duly dismissed and departed with my tail between my legs, fuming at what I perceived as the iniquity of the judgement! What sort of progress, I rather dismally reflected, had been made over the last twenty years. We might just as well have been aboard the *Orion*, he in his Captain's cuddy and me a lad of nineteen quaking before him. Was that the way my boys saw me?

Poland sent for me the next morning to find out how I had got on. He showed a complete understanding for my feelings and I was very grateful to him. In the warmth of the moment he unburdened a few tales to me. In spite of the greatest respect and loyalty he commanded on this station through skilful and friendly handling of personnel, he too had had some bitter pills to swallow. This exchange of confidences made me feel a lot better and I determined to persist with my approach to leadership. I had always felt the personal touch to be the key. Poland agreed with me, commenting that history bore this theory out. He consoled me over the regatta, saying that he and Mrs Poland had thoroughly enjoyed themselves. He remarked on the curious amnesia which crept over people on this station. Things became far more difficult to remember and the effort required to keep up to standard increased the longer one served here. It applied particularly to Hong Kong where the climate was very enervating. He singled out the ideas of the *Bruce* Trophy and the ill-fated regatta as events which had helped to banish this lethargy. They had also increased the men's *esprit de corps*, general pride in their appearance and willingness to put up with some of the more tedious jobs they had to do. My hackles subsided under this sympathetic panegyric and I once again counted myself extremely lucky to benefit from Poland's sensitive and wise leadership. The gods, spearheaded by Our Father, seemed to be doing their damnedest to torpedo the Dairen cruise completely though. Even the native deities were keeping a little something up their ample sleeves for me as we steamed south to recover both dignity and equilibrium. The final call was to Chefoo where our berth lay cradled protectively inside the breakwater. The Chinese pilot was brought on board, a tiny black speck ascending the Jacob's ladder, and came on to the bridge where we bowed and greeted each other with the proper decorum. After a brief consultation I said, 'Right you are, Pilot, you take her in.' 'Very good, Captain!' came the thickly accented response and then, somewhat to my surprise, a command to the engine room of, 'Full speed ahead both!' The engine room, quite naturally, obeyed and I found myself practically dismasted as we suddenly shot ahead at thirty knots. The look of terror on the poor pilot's face was something to behold as he beseeched the galloping *Bruce* with shouts of panic to go 'Full astern, Captain! Full astern!' The engine room must have been pretty astonished too, although we were in no danger at all because there was plenty of room in the wide bay. The pilot who, it later transpired, was accustomed to handling ships with a top speed of about 8 knots, suffered considerable loss of face not to mention loss of balance. The incident had its funny side of course, but, coming as it did on top of our recent adventures, it made me groan inwardly and long for the blessed peace of Liukung golf course.

I was very proud of the *Bruce*. I think the men were too. Ship appearance was one thing that had struck me when I arrived on station. Not that I had taken over a shoddy vessel. Not a bit of it. But she had been refitting, the crew had had time to move one or two points off the wind and there had been a lot changes. No one out here seemed to mind as much as they did at home. Ships were clean, but they were allowed to get slovenly. There was a noticeably more casual attitude towards the men's dress. Gym shoes were freely worn and blue shirts were almost a working uniform. In the weeks spent exercising before the summer cruise the men had pulled together well and got themselves and their vessel looking very shipshape. Even at play now they were displaying some pride. They had all gone ashore in Hong Kong and kitted themselves out with silk football shirts in their respective colours so that the field became a blaze of red, blue, orange and white on fixture days. They also sported cricket caps quartered in the ship's colours, red and blue, which added to the polycromatic discord. Poland and I were both somewhat at a loss to understand why an officer should be reproved because his men showed a bit of spirit in activities which were after all sporting, not bellicose. I could not get free of the aftershocks of the Dairen incident though. Weeks after we had got back down to Weihaiwei a retired Chinese Admiral who lived on the mainland and who had amassed great sheaves of cuttings from the Chinese papers collared the C-in-C. The newspapers had so grossly exaggerated events, reporting almost daily armed clashes on the streets of Dairen, that the poor little Admiral was quite convinced we were going to war with Japan. The Chinese community was awash with rumours of the imminent outbreak of hostilities!

15

Piracy!

THE SNOTTIES' (and, therefore, Commanders') seamanship exam loomed. In a last-minute bid to gain enough collective knowledge to avoid being bounced by the eager young candidates, the examining board met in the *Cornwall*.

Tension was in the air. In his own inimitable style, the Lord Almighty had decided to inspect the *Medway* that morning at short notice. So far there was no news of the result. The *Berwick*, however, had received a very laudatory signal from Himself after completing a most spectacular efficiency test. They had managed to fire thirteen broadsides in two and a half minutes. I was delighted for her Captain, Dick Lindsell, who would be returning to England with the *Berwick* in July. It must have been very satisfying to know that one's commission was ending, literally, in a blaze of glory. However, this fine display of warfare by the *Berwick* did little to help our gently perspiring quartet of potential examiners who, by tradition, were required to know more than their unfortunate examinees.

Eventually, feeling like a bunch of defeated schoolboys, we gave it up as a bad job and went ashore to the club for a game of bowls. We had scarcely finished the first end when messengers started dashing in with orders for sundry officers to return on board immediately. The *Bruce* was not apparently in demand so, in the approved Drake style, I continued my game. Dusk blackened into darkness and we were still none the wiser as the hubbub gathered momentum. It was not difficult to picture the consternation in the hotel down the road as torch-wielding marine orderlies hastened officers away from the embraces of their ladies. The wives must have found it pretty nerve-racking too, being left all of a sudden in the night with no information and nothing to alleviate their anxious thoughts through the long dark hours. They were probably imagining most dire war in all directions.

All was revealed on my return on board. Apparently the new Butterfield ship the *Shuntien* had been seized by pirates and taken off. Among the complement of passengers were two young submarine officers returning from leave, Luce and Field. The destroyers *Veteran* and *Whitsed*, with air cover from the carrier *Eagle*, went off in hot pursuit that same night, followed by *Wren* and *Witch* the next day. It seemed incredible to us at the time that piracy should have been possible at all in 1934, let alone under our very noses. The story which emerged was extraordinary.

On the afternoon of Sunday, 17 June the *Shuntien* sailed from Tongku, expecting to put in at Chefoo early the next morning. Of the fourteen passengers in the first class saloon, one was Japanese. The rest were either English or American. Among them were five ladies and three children.

Field and Luce, both somewhat jaded after several late nights ashore in Peking, were looking forward to turning in early. In fact all the first class passengers had gone to bed by half past ten and Luce was reading in his cabin when he heard the patter of feet overhead. The light but distinct footfalls came from forward of his cabin and disappeared aft. He didn't pay much attention at the time, thinking that the crew might quite possibly be furling the boat deck awning. The weather had been threatening a change and it was blowing up quite a bit.

A few minutes later three revolver shots rang out quite close at hand. They seemed to come from the passage outside Luce's cabin. He immediately thought of pirates but could not really believe the *Shuntien* had been boarded until Field slipped across from his own cabin seconds later saying that there was a very nasty looking specimen outside with a gun. The two young submariners peered cautiously out of Luce's cabin door only to come face to face with the gunman who waved them back, brandishing his pistol. Field and Luce hopped inside and slammed the door with alacrity.

It was quite obvious then that the ship was being pirated and they heard one more shot, but some way off. They extinguished the light and waited for events to develop. A terrible pandemonium broke out in the passages outside. Doors were being slammed, people were dashing up and down the deck chattering like monkeys and yells were heard from the second class accommodation where Chinese passengers were being harassed by the looters. It was all rather unpleasant.

The hubbub gradually died down and the boarding party started doing the rounds of the cabins. They started with Luce's as it was the first occupied one. The door was thrown open and a torch shone on the two men. There were several pirates but they would not advance any further until Luce had switched on the light. Then three of them shouldered their way in, fingers at the ready on their pistol triggers.

They made the young officers sit up while they searched them by patting them all over. The whole thing was executed roughly but efficiently to sudden bursts of jabbered commands. They took watches and rings and any money they could lay their hands on before wrenching open the suitcases and turning them all upside down.

The object of their search at this stage seemed to be firearms. It was only later that the really serious looting began. Finding nothing more of use to them just then, the pirates locked Luce and Field in and moved on to the next cabin. By now the tension was beginning to tell and one or two of the ladies were getting rather hysterical. There was little anyone could do for them since, cabin by cabin, the passengers were being locked in for the night and visiting was strictly forbidden.

The cabin search completed, the pirates dowsed all lights and left their prisoners in peace. It was hardly surprising that no one got much rest. Not only had the passengers been taken prisoner in their own cabins, stripped of their possessions and left in miserable darkness and uncertainty, but they were also aware of the ship's engines continually stopping and starting throughout the night. This usually reassuring bass rumble now punctuated their edgy dozing with taut silences betokening goodness only knew what.

In the grey false dawn the engines stopped once more, this time for a longer spell. It was by now Monday morning and the *Shuntien* would shortly be overdue at Chefoo. The engines stayed silent, thereby raising the passengers' hopes that the pirates were picking up their junks and would shortly be leaving the ship. Such hopes came tumbling down when a series of staccato orders ricocheted along the passages and doors began slamming all over again.

It was near six a.m. when Field and Luce were turned out, still in night attire, and escorted down to the second class saloon. Here they found some of the Ship's Officers and were soon joined by the Captain and the remainder of the first class passengers. The Captain was able to bring everyone up to date with events and wasted no time in doing so.

He had been asleep when the ship had been taken, held prisoner in his cabin all night long and allowed nowhere near the bridge. Third Officer Ross, who was on watch at the time of the incident, had tried to disarm one of the pirates. He had been shot for his pains — three times in the arm and once in the back of the neck. This news naturally caused some consternation and served to lower morale among the passengers, one of whom stepped forward at this point in the Captain's narrative to identify himself as an Army doctor and offer assistance.

He was hurriedly bundled away between a couple of particularly bloodthirsty looking characters to attend Ross up on the bridge. Relief at the discovery of a fellow-passenger permitted to help the wounded Officer was tinged with unease and the company assembled below waited somewhat anxiously to hear of Ross's condition. The hoped-for news never came as all contact with the bridge was strictly forbidden. This put an even bigger damper on what was already turning out to be one hell of a Monday morning. In mitigation it must be said that the pirates were very apologetic about shooting Ross and hoped that he had not been too badly hurt!

It was the usual practice for pirates to keep one Officer on the bridge to navigate the ship. In this case, with Ross incapacitated and the Captain denied access to his domain, no one had the faintest idea where the ship was. This, of course, was precisely what the pirates intended. Although those aboard the *Shuntien* were very much 'at sea' as far as navigational information was concerned, they need have had no qualms what'soever about their maritime safety. The pirate left in command certainly knew how to handle the ship and demonstrated his skill with consummate artistry when he got alongside a small fleet of five sampans and captured them with the accuracy and grace of a thirty-foot whaler turning onto a mooring at the end of an annual regatta.

By this stage the rest of the brigands had been through the *Shuntien* from stem to stern, stripping both first and second class accommodation of loot. This was quickly transferred to the captured sampans. Pirate crew were put aboard and the whole jolly lot sailed off over the horizon. The Chinese in the second class cabins which opened onto the saloon were then turned out and sent forward. There were two poor wretched females who were so frightened that they could hardly walk.

The assembled company spent a very uncomfortable time in the saloon, nobody knowing what was going to happen next. The subject of hostages was not discussed but it crossed Luce's mind that he and Field, as the two youngest, would be the first to be taken. Most of the passengers had no clothes, having been roused from their bunks and brought directly to the saloon. They were allowed to send the boys to fetch whatever they could find in their cabins. A pair of grey flannel trousers, a shirt and evening shoes were produced for Luce but he was unable to get his socks.

The Captain, very much aware that ignorance strengthens fear, especially when people are tense and exhausted, encouraged the other Ship's Officers to speak out and relate the events of the night hours. A more complete picture of the taking of the *Shuntien* now unfolded before the passengers and crew huddled in nervous groups around the second class saloon.

It transpired that the Chief Engineer had been caught in the engine room with the Fourth Engineer who was on watch. Together the two men kept a 14-hour watch at pistol point, obeying the only two telegraph orders which were used for the duration: FULL AHEAD and STOP. This would account for the fitful stopping and starting which had so stretched everyone's nerves during the hours of darkness. It was not until well into the forenoon that they were relieved by the Second and Third Engineers.

This therapeutic recapitulation of events, although doing little to alleviate the obvious anxiety of the passengers, at least served as some form of distraction. The Captain maintained an aura of compassionate command among his miserable and confused passengers in the cramped saloon. Morale was re-kindled, hysteria was diverted. The torpor which comes from shock and fatigue began to settle over the assembled company until, at about four o'clock in the afternoon, it became obvious that the pirates would shortly leave the ship. She had been brought close in shore and there was a slight bump as she was put on the mud.

The Number Two pirate opened the next act in this drama on the high seas by bursting into the second class saloon and saying that he wanted three passengers and two officers to go with him. At last Luce's unspoken fear of the hostage question had become a reality. It was obvious that he and Field would have to go. As they got up, another passenger by the name of Nicholl said he would go as well. From the crew of the *Shuntien*, the pirates chose the Second Officer and the Fourth Engineer. The sole Japanese passenger from the First Class saloon completed the hostage party which then became somewhat embarrassed as a missionary lady started to pray aloud for its members in no uncertain tone. Field, by some fluke, still had his money on him and he tried to pass it to this devout woman. Receiving neither acknowledgement nor response to his furtive gesture, and being rather pressed for time, he shoved it down the top of her dress while she was still at prayer. He apparently got it all back again afterwards.

The hostage party was put down in a junk but as the Number Two pirate did not cast off at once, Field and Luce asked for hats and blankets. These were passed down, also some soap, some glasses and finally a bottle of whisky. The junk then cast off and sailed away. The *Shuntien*, under the command of the Pirate King, got off the mud very quickly and soon disappeared over the horizon.

It was not long before the junk, full of hostages and booty, came up into wind and dropped anchor. Summoned by the domestic clatter of the mains'l being dropped, the little sampans which had been captured to ferry the spoils busied themselves alongside. The pirates, evidently well-satisfied with their night's work, got on with their chores and left the hostage party to its own devices. There was a good deal of chatter flying back and forth among the little boats but it sounded good-humoured enough. The Japanese passenger, who could speak Chinese and a little English, eventually relayed the pirates' plans to the rest of the captives. The idea was to send one Englishman, one Chinese from the captured sampans and the Japanese himself to Tsinan with letters addressed to the various consuls. The English were not being held for ransom but as a protective measure. If Chinese soldiers were sent against the pirates the English would be shot. Through the Japanese interpreter, Field and Luce asked when these letters would be written and were told, 'Not for a few days'.

Just before dark the hostages were paired up, taken off the junk and put into separate sampans. Nicholl and Luce were told to sleep in the fish hold of theirs. It was minute and smelt like nothing on earth, so they argued the point with their captors for some minutes, but eventually had to get below. By wrapping themselves up in their sheets and blankets and jamming on their hats they managed to make themselves fairly comfortable among the nets and other spikey bits of gear. The main difficulty was keeping clear of the fish which lay fragrantly in the bottom of the hold. There was a good deal of competition during the night to see who could manoeuvre his head furthest away from the ghastly pong. The hatch was lashed down with only a small hole left for air.

The sampans sailed all night dropping anchor for the second time in the early morning. At daybreak each cargo of hostages was allowed up on deck. While they breathed in grateful draughts of clean air, saluted each other across the water and tried to get the circulation restarted in their cramped and aching limbs, the sampans got under way again and turned in towards the shore. The only land visible was a low, desolate expanse of mud flats punctuated by occasional clumps of reeds. It was a godforsaken spot and an ideal hiding place as the water was so shallow that only sampans and very small junks could possibly approach the land.

As the shoreline emerged from the general murky gloom, the hostages espied a small river with seven or eight junks lying a few hundred yards off the entrance. It was towards these that the sampans were heading. They secured alongside each other with their bows into the shore. Their arrival caused a good deal of excitement and they were greeted by about fifty awful looking ruffians who, on catching sight of the hostages, made a tremendous hullabaloo. Luce and Nicholl were joined in their sampan by Field and the invaluable Japanese interpreter. On comparing notes it seemed that they had spent an equally uncomfortable night, if marginally less smelly.

After the swashbuckling excitement of the initial capture, settling down to a hostage routine ashore was rather dull.

Endeavouring to establish rapport and enliven proceedings, Luce offered to demonstrate part of the looted booty, a shotgun, which completely baffled the ruffians because there was no apparent means of firing the charge. The firearms tucked in to the pirates' belts when they had boarded the *Shuntien* were rather obsolete models. They were muzzle-loading percussion pistols. A charge of powder was poured into the barrel and the shot rolled down on top. This was secured with a wad of paper, hemp or some such similar material to avoid the inconvenience of a trouser-leg full of explosive. When released, the clearly visible external hammer struck a small cone with a hollow centre. Seated in this cone was an inverted copper or brass cap containing the tiniest speck of mercury which ignited on impact to fire the powder which then discharged the shot.

A hammerless shotgun was a complete novelty to the brigands who, due to the difficulty of obtaining cartridges, were still using 19th century weapons which relied upon freely available powder and shot. Luce dismantled the shotgun to demonstrate the firing mechanism and the cartridge. This thrilled the audience to the core. He then fired a couple of rounds and Number One pirate thought he would have a try. He stood with his legs very far apart, pointed the gun horizontally in the manner of a pistol, fired both barrels at once and fell over backwards to great applause. After this success they brought along a Very Light Pistol, which had belonged to the *Shuntien*. This had completely mystified them but when Luce fired a round it absolutely brought the house down and they immediately fired about twenty more.

On Tuesday, the hostages were moved to a different junk where the pirates were a lot less friendly and altogether rather unpleasant. As they threatened death by firing squad if anybody interfered with them, Field was not best pleased to hear the drone of an approaching aeroplane. The others caught it long before the pirates did and eventually picked it out of the haze flying low over the horizon, apparently straight past. About to sigh with relief at not being spotted, the hostages held their breath when they saw the plane bank, turn and come flying in towards them. The pirates got very excited at this and started firing, but the machine only circled once and then went away. Luce convinced the pirates that it was a Chinese aeroplane carrying mail. It was, of course, from the *Eagle*.

The arrival of the aeroplane had the effect of hastening Nicholl's departure for Tsinan. A letter was written and signed by all the hostages using a paintbrush. Nicholl and one Chinese prisoner from the captured sampans then pushed off the mudflats and set sail. None of the pirates went with them. They just had the two fishermen who owned the boat and $30 in silver to help them on their way. They had only gone a few hundred yards when the aeroplane was seen to be coming back. All was excitement again, the pirates readying their antiquated rifles and scattering overboard among the reeds. They started firing long before the machine was within range. Field, Luce and the rest were hastily pushed on to the mud with pistols in their backs and made to wave. They waved their blankets like mad in the hope of being recognized, but as the aeroplane approached she dipped down towards them and opened fire.

Things really started warming up then. The pirates, who had learned to keep a good lookout, observed four planes approaching. They adopted the usual practice of scattering on the mud and taking cover in the reeds. Luce just had time to see that three of the machines were fighters while identifying the fourth as their old friend. She was presumably leading the others over. He took cover under the thickest piece of wood he could find in the sampan just in case. When the fun started it was quite obvious that the vessels were not the target so he poked his head up to see what was going on. It was very thrilling watching the fighters diving on the miserable pirates and banging away at them with their machine guns. The roar of the engines, the pop-pop of the machine guns and the rifle fire from the pirates were very awe-inspiring and the whole spectacle had Hendon beat to a frazzle.

During the afternoon two seaplanes landed near Nicholl's sampan out to sea. This was just visible from the river mouth, so the hostages quite rightly assumed that Nicholl and the Chinese were being taken off to the *Eagle*. Once they were safely on board there would be no more shooting without warning and the hungry and somewhat dehydrated hostages could look forward to the possibility of someone coming over and dropping some beer and food. While Field, Luce and the others were contemplating the prospect of a decent meal, an argument broke out among the pirates. Eventually a party went out to bury the dead who still lay sprawled in the reeds on the mudflats where they had fallen. The gravediggers took good care to strip the bodies. Nothing of value remained.

The sticky afternoon heat encouraged the waiting prisoners into a doze. Suddenly four aeroplanes were sighted by a pirate lookout who leapt to his feet, reeling off a burst of orders. The usual excitement ensued, but this time all the pirates got under cover and the hostages were made to stand on deck and wave. Just in case they had any ideas about fleeing into the cover of the reed-clumps to avoid the odd burst of machine-gun fire the pirates held them at pistol point. One machine came round very close and one or two pirates took pot shots at it, but the hostages managed to stop them firing by telling them that these were British aeroplanes and would not open fire at them. The observer in the lead machine acknowledged their frantic waving and then dropped a small package about a hundred yards away on the mud. Luce, obviously stirred from a pleasant dream of beer and sandwiches by all this activity, immediately wanted to walk over and pick it up but this was not permitted. He then tried to make one of the pirates go but they would not agree to that either. The story about British aeroplanes holding their fire had obviously not been very convincing and they were frightened of being picked off from the air. A compromise was eventually reached with Luce and a pirate going out together.

The message contained therein was written in English and Chinese and read as follows:

By order of His Excellency the British Commander-in-Chief. Unless you give up prisoners you will be bombed and shot with machine guns. Next time the bombs will hit. Put all prisoners in sampan and send them to sea. Display a large white flag to show you understand. If not you will be fired on.

Luce was led back to the sampans and the message was relayed to all and sundry. It caused considerable consternation. Just as the performance came to an end the aeroplanes, which had been flying round all the time, dropped their bombs about a mile away, sending up a cloud of mud and water. The timing could not have been better. The bombs made plenty of noise and were even heard in the *Eagle* thirty-five miles away.

A second message was dropped, but written in English only this time. It said that a destroyer was lying four miles off the mouth of the river waiting to pick up the hostages. The pirates were very worried by this message as they did not know what was in it. Field said that it was the final warning before the bombs came. After interminable internal disputes between the lieutenants of this nefarious crew, an agreement was eventually reached. The threat of direct air bombardment had clearly put the wind up them and, towards sunset, the hostages were put on board a sampan and released.

The darkening horizon was quite empty. They very wisely decided to sail straight out to sea, thereby putting as much distance as possible between themselves and the pirates. It was not long before they sighted several ships and shortly after midnight they fetched up alongside the *Whitshed*. The sampan men who had been captured by the pirates were only too delighted to be free. They were given food and water and were last seen sailing away smoking the Fourth Engineer's cigars.

While part of the fleet was dealing with piracy on the High Seas, the rest was having its customary diet of routine exercises and inspections, livened up by preparations for a Ministerial Visit. There is some kind of Naval Law which states that Visiting Firemen shall arrive at times least convenient and most disruptive to the business in hand. I was having to mediate in a rather awkward situation which had arisen between *Medway's* Signals Officer and some of the submarine COs. Paradoxically this had resulted almost in a breakdown of communications – a farcical state of affairs. It was partly a question of personalities and partly a matter of residual grievance over various trivial points in wireless organization. The whole thing had been allowed to go on niggling for far too long and the air needed to be cleared.

My head needed to be cleared as well. The snotties' examination day had been long and exhausting with eight young gentlemen appearing at intervals of an hour and a quarter. They did not seem to be nearly as nervous as I had felt years before when facing the same ordeal. I expect they were faking it. Their studied ease was a shade too perfect. The day stretched out interminably. Only one candidate was obviously indifferent in seamanship knowledge but none of the others, although adequate, struck me as being really all about and bright. There was no exceptional sparkle to lighten the darkness of the four rather jaded examiners! We gave one 1, six 2s and one 3, finishing at half past six in the evening. After dining, we escaped ashore to the club only to find it full of very intoxicated snotties and friends celebrating their achievements. The ones we had examined earlier were very keen to buy us gins. We tried our best to maintain an air of tolerant empathy towards these uninhibited youngsters, but it was sad to note that our very appearance put a damper on the party.

Parties were the order of the day thenceforward as the Ministerial visit got under way. The poor man was actually taking his wife and three daughters on a short holiday but a meticulous programme of entertainments swung into action as soon as the *Falmouth*, bearing its precious cargo, came into harbour. All thought of rest — for anybody — was completely dispelled. The various Captains were each told off to do their bit — lunch: *Cumberland*, dinner: *Cornwall*, and so on. As one senior officer cogently remarked, high tea aboard the oiler *Francol* appeared to be the only omission. I gave a small dinner on board the *Bruce* which did not include the Minister but which did include members of the party invited to join him at the C-in-C's dance in the *Suffolk* afterwards. The Flag Lieutenant had done his level best to round up enough ladies but even so there was a large preponderance of men forced to wait their turn for a dancing partner. The poor ladies must have been totally exhausted by the end of the evening. The C-in-C, with grave ceremony, approached me at about half time. Bracing myself for lord knew what to break over my bows I was brought up all standing to be greeted with a smile. 'How do you do', he intoned in deep bass tones. 'Are you fond of dancing?' On being assured that I lived for it he took me by the arm and practically frog-marched me down the deck. 'I will introduce you to the Minister's daughter.' This was no invitation, it was an order. 'Affecting an air of studied disinterest, you will ask her to dance.' The merest shadow of a grin flickered in my direction as he left me with the girl — a pleasant enough young woman of about eighteen. Perhaps there was a grain of humour yet in the bottom of the scran bag.

The Minister's holiday was brought to a close with a demonstration of Naval might which included flying from the *Eagle*, a shoot in cruisers, a surface trip in a submarine and an attack in destroyers during which each daughter fired a torpedo because a previous Very Important Daughter had done it the year before. The Fleet swept majestically back into harbour in two divisions, both hopelessly far ahead of *Bruce*, the Flotilla leader. Division One went full astern to rectify matters while Division Two, which included *Eagle*, performed a very elegant serpentine to get themselves back in step just as the Flag swept upon us. I foresaw *Eagles* Captain, blue-eyed though he was over the *Shuntien* affair, getting a roasting as soon as the Ministerial visitors had left our sea area. He would have to exercise all his considerable powers of tact to smooth ruffled plumage.

The returning heroes of the piracy, Luce and Field, had one final ordeal to endure. Their presence was required at an official reception to meet the Minister. The party consisted in much hand-shaking, conversation and champagne − all rather sticky. The two poor captives were lionized. They were nice lads, both very tall. They clung pathetically together as though still manacled.*

Released from the ardours of obligatory hospitality, *Bruce* and the submarines plunged back, with great relief, into the relative obscurity of our designated exercise programme. After all the ups and downs of the cruise north, the alarums of the piracy episode and the considerable stresses and strains surrounding the Official Visit, a bit of peace and quiet to let us get on with our own business was very welcome. The exercises, for once, went like clockwork. It was as though some unspoken rule moderated the men's behaviour, urging each one of them to put aside any pettiness or irritation lurking below the surface in favour of the greater satisfaction of a job well done. *Esprit* could not have been higher and our performance confirmed it. We returned relaxed and rather pleased with ourselves.

As we secured to our buoy a Chinese naval launch went by, loaded to the very gunwales with cadets from the Naval School. She looked definitely crank and was wallowing somewhat under this vast cargo. Elwin remarked on the apparent lack of regulations controlling the overcrowding of ships and I had to agree with him. Many's the time we had witnessed hordes of passengers, clustered like fleas on a stick clamped firmly between the jaws of an afflicted dog paddling valiantly against the current for the shore. Disaster was often only averted by the greatest good fortune: good seamanship simply did not come into it.

I left the bridge to go below and pursue my leisurely ablutions before dinner. I was just pouring myself a well-deserved gin when there was a knock at my cabin door which heralded a signal informing me that the naval launch had capsized and sunk. Boats from all our ships, particularly the *Francol*, went immediately to the aid of the stricken vessel but despite their efforts seventy-two boys and two officers were drowned. A young submarine officer who was standing OOW in the *Medway* showed remarkable initiative by getting himself relieved and going off with two DSEA** instructors to the wreck. All three of them dived and walked all over it in four fathoms of water − one actually going inside. That they were unable to find any bodies in no way detracted from the outstanding originality and determination they displayed by their actions. This was in stark contrast to the tight-lipped impassivity of the Chinese naval authorities who seemed strangely

* Luce went on to become Admiral and C-in-C Far East. Field was shot down on 16 December, 1941, on a plane bound for Gibraltar carrying Leslie Howard. He was at that time Captain of the *Seahawk*.

** Davis Submarine Escape Apparatus.

unconcerned by the tragedy. Such an event at Portsmouth would have led to a hornets' nest of enquiries, reprimands and disgrace.

The only disgrace to be publicly acknowledged in this case was, I found to my astonishment the following morning, our own. The poor old *Bruce* was splashed across the headlines of the Chinese press, accused of causing the capsize with her wash. Since we were actually on our mooring more than a mile away from the incident when it occurred and since there was an abundance of eye-witness reports attesting to the overcrowded conditions on board, this calumny was soon scotched. After the inevitable enquiry, which was convened aboard the *Cumberland*, a wire was sent to the C-in-C in Peking with the evidence which cleared us unequivocally. It was a tragic event none the less, made all the more poignant by the extreme youth of most of the victims who, in their somewhat undisciplined exuberance, had rushed *en masse* to the starboard rail of their launch to cheer on a Chinese wedding party as it passed in full regalia. The boys' utter disregard for boat sense led to a predictable and devastating result. The joyful confusion of clashing gongs and celebratory shouts rising from the gaudy red and gold wedding spectacle took on the hard edge of panic and soon all was wailing chaos. The *Cornwall* eventually succeeded in raising the sunken launch and getting her on to the beach.

I spent my fortieth birthday preparing an analysis of the work done by the submarines at Weihaiwei. By deducting weekends and cruising time from a gross total of 157 days, I got the net figure for which each boat had been available for exercise. *Odin* came out on top with 67. Some of the others dwindled right down to 22, which was very low indeed, but, as Elwin pointed out as he glanced over my shoulder and wished me many happy returns of the day, there had also been a certain amount of refitting. Overall, we were well ahead in our preparations and could afford a stand down in Hong Kong as we waited for the flotilla to come south for the winter.

This formal review provoked a few personal thoughts on my own progress through the commission of life. One tends to become more conscious of the set of the tide as one drifts past these lighthouses, although at forty I felt a jolly sight younger than I had for some years past, despite the fact that anno domini seemed determined henceforward to place me in the 'elderly' category. I remarked to Elwin that on reaching this great age I felt like transferring my position to a new chart. He, with the lighthearted cynicism of youth, retorted that it was not a new chart but a new folio that I was starting!

16

Trans-Siberian

LEAVING THE *Bruce* was a sad affair for me. I had enjoyed my second stint in South-East Asia enormously and had been privileged to serve with some outstanding sailors and submariners. But it was back to England and a new job now. My promotion had come through and I would return as Captain.

The voyage home from Hong Kong began in the relative security of that familiar element – the China Sea. Arriving at the port of Dairen about noon, I found myself with plenty of time available to suffer the minute and officious scrutiny of the Japanese Customs, a procedure repeated throughout the traversal of this occupied zone. I felt quite unreasonably harried at having to pay a small duty on spirits, freeport notwithstanding. Departure for Harbin was scheduled for nine the following morning on the Asia Express. We were expected at our first staging post some thirteen and a half hours later. Thomas Cooks had wired ahead for overnight accommodation. Entry papers were completed. Visas for crossing Manchuria were eventually deemed in order. The initial administration of the journey was so long and drawn-out that a brief period of recovery was necessary before setting out to shop.

The overland journey to my new appointment in command of the submarine depot ship *Lucia* at Devonport started with a shattering drive just after breakfast the following morning. There were three of us squashed into the back seat of the car – my wife, myself and a friend of ours from Hong Kong who was a wine-merchant. It had been his bright idea to gather a couple of companions about him for the trip. I suspect the plan had been hatched in the glow of one or two of his excellent bottles after a suitably seductive dinner. The end of my commission in the *Bruce* coincided with his travelling dates and thus we found ourselves hurtling through the streets of Dairen in the general direction of the railway station.

Our driver was a pimply youth, expert in little other than blowing his horn. Sick with apprehension, my wife cast anguished looks at the pair of us as we attempted to relieve him of his command and drive from the back seat. At bends we were forced to take charge physically. Our eccentric progress attracted not the slightest attention from any of the other motorists in the town who were all stalwartly fighting for their own road space. The

Manchurian highway code obviously credited the other driver with no rights whatsoever and God help the third party. Almost all the cars were American, with horns tuned to the same note. The consequence was extreme difficulty in distinguishing one's own voice from that of the enemy in the continual blare.

Utterly exhausted, with hardly half the morning spent, we lurched alongside the station building and hove to with engines full astern, narrowly avoiding the vehicle athwart our hawse. All faith in the efficacy of any kind of travel arrangements had by now been shaken out of us. There had been a general but unspoken fear weighing on our little party as it prepared to leave the domestic security of the hotel. We were about to cross Manchuria, Russia, Poland, Germany and the English Channel. We had been informed we should put into Liverpool Street Station eight days hence. (This, incidentally, would have taken us as far as Singapore had we opted for the leisurely sea route home via P and O.) Luggage was something we should probably never see again and our reservations had surely evaporated into the gentle haze hovering over the sunlit alleyways. We were pathetically relieved to find on arrival at the platform that the hotel porter had secured both seats and suitcases.

Our doubting hearts were further gladdened by the smart and commodious appearance of our train. The Asia Express came up to even the laudatory remarks of its propagandist booklet and we travelled in great comfort. It was air-conditioned and cooled, which made us wonder why the railways in England were so slow to adopt this technology. It improved the cleanliness and comfort of the journey to an astonishing degree, especially in the heat of early summer. With the exception of the main carriage frames which were German, the whole of the train was built in Dairen. It was an eye-opener to me. I had not realized how efficient the Japanese were. Indeed the entire operation of the South Manchuria Railway Company was most impressive. Count Hayashi's stewardship was clearly of the best. We boarded our streamlined transport with rising spirits, gradually restored to normality by the contents of our friend's hip flask, an essential accessory when travelling unknown routes! The only slight disappointment was the rather ill-kempt appearance of our engine, grubbily getting up steam. It rather let the rest of the sparkling rolling stock down.

Revived in flesh and spirit, we busied ourselves organizing our twenty-two pieces of luggage into the space available around us. We had been forewarned that victualling for this particular journey across half the world's landmass was not to be undertaken lightly. Indeed, it would have tested the imagination of the most ingenious quartermaster, faced with a non-stop circumnavigation. We had provisioned accordingly in Dairen, not forgetting to purchase an abundance of soap which, we were assured by veterans of the route, was to be had for neither love nor money once one was embarked. Amidst a welter of frenzied porters, late passengers and clanging carriage doors we positioned our perishable goods to hand and settled back into surprisingly comfortable accommodation. Our fellow-passengers were few. One, a Nipponese General, delicately removed his footwear and prepared to undertake his journey in stockinged feet. This by now no longer dismayed me. A whistle sounded, there was an answering toot from our disreputable engine and we squeaked into motion on our six-hundred-mile run north to Harbin.

The hilly countryside trundled past our windows at a steady forty-four miles an hour, no mean speed for the Orient. We learned that at this pace there was a daily service up and back to Harbin, another example of Japanese efficiency which took us somewhat by surprise. We passed through Anshan during the forenoon — some five miles of iron smelting works. As we dipped into our luncheon basket of bread, cold meat and fruit, the view began to change. The fertile Manchurian Plain spread itself around us in well-cultivated swathes. Our stops were at Tashikao, Mukden, Szepinkai and Hsinking (Changchun). We saw very little of Mukden, a rather ramshackle town in the middle of the plain, swept by clouds of dust. Hsinking was hardly more impressive from the train but a large amount of building was evident and the place seemed surrounded by wireless stations.

The line after Hsinking became noticeably more bumpy as we reached the old Chinese Eastern Railway. At Mukden our Japanese General exchanged felt slippers, thoughtfully provided by the railway company, for field boots with spurs and politely took his leave. We congratulated ourselves on our passage planning as the food provided on board was disappointingly unappetising. Drinks were abundantly available throughout, but to the horror of our wine-merchant expedition leader, no Johnnie Walker. Drastic action was called for. We rationed the hipflask. The Asia Express drew in to Harbin station a few minutes after eleven that night. We felt entirely satisfied with the journey thus far and, though somewhat stiff from prolonged sitting, yawned ourselves into wakefulness and a pleasant sense of anticipation for whatever might happen next.

By midnight our spirit of adventure had fled. Our hotel was full and we were thrust into a car by alien porters who shouted unintelligible commands at the driver. He took off at Dairen speed into the night, rattling us over potholes on a switchback ride which seemed to cover just about every possible compass point. Tired, depressed and completely disorientated, we eventually fetched up in a row on a sofa in a dirty hotel bedroom waiting for the luggage we were still more firmly convinced we would never see again. 'Travel as light as possible,' we had been warned before leaving Hong Kong. 'There is ample accommodation for baggage on board the train but under no circumstances take more luggage than you can fit into your compartment.' This was good common sense and a fairly basic security precaution. What we had not bargained for was being suddenly cut adrift from our belongings. We had gone aground in the Hotel Moderne, an establishment well past its prime. In fact not the slightest hint of modernity remained. It stood silent and deserted beneath a thickening film of neglect. There was no one to greet us, nothing to drink and the hip flask was empty.

Even the least promising situation looks better in a morning light. The Moderne turned out to be the only hotel in our collective experience which actually looked better by day. This encouraging observation rekindled our sense of touristic fantasy which was heightened by an impressive Russian blonde selling exotic sounding things in tins. We came across her in a Jewish department store where she presided over a counter groaning under the weight of comestible pyramids. Sighting our wine-merchant a good cable off, she closed him in next to no time and, adding sex to salesmanship, persuaded him into making expensive purchases of an indiscriminate nature. Signs of improvement on the mess deck for the onward journey!

The reason for this second provisioning call, which occupied most of the forenoon, was the growing complication of victualling on board as we approached new and more remote frontiers. We had listened to dire reports from veteran travellers who had suffered acutely from the quality and/or scarcity of meals provided. Also, foreign exchange transactions seemed liable to trigger a diplomatic incident if clumsily handled. Caught unprepared, one was left entirely at the mercy of a black market whose implications were dangerously unclear. In the light of this alarming intelligence we stocked up on loaves of bread and plenty of butter to go with the delicacies pressed upon us by the beautiful Russian blonde.

Our next concern before plunging across Central Russia was travel documentation. We rendezvoused with the Cooks' man who reassured us that our tickets were in order. In answer to our enquiry about Harbin amusement — we were not due to depart until the following day — he assured us that after 40 years' experience he recommended the museum!

With a ridiculously naive sense of achievement we decided something a little more self-congratulatory than the museum was in order. We steered course for the yacht club which had been taken over by the Wagon Lit Company and now specialized in Russian food. We sat in warm June sunshine on the banks of the broad Sungari River. It was difficult to visualize this majestically serene sweep of water as it had been only a few short weeks before, frozen hard and dusted with snow. We feasted on an enormous lunch of zakouska, bortsch and chicken Kiev. Despite our 'wise virgin' morning there was evidently a lurking paranoia in all of us that we should be stranded in Siberia with no tuck box. We ate far too much and felt in need of sodamints afterwards. The evening brought fresh gastronomic delights in the form of sturgeon soup and mutton cooked on a sword as done over the camp fires of Caucasus. This quite delicious dish was called shashlik and had to be washed down with copious draughts of roughish Caucasian red wine. The two large and bearded Russian owners of this traditional establishment, where we had been taken by the British Consul as a prelude to an evening out in Harbin, stood quietly but firmly by as we downed the first glass. I found it quite palatable. Not so our wine-merchant friend whose complexion underwent a number of interesting colour changes before we managed to revive him with a bottle of Pommard.

The Consul was very interesting on the subject of Manchukuo. I of course had heard much about it from the point of view of the occupiers but little from the other side. While the three of us ate in appreciative silence he painted a picture of a city dying in fear and poverty. Like most people who had much to do with Japanese officialdom, he cordially disliked it. Harbin's mixed population lived under ever-tightening control by the Japanese who, despite repeated assertions that Manchukuo was an independent state, clearly regarded it as nothing of the kind. Even their pretence of interviewing Chinese officials and acting in concert with them had gone completely by the board. All state business was quite openly being carried out by the Japanese. The Japanese Military Mission were de facto rulers of the province. They arrested, tried and executed prisoners without reference to the Manchukuo government. Arrests were becoming so numerous as to be almost uncountable and perfectly innocent people were being kept in gaol whilst trumped up charges were examined.

The sale of the Chinese Eastern Railway had forced over 20,000 Russians into unemployment. Rather than face starvation in Manchukuo, they had gone to the USSR. Many of them were former white Russians. It was a question of survival. For them, politics played second fiddle to expediency and they became 'Radishes' (red outside, white within). Of the remaining 40,000 Russians in Harbin, the Consul told us more than half were currently without jobs and their situation was fast deteriorating. Their reaction to the occupation had been to split up into small groups. These groups had become secret societies and their members so confused and frightened that they had begun informing on each other with disastrous results. The Japanese spared no pity on these unfortunates. They were simply regarded as a nuisance near the prospective Japanese front line. The position of any professed Red Russian was of course untenable.

To add to the general discomfort there were five different kinds of police: Manchukuan, Manchukuo Army, Japanese Railway Guards, Japanese Army and Japanese Military Mission. Bandits were active in Northern Manchukuo and had begun operating politically as terrorists. They were known to slaughter any Japanese who came within range. The Japanese were understandably scared stiff of being ambushed under these circumstances, hence the vast number of security forces. The remaining 600 miles of our trip across Manchukuo from Harbin to Manchouli didn't sound as though it was going to be much fun.

Our host for the evening, fearing he had cast a pall of gloom and despondency over his well-fed guests, suggested a night club to add a bit of sparkle. We visited two fairly conventional places which persisted in spite of the obvious poverty of the town. It was a strangely unreal night out and as we took our leave of the Consul outside the hotel about dawn, we felt a great deal guiltier than our extremely correct behaviour warranted!

We were eager to be away the next morning. Harbin's atmosphere of tension and despair was slowly seeping into our bones. The hustle and bustle of departure soon swept these anxieties away and we found ourselves once more installed in a reasonably comfortable but very dirty train. There was hardly space to turn around. Passengers of all nationalities kept on tumbling into the carriages. We were engulfed in a multilingual babble as Swedish, French, German, American and English travellers boarded. There was a sudden crescendo in the general hubbub and a swathe was cut through the crowd on the platform for a large party of Japanese athletes on their way to Berlin for the Olympic Games. Like our General on the ride up from Dairen, they all removed their footwear once suitable accommodation had been found. The timetable advertised the Harbin/Manchouli stretch as taking 22 hours. We had been advised by Cook's man that the present service was extremely inefficient due to the deplorable condition of track and rolling stock. Heavy delays were inevitable. Having completed all housekeeping arrangements for the journey, we drew a deep mental breath and braced ourselves for a further 600 miles and thirty hours of endurance. The hip flask was checked several times.

A series of bone-chilling squeaks announced our departure from Harbin and we juddered slowly out of the city into the dead flat plain which lies to the north-east. We spent the whole day crossing this land — so flat and green it might have been the sea. The weather was perfect and the sun shone continuously out of a cloudless sky making it rather hot in the middle of the day. About every 10 miles we would stop at a station around which clustered a handful of mud huts. A detachment of Japanese Railway Guards hovered at every one. Most of the country looked excellent grazing land but we saw little evidence of husbandry. Duck and heron inhabited large stretches of swamp and I spotted a brace of silver pheasant after one stop. Towards dusk the temperature dropped sharply as we climbed into a wilder hilly country which glowed in the evening light.

Our train had sleeping cars which could be reserved in advance. Also we

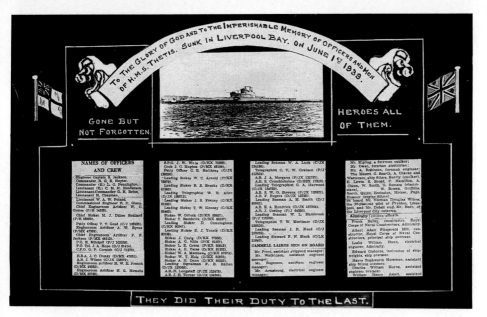

20. From Victorian times, any disasters befalling HM ships were commemorated by postcards showing the vessel and roll of honour, sometimes embellished with poetry, garlands of flowers, etc. *Thetis'* memorial postcard is one of the last in that tradition. The onset of war made their production a practical impossibility, since so many ships and men were lost and the information on their passing was confidential.

21. Captain Oram at the Requestman and Defaulter's Table. In most ships the First Lieutenant or Commander dealt with almost all cases, but for the more important ones - promotions, medal presentations or requests for compassionate leave etc - the Captain woud preside. He would also dispense justice where crimes were more serious than leave-breaking, being drunk ashore or missing from a place of duty.

22. Whilst accompanying Rear-Admiral Harwood, victor of the Battle of the River Plate, on his round of farewells in South America, Captain Oram had the opportunity of seeing the wreck of the German pocket battleship the *Admiral Graf Spee* which was blown up by her own crew after the fight with the *Exeter*, *Achilles* and *Ajax* on 13 December, 1939.

23. The aircraft carrier *Formidable*, at speed, taken from the *Hawkins*, en route to the Mediterranean via the long haul round Africa to replace the *Illustrious*, badly damaged by German aircraft on 10 January, 1941, in the Sicilian narrows while escorting Convoy Excess which was taking supplies to Malta.

24. Survivors from a sunken ship, the tanker *British Premier*, wait to be picked up by the *Hawkins*. The nine people in the oil-stained boat were the only survivors from a crew of over forty. The tanker was sunk by the German *U65* 200 miles off Freetown on Christmas Eve, 1940. The *U65* survived her victim by only a few months, being lost with all hands when she was sunk by the British corvette, *Gladiolus*.

25. The wind 'creaking in the rigging again'. Captain Oram Rtd. (second from right) on board the Outward Bound training ship *Danmark* at Dover, 1955. Members of the committee, among them David James, Gerald Emerson and Vic Feather, accompany the Chairman, Sir Spencer Summers (with cap).

26. Old memories rekindled. Lt David Hubbard, one of the Submarine Escape Tank staff, explaining the latest techniques and equipment as Captain Oram looks on during his final visit to HMS *Dolphin* in February, 1986.

had been advised to travel first class on the Harbin/Manchouli leg, although second class up from Dairen had been most acceptable. We had taken this precaution and were very glad of it since we were carrying swarms of military from Harbin to Hailar near the border. It was virtually a troop train. They pinched all the best bunks regardless of reservations. This behaviour precipitated a series of storms which broke somewhere abaft our beam. The most spectacular featured a grizzled grandmother and a bearded Frenchman both of whom, for reasons best known to themselves, objected vehemently to being placed in the same sleeping compartment. Fortunately our coach was not invaded until early the next morning after we had managed a few hours' sleep. The Japanese Military Guards then proceeded with great officiousness and lack of courtesy to throw open all compartment doors and pull down all blinds as we entered the region between Hailar and Manchouli. Shrouded thus for twenty miles we ran through what one imagined to be extensive fortifications. Perhaps it was all bluff and there were none. I imagined though that this area must have been chosen for their fortified railhead.

Manchouli had always conjured up for me a desolate outpost of civilization on the edge of the wastes of Siberia. Certainly in itself it was desolate, standing alone on high downland and existing only by virtue of its two railway termini. With our twenty-two pieces of baggage we eventually paraded in the customs shed. According to the timetable there were seven hours to spare for the Japanese officials to deal with our innocuous belongings before our journey continued. This seemed ample time and we relaxed slightly. The Japanese Olympic team naturally went to the top of the queue, was swiftly processed and departed singing and waving banners. This signalled the shutdown of customs business for the time being and we were told that we would be done in two hours.

The likelihood of any of us ever having the opportunity of tourism along the Sino-Soviet border again was fairly remote. After a short conference we decided to go off and explore our surroundings, attempting in the process to procure both lunch and a bath. Manchouli's main street was reminiscent of comic book pictures showing old-time American frontier towns. It was lined with untidy wooden houses where bedraggled horse carriages and water carts were drawn up in tangled heaps. This architecture did not bode well for the bath so we repaired to the station buffet for a very passable lunch and returned to the customs shed at our appointed time. More delay. No one could tell us when our bags would be looked at but it would not be for some time. We made another foray in search of toilet facilities and stumbled upon the Hotel Nicitine more by luck than design. This excellent hostelry provided us with a bath in which the boiler was part and parcel of the tub, making one's ablutions a trifle overheated in summer but probably quite delightful in winter. We speculated on conditions at this Central Asian latitude of 50 degrees north when arctic winds swept the plain, blistering the snow-covered countryside. Grim indeed, and even in summer Siberia could be chilly, so, along with an extra loaf for the larder, we each bought a fur hat, just in case.

Ready to proceed on our journey through to Lake Baikal, Irkutsk, Novosibirsk, Omsk, Sverdlovsk and Moscow, we presented ourselves once more in the customs shed. Time was growing short and we were beginning to panic. We could hear our 'Lux' express being prepared for departure. A couple of languid officials strolled in and beckoned us over to undo our luggage. Every single package had to be opened and examined. The inspection went ahead arrogantly and in slow time while our horseless carriage snorted impatiently outside.

We just made it as the train drew away from the platform. We sank onto our luggage to await the border crossing into the USSR. It took about twenty minutes to reach the Siberian frontier station of Otpov where cameras and field glasses attracted disapproving glances. The no-man's-land we passed through near the border looked unkempt and I felt an ominous sense of foreboding which was increased by trenches and barbed wire. Under an arch over the railway we passed into the USSR — to me an unknown country. We were relieved of our passports which we did not see again until we got off at Berlin. This left me feeling distinctly uncomfortable as the Russian immigration official gave me a long hard stare when he got to the bit in mine which said 'Naval Officer'. I didn't fancy being dropped at Omsk without a passport so I kept pretty close to the carriage for the whole trip. We had to go through customs all over again. The Russians removed everything and everybody from compartments. We had to pay the porters 80 kopeks a package for the privilege. Since we knew there would be a repeat performance of all this as we crossed the western frontier into Poland at Niegeroloje, we had taken the precaution of re-packing of our suitcases. Those 'not needed on voyage' were sealed by the Customs on entry and this saved us considerable trouble at the other end.

We had placed all reading matter on top of our three unsealed bags. The examining officials were particularly interested in this and we were carrying a fair amount to while away eight days of rail travel. As they scanned titles and even pages, apparently at random, we started to feel quite furtive about our totally innocent library! Jewellery, watches and anything made of gold, together with cameras, had to be declared and signed for, also any credits, drafts or foreign currency. We received receipts and were told that unless we produced them on leaving Russia, our goods would be liable to confiscation. Though brusque, the officials were courteous and they did not make our hackles rise as the Japanese had done.

As soon as we were allowed back on board we got on with the business of putting our small house in order. The luggage disappeared aloft and we settled into our two adjoining first class *wagons lits* with washbasin between. On this train there were two classes and two divisions of the first class accommodation. It all sounded rather complicated until one realized that the class difference concerned density of passengers and the divisions in the first class signalled facilities available. We were travelling first class, first division which meant that only two of the four berths in each compartment were occupied and that we had a minute washroom between our adjoining compartments. Had we been in the second division we would have had to use one of the communal basins at either end of the car. If our accommodation had been second class then there would have been four travellers in each compartment. WCs were at either end of the carriage, not in our washroom. Thus we were three travelling in two four-berth compartments. We used one as a kitchen and living area and the other as a dormitory. By keeping scrupulously tidy we were not at all cramped. Indeed, we travelled in relative luxury. Our accommodation was clean and fresh looking – a welcome relief from the squalor of the train we had so recently left.

We were all tired out by the administration and endless shunting about to get us out of one country and into another. Here we would live for a week. Our next change was too far off to worry about. Relaxation crept over us, encouraged by the comfortable heating in the carriage and the hip flask. We prepared for bed, carefully extracting a full deck of playing cards from inside our shoes where we had stowed them, on advice, after bathing at the Nicitine!

The morning brought glorious sunshine filtering through woodland. We were climbing steeply. Hitherto my railway journeys had all been short ones arriving sometime today, or at the latest, tomorrow. This was different. Here we would live for seven days, trundling through places so completely remote they might well not exist at all. The end of the journey was unimaginable. I am a doer, not a passer of time, and as I woke to the stippled light flickering across the ceiling of the compartment I wondered how soon the restlessness of inactivity would pass.

We were stewarded on our journey by two monolingual Russian carriage attendants who were courteous, grubby and responsive to tips. The customary tip per passenger for the trip Manchouli/Moscow was U.S. $2 per attendant. The attendants were changed at Moscow. Since our party elected to dine mostly in its compartment and had additional service from this pair of heavyweights in the form of clearing up and cleaning, we proffered $3 and benefited by offering half of this at the start of the journey. I slipped up seriously in my first set of negotiations with the heavyweights by pulling roubles out of my wallet. The already puddingy faces blanched and ossified. 'Try dollars!' murmured my wife under cover of re-packing her overnight bag. This had the remarkable effect of demolishing the language barrier at a stroke. Presumably the locals got a much better rate on the black market then the official rate we were offered. Our car attendants kept us constantly supplied with drinking water from the samovar at the end of our carriage. It was not very appetizing, even for toilet purposes, and we had a small spirit kettle upon which we boiled it up in our 'galley' just to make sure.

We also carried a Intourist official charged with interpreting and nannying. He was a very well-informed man, though not a rampant propagandist. If courteously treated he was most obliging. It quickly became apparent that any complaints or additional requirements should be referred to him rather than to the attendants whose palms we had so liberally crossed. Their scope was definitely limited and we were not equipped with pocket dictionaries.

The food on offer was plentiful and fairly good, though heavily Russian. If one needed building up, additional poundage could be achieved quite successfully on a trans-Siberian journey. This assumed that one was first able to crack the bureaucracy of purchasing the wretched stuff. Naval requisitioning is not known for its speed or simplicity but never in my life had I come across such a complicated procedure. It needed kid gloves and massive advance planning. There was the option of a complete set of meal tickets for the 7-day journey giving three meals a day. These were priced according to the category of one's travel and were only obtainable outside Russia. Neither single tickets nor books could be obtained on board. The problem was that not many people outside Russia knew about this scheme with the notable exception of hungry veterans who had learned the hard way. The price per set was £4.7s.1d. for first class category. Without this set of tickets, precisely the same food was available *à la carte* at three times the price in roubles. An awful lot of life seemed to work on the 'all or nothing' principle in the USSR. A whole set of tickets entitled one to huge indigestible meals of lumpen consistency. Hence the dimensions of our two attendants I suppose. The Intourist official tactfully informed us that 'Administration' would buy back any unused tickets at cost when we left at the further frontier. The refund would presumably be in roubles and since roubles were useless outside Russia this offer was rather puzzling. There seemed no objection to travellers bringing all their own food with them and many people had done the same as us, merely topping up from the restaurant car as the need arose. There was a tendency for the soda water to run dry but other than that we were quite well served.

With political uncertainties of such huge dimensions overhanging the whole of eastern Europe, the USSR and South-East Asia, currency regulations were constantly changing. One had to check almost from day to day what was and was not permitted. It was all too easy to find oneself stranded with no acceptable currency although one actually had plenty of money. No foreign currency at all was accepted on the Russian train. We had to estimate pretty accurately how many roubles we were going to need and buy them at the rate of 25 roubles to the pound or 5 roubles to the US dollar. This was done on entry at the border. We estimated 50 roubles each for the trip and an extra 25 for Moscow, where we would make a brief call. We could change more there if we needed it. The trick was to avoid having pockets full of roubles at the western frontier because they were unsaleable. Single US dollar notes were the most convenient sort of foreign currency to have about one's person. Travellers' cheques were only cashable from Moscow onwards. We had reckoned on fifty dollars-worth apiece plus five pounds in sterling and 50 yen in cash for the whole journey. It came out about right.

There was considerable work going on on the railway which was, I think, in connection with the laying of a second track. As far as I could see the double track now reached as far as Karminskaya — about 200 miles west of the border at the junction of the Vladivostok line. We halted for a while at Chita, the regional capital of the USSR in the Far East. All the buildings were of wooden logs, in fact everything was constructed from wood.

The people for the most part looked poor, dirty and sad. Their general appearance would have indicated starvation anywhere else. They either worked with grim expressions of set purpose or idled listlessly. No one smiled. There was no skylarking. The arrival of a train full of foreigners provoked some interest but the stares which greeted us were sullen and immobile. A lot of the men wore the railway workers' uniform — a crossed hammer and spanner embroidered on the collar.

A station platform is perhaps not the best place to get a true picture of any country but it is usually filled with representative types. Going through Russia we got a series of ten-minute vignettes. The lack of professional types was noticeable. There were almost no citizens with clean hands. All were manual workers and looked a dull unsavoury crowd with no spark of life about them. The few who appeared to have an educated air of fastidiousness were in Russian army uniform. They were clean, smart and well-turned-out with an authoritative air of command. This surprised me. I had imagined the Red Army to be led by officers as sloppy and unkempt as their brethren. Our snapshot views of the Russian people were interspersed by longer sequences of glorious countryside, wooded with shining birch and beech trees, wild iris and marigold carpeting the meadows. This enchanting fairyland was so unlike the Siberia of our imaginations, all frozen wastes and glowering pine forests. Rafts of logs floated down the rivers. Cattle grazed along their banks. The Baikal Mountains reared, still snow-capped, against a sapphire sky. The lake lay peaceful beneath, stretching to the horizon. It was the size of southern England and a thousand fathoms deep.

We read our books, we played cards, we stretched our legs when stops permitted and we embarked upon several long conversations which lasted the whole trip, getting becalmed from time to time, then picking up again and finding a second wind. It was an oddly pleasant way to spend time. We were late, of course, almost everywhere and so had, literally, a whistle-stop tour of Moscow. Lenin lay in his tomb — a shrivelled looking little figure. The Hotel Metropole fed us and then we were back on board, heading for the western frontier at Niegeroloje and another episode with the Customs. We changed trains at Stolpce, the Polish frontier with Germany, on to an up-to-date European *wagons lits*. We ran along close to the Baltic Sea and soon found ourselves turning south to Berlin where we arrived at half past seven in the morning. We had the scent of home in our nostrils now and started to feel quite excited as we set off on the final leg via the Hook of Holland for the boat train and Harwich. Already the deserted wastes of Siberia were slipping away.

Manchuria was long gone and the past seven days seemed like a dream. One more night at sea and then England. We puffed majestically into Liverpool Street twelve hours later and could not resist letting out a cheer!

17

Thetis

THE YEARS BETWEEN my return from China and the outbreak of the Second World War could not have given me greater job satisfaction. I was back in home waters and so relieved somewhat of the stress of being away from my family. I was doing a job I adored, working in an element I had been obsessed with since boyhood, an element whose inspiring vastness and terrifying ferocity I had once thought lost to me after the long-ago disappointment of missing out on a career in sail. To have discovered an equally passionate interest in a totally different aspect of maritime work - submarining - was fortunate indeed and I rejoiced in the comradeship of that society. The best thing one man could say about another was, 'He's my raggie.'* Compliments didn't come any higher than that. I am perfectly sure that a lot of the men who served in boats found a great deal more affection and spontaneous happiness among their mateys than they did in their homes ashore. The tug between family life and Service life became intolerable for some of them. There is a good deal of truth in the saying that a man marries the Navy first and his wife second.

After summer exercises with *S2* and the Home Fleet off Denmark I found myself once more back at Blockhouse, this time in command as Captain (S) with the Fifth Submarine Flotilla. By the early summer of 1939 things were starting to liven up and I had a fair amount to do, but there were no particularly difficult problems. Then things suddenly changed. Disaster struck in an entirely unexpected way.

At any one time the Navy had a number of submarines building in various shipyards throughout the United Kingdom. They were built to an Admiralty design which was prepared and worked on by the Naval Construction Branch. The building drawings were prepared by the shipyard which, after consultation with the Naval Construction Branch, was then instructed to proceed with the building of the submarine. It did not become the property of the Admiralty until the day of commissioning. No ship could be commissioned until she had completed trials at sea, which, in the case of submarines, included diving trials.

* An engine-room term derived from the working practice of men side by side sharing the same 'rag'. It therefore came to mean a trusted shipmate and friend.

Shipbuilders, although expert in their building skills, were not trained to act as submarine crews. It was therefore the custom for the Navy to provide a crew when submarines did their diving trials. It was the general rule to send the crew to the shipyard some weeks, or even months in the case of the engineer, before commissioning. They lived in the shipyard port and watched the submarine building. This enabled them to familiarize themselves with every detail of its construction.

In 1939 we had three submarines of the T class under construction at Cammell Laird's yard in Birkenhead. This was a new class of submarine with ten twenty-one inch torpedo tubes. The first in the class, *Triton*, had been launched from Vickers' yard in Barrow in 1937. T class submarines had twice the displacement of the U class, which had been designed as small coastal patrol vessels and were therefore economical on manpower. The Ts were altogether bigger with a crew of 53. They were a force to be reckoned with during the Second World War and were very popular with their crews. Of the 53 constructed, 15 became war losses, including the *Thunderbolt* which had started life under a different name. It so happened that in 1939 Cammell Laird was also putting the finishing touches to a new aircraft-carrier called the *Ark Royal* and the Captain's wife, Mrs. A. J. Power, was invited to name one of the new submarines due to be launched from the same yard. On 29 June, 1938, she glided gracefully down the slipway to time-honoured ceremonial as Captain Power's wife pronounced the benediction: 'I name this ship *Thetis*. God bless her and all who sail in her.'*

It was my duty as Captain of the 5th Submarine Flotilla at Fort Blockhouse to provide crews for submarines under construction. Normally they went out for their preliminary dive in an area close to the port of construction, although on some occasions they went to the Firth of Clyde. In 1939 I had three submarine crews detailed for the three submarines under construction by Cammell Laird's, including the *Thetis*.

Preliminary trials carried out in Scotland had revealed a problem with the hydroplanes. This had been corrected at Cammell Laird's and she was now ready for further trials in Liverpool Bay. The assigned date was June 1st.

I had never been to sea in a T class submarine. Since I was providing the crew and the *Thetis*, when commissioned after acceptance, would be joining me in the Flotilla at Fort Blockhouse, I decided to go to Liverpool and observe the trials. It would be a golden opportunity for me to familiarize

* The first Thetis, a 28-gun 'wooden waller' was built by the early Naval Constructor Henry Adams at Buckler's Hard in Hampshire. She and her sister-ship, *Triton*, were launched in the Beaulieu River in 1773. The working drawings for *Triton's* figurehead can be seen in the Maritime Museum at Buckler's Hard.

myself with the construction of this new class of submarine and see the crew in action.

It was a fine morning, very little wind and the beginning of a hot summer's day. The light grey profile of *Thetis'* bulk lay peacefully alongside, sleek and warlike. As I strolled down to embark in the early morning sunshine, the *Regulus* trials came to mind almost exactly ten years before. A momentary shiver went down my spine as I recalled the bleak November chill. Not a bit like today. The calm, bright morning augured well for *Thetis*, glistening and eager to be put through her paces. We would carry out surface trials on passage to our diving area and diesel trials on our way back after the dive. We were due to return to the basin at about half past ten that night. It was to be a busy day. There was a lot to get through. I began to feel the excitement of taking a brand new submarine to sea again. It was just after seven a.m.

We sailed for Liverpool Bay shortly before ten. Conditions were ideal and the forecast good. None of us could know then that the anticipation and excitement which lent a faint air of carnival to the day would end in catastrophe. The *Thetis* was destined to be the victim of a calamitous disaster. Within a few hours she would be on the bottom and out of control. More than that, she would be out of contact with the surface and we, imprisoned and utterly dependent on mechanical signals to indicate our predicament, were not to realize for several vital hours that these had failed.

The boat's normal crew of 52 was under the command of Lieutenant Commander Guy Bolus. We also had on board a Mersey Pilot, Mr. Willcox, and the Captains of two of the other 'T' class subs who were there to gain experience of the vessels they would be commanding for me in the Flotilla. There were representatives of Cammell Laird and Vickers Armstrong on hand for any minor repairs or adjustments during the trials, together with several Admiralty officers. One of these was a senior constructor, Mr. Bailey, who had been concerned with the design of T class boats. Last but not least there was a small catering staff which carried the important responsibility of the welfare of the 'inner man' during this busy day, and of course myself. Since I was there in the capacity of an observer I was not in uniform and naturally had no authority of command. The boat was uncomfortably crowded, having a total complement of 103. This doubling of personnel had significant consequences in the ensuing hours.

Although *Thetis* was flying the White Ensign, she was still the property of Cammell Laird. The Naval crew was therefore in the position of being seconded to Cammell Laird's for this particular service. On commissioning it would come under my full jurisdiction at Fort Blockhouse but at the time of the trials I had no authority over the crew. They took orders from Captain Bolus who held sole command at sea. The crew was technically 'on loan' to the builders because they couldn't actually take her out themselves. Whatever they needed, they passed on to the Captain and he briefed his crew accordingly. The only thing I did at this stage was to pay them.

The passage to the area set aside for diving trials took between two and three hours. We were accompanied by the tug *Grebecock*. It was customary for submarines carrying out trials to have a tug in the vicinity flying a red flag to warn other ships in the area to keep clear. Lieutenant Coltart was on board our tug acting as Liaison Officer between the tugmaster, Mr. Godfrey, and the Admiralty. Coltart himself was a submarine officer of five years' experience appointed to one of the other submarines currently building at Cammell Laird. He and Bolus had discussed communications between the surface vessel and the submarine at a briefing the previous day. Once dived the submarine would be 'shut down' and out of radio contact. If a ship should happen to come near when *Thetis* was below periscope depth, there were only two options available to Coltart. One would be to drop explosive charges and the other would be to tap on the tug's hull thus transmitting a signal which could be picked up by whoever was on listening watch on the *Thetis'* hydrophones. These were located forward in the ballast tanks on either side of *Thetis* bows.

Bolus listened carefully to all this and after some consideration decided to dismiss the idea of such communication altogether. He told Coltart that he would have a good look round with the periscope before going below periscope depth and would not stay there long enough for a surface vessel to get dangerously close. He then handed Coltart a programme of events for the dive.

H.M.S. *Thetis*
Programme for Dive
Take draughts. F.A. Disembark men not required for dive.
Open up for diving. Make diving signal.
Test H.P. blows on main tanks fitted. L.P. blowers on all
tanks.
Vacuum test. Slow G.U.
Submerge and obtain trim
Test battery ventilation outboard trunks, W/T deck tube, all
T.T. drains, W.C.s and look through ship for leaks.
Surface and blow main tanks on blowers.
Stop. G.U. slow.
Dive to periscope depth. Time.
Lower periscopes.
Dive to 60 feet. Close W.T. doors at 60 feet.
Auxiliary drive.
Fire smoke candles.

Periscope depth 4-5 knots. Check by log.

Raise and lower W/T mast.

Blow main tanks to put forward casing just awash (15' on gauges).

Full speed. Check on log. 380 revs.

Forward hydroplane trials.

Dive to periscope depth.

Stop and obtain trim.

Release indicator buoys.

Surface with L.P. air — take time for each tank.

Take draughts and condition of all tanks.

We arrived in Liverpool Bay without incident. The trial of the engines was of course carried out on the surface. Once dived, *Thetis* would rely on her 336 electric cells for propulsion. We achieved the desired surface performance without difficulty. Steering trials were satisfactory and a number of trials of equipment were also completed without any serious defects being found. We also carried out a test blow on the main ballast tanks.

A submarine's ability to dive rests on the efficient working of the main ballast tanks and speed from the motors to force the boat down, guided by the forward and after hydroplanes. To surface the boat, main ballast tank vents are shut and high pressure air from the numerous air bottles stowed about the boat is admitted into the tanks. The hydroplanes and motors are used to glide the boat to the surface. Part of the surface trials involves checking that system to make sure that all valves operate correctly and that you can get HP air into the main ballast tanks when you need it to surface.

We reached the Bar Light Vessel at about noon. The pilot cutter was waiting there to disembark Mr. Willcox but, with the Captain's permission, he remained on board and had lunch with us. Sandwiches and hot coffee went down very well after a brisk morning's work. Even a light summer breeze can just put a nice edge on one's appetite, sharpened from the vantage point of the bridge. We signalled *Grebecock* to follow us at about 9 knots while we completed our steering trials and tests on main ballast tanks.

By about half past one we were ready to start on the diving programme. This was to include a test of safety equipment as well as the general performance of the submarine. The tide was at about one hour of ebb. Draughts were taken, fore and aft. We called the *Grebecock* alongside to disembark any personnel not required during the diving trials. This was a purely voluntary procedure. The rare opportunity to dive in a submarine was too tempting though, and as it happened no one elected to go. Captain Bolus picked up a megaphone and called across to the tug, 'I shall not be disembarking anyone.' *Grebecock* was ordered to stay in the close vicinity and informed of our diving course. We then went ahead and *Grebecock* shadowed us at about half a mile on our port quarter. I heard Bolus call down the voicepipe and give the order for our diving signal to be sent, then we left the bridge and went below into the control room.

The purpose of the diving signal was to appraise all interested authorities of *Thetis'* intentions. This was accepted practice for all submarines to indicate they were about to dive in a certain position and that they expected to surface again after a stated period. *Thetis'* diving signal was transmitted to Captain (S5) (in other words, me) at Fort Blockhouse and repeated to the Admiralty and C-in-C Plymouth, who at that time was Admiral Dunbar-Nasmith. We told them we would be dived for three hours. We still had our mast up at this point of course so we were able to use our transmitter. The message was sent at twenty minutes to two and as soon as it was acknowledged by the Naval Wireless Station at Plymouth some fifteen minutes later, Bolus gave the order to lower the wireless mast. *Thetis* was ready for diving with her crew assembled at 'Diving Stations'.

'Diving Stations' means all personnel take up their various positions ready to dive or surface the boat and the order is always swiftly obeyed. Surface routine and diving routine are quite different. On the surface the submarine is driven by its diesel engines under the supervision of the Engineer Officer, a Chief Engine Room Artificer, and a team of three stokers and a leading stoker under a stoker PO. To dive, personnel are needed to actually guide the submarine below at the correct angle and then maintain it at the required depth by means of the hydroplanes. Dived or on the surface, there is always one rating on duty in the motor room at the after end of the engine room to oversee the charging of the batteries on the surface and, in an emergency, to throw the switch to put the boat astern. *Thetis* could not go astern on her diesels. Diving routine means that the mast is down and wireless communications are no longer possible so men are needed on the listening apparatus. *Thetis* had ASDIC which was sending pulses out that would bounce of anything in the vicinity and tell us about 'enemy' shipping. The ASDIC dome and hydrophones were on the forward end of the keel, about twenty-six feet back from the bow.

Most importantly, the submarine has to get below the surface. Men must be standing by to flood the tanks. Calculating the amount of water to be let into the tanks so that the submarine submerges and then maintains the correct depth with the proper buoyancy is called 'putting on the trim'. The outside ERA (so-called because he is responsible for all machinery 'outside' the Engine Room) and his mate, a stoker, are standing by in the control room near the valves which they operate when the order to dive the submarine is given. Each man has a specific job to do at diving stations. He must concentrate on that job, do it when he is told to do it and report that he has done it. Submarines are designed to sink, but under controlled circumstances. Submariners are very much aware of the enemy without and the importance of not letting it in through the wrong hole.

Picture the Control Room crammed with people. Under normal conditions the Captain would have been surrounded by his First Lieutenant, Navigating Officer, two hydroplane operators, helmsman, ASDIC operator and his mate, the Electrical Artificer, the outside ERA and his mate, the Control Room messenger and the signalman. That adds up to a ton of men according to the old submarine saying. In *Thetis'* Control Room that day we were nearly a ton and a half, including the two other submarine captains, the Admiralty Constructor Mr. Bailey and myself. Conditions were undeniably cramped and it wasn't long before we were all sweating a bit as the ventilation system struggled with the extra load. Bolus was standing at the periscope and I was somewhere near him just watching what was happening. There isn't all that much space in a submarine control room even under normal circumstances and of course the Captain needs to have an overview of everything that is going on. He must also be able to communicate rapidly and clearly with his First Lieutenant. We made ourselves as inconspicuous as possible. Then came the command: 'Open up for diving'. A businesslike hush settled through the boat as the senior ratings in each compartment began the checking procedure. Lieutenant Chapman took the forward end and Chief Engine Room Artificer Ormes went aft. One by one they ticked off the items on their checklists, waited for the crisp response from the senior rating responsible at each station and then moved along to the next compartment.

Lieutenant Woods, the Torpedo Officer, and the fore end man under the direction of Torpedo Gunner's Mate Mitchell had already started making their preparations in the tube space forward and Woods had ordered the starboard door in the bulkhead between them and the torpedo stowage space to be shut. The port door was latched forward in its open position and TGM Mitchell was on the telephone just abaft the bulkhead. ERA Howells was with him. Leading Seaman Hambrook, Mitchell's immediate subordinate, was in the tube space with Woods and Lieutenant Jamison, the Engineer Officer from *Trident* who was along for the day to get some experience. Half an hour later Chapman was able to report to his Captain, 'Submarine is opened up for diving, Sir. Permission to flood Q tank.' The Q Tank is a large tank which, when flooded, adds negative buoyancy when the main ballast tanks are flooded and ensures a rapid dive in times of emergency or enemy engagement. It is located about one-third of the way down the submarine from the bow and is usually maintained flooded during surface steaming in time of war. All one then needs to do to execute a quick dive is to flood main ballast and down she goes. At a given depth, the Q tank must be blown to regain neutral buoyancy. During submarine trials the Q tank is sometimes used when the boat is 'light' and needs to be forced down.

'Flood Q!' came the order, which was repeated and followed by, 'Q tank flooded, Sir.' The rating operating the Q tank lever refrained on this occasion from making the traditional Anglo-Saxon response which could hardly be distinguished from the 'Flood Q!' order. His poker face was exemplary! Decorum had to be maintained, especially given the brass hats in attendance.

'Dive the boat Number One.' The motors were put to half ahead group up and the hydroplane operators put ten degrees of dive on their wheels but *Thetis* stubbornly refused to comply. We found that we were very light forward. At least a quarter of an hour after the order to dive had been given we were still on the surface. This did not alarm anybody. A light submarine is very difficult to get under water. Bolus ordered most of the auxiliary tanks forward and midships to be flooded but still *Thetis* lay stubbornly clinging to the surface with her gunshield just awash.

After a few minutes Bolus turned to Mr. Bailey and asked, 'Why do you think she's so light?' The Constructor stroked his chin thoughtfully. 'I don't know,' he replied. 'She shouldn't be. The trim was calculated to compensate for the lack of torpedoes.' Eight of *Thetis'* ten torpedo tubes were located forward. The top two were externals and could be fired but not re-loaded at sea. The remaining tubes were located one on each side of the conning tower. Making your way forward from the control room through the accommodation space, you stepped over the coaming of the watertight door in bulkhead number 40 into the torpedo stowage compartment. At the forward end there was another bulkhead, number 25, with port and starboard watertight doors giving access to the tube space itself. There you were faced by two vertical stacks of tubes with three in each stack. The tubes were numbered, even numbers to port and odd to starboard. This numbering system identified the tubes on a panel which was operated by the Torpedo Officer. On trials a submarine did not carry torpedoes in her tubes and this naturally altered the displacement of the vessel. A torpedo weighs about a ton. That sort of difference would have a considerable effect on the trim, so, when a submarine was not carrying torpedoes, the trim was adjusted by letting water into the required number of tubes. This was done before the boat left the yard.

Well, there we were, trying to get down and nothing was happening. Bolus enquired about the trim. 'In the trim, which tubes should have been filled with water to compensate for the lack of torpedoes?' Chapman, checking the trim which had been prepared under the supervision of one of the Admiralty Overseers that morning, answered, 'Five and six should be full, Sir.' Bolus then said, 'Ask the tube compartment if 5 and 6 tubes are full of water or not.' The fore end was connected to the control room by telephone. The message was relayed to Lieutenant Woods and we stood chatting and waiting for a reply. By now it was nearly three in the afternoon and we had spent almost an hour trying to submerge.

Suddenly there was a sharp rise in the air pressure. We felt it on our eardrums and it told us immediately that there was something terribly wrong. There was a tremendous rushing sound. The bow lurched steeply down. We all grabbed something solid and looked around in alarm. Unsecured gear crashed forward as the angle quickly increased. Almost simultaneously a message to 'Blow main tanks' came through on the telephone from Mitchell, but Bolus had already given the order. There was a thud as our bow hit bottom. We hung there at an angle of 40 degrees. 'Shut all watertight doors!' came the order from the Captain. I caught sight of the barometer. It had jumped three inches. The control room depth gauge read 128 feet.

Whatever had gone wrong had done so in the tube space itself. The fore end was a lot heavier than it should have been and the only thing which could have made it that way was an accident that had let in the sea. The crucial steps now were to stop any more water getting in and to surface as rapidly as possible, but *Thetis* was not responding to the HP blow.

Meanwhile, water was cascading uncontrollably into the tube space. The force of it knocked Leading Seaman Hambrook off his feet and Woods had to help him scramble back through the port watertight door in No. 25 bulkhead. Lieutenant Jamison hauled the two men over the coaming and then set about trying to shut the door but it wouldn't budge. They had forgotten the latch. Jamison and ERA Howells jumped back down into the swirling water, got behind the door and released it. They could hardly keep their footing in their desperate fight to drag the lump of heavy steel up behind them as they clambered out of the tube space for the second time. It was a miracle they did it at all and they showed great courage.

Water was now lapping at the coaming and beginning to slop relentlessly over into the stowage compartment. Speed was of the essence. There were eighteen butterfly nuts to be clipped into place and secured. They couldn't seem to get the first one on properly. Something was jamming the door open and water continued to spurt in under it. Suddenly the lights went out. Now it would be impossible to see what the obstruction was.

Thetis could surface with one compartment flooded but not two. Beneath our feet, her life-giving batteries extended under the floor from the forward end of the accommodation space to the after end of the control room. If they became contaminated by seawater we would have the added problem of chlorine gas. From the control room Bolus ordered Woods to leave the watertight door in No. 25 bulkhead and get his party clear of the stowage space where the water was already gaining a hold. With some difficulty they climbed out along the torpedo embarking rails, pushing their way through tables, stools, boxes of food and other gear which had catapulted on to the forward bulkhead when we had nose-dived. The watertight door in No. 40 bulkhead had one quick-acting lever. The men were through it just in time to prevent the water getting any further. Woods, drenched and breathless from his exertions, appeared in the control room and reported events to Bolus.

When it became clear that blowing was not giving *Thetis* positive buoyancy, Bolus ordered the outside ERA to stop and motors half-speed astern but the only effect this had was to slightly increase our angle. Bolus called for silence. Every ear strained for sounds of leakage. The boat shifted and creaked eerily as she hung in the water. With every movement the angle eased down slightly. Although *Thetis* had failed to respond when Bolus had given the order to blow, he was at least sure now that no more water was coming in. It seemed an eternity until we were able to stand upright without keeping a firm hold on something. In fact it was only about half an hour.

Bolus needed to know the precise situation forward. He took a torch and went to have a look. At that stage we still had lights working in the rest of the submarine. He found the bedraggled escapees shivering beside the bulkhead at the forward end of the accommodation space. They were drenched, exhausted from wrestling with the heavy watertight doors and somewhat shocked. They said that the two forward compartments were full of water. The water had come in through No. 5 tube when the rear door had been opened. Remember, there had been an order requesting verification of the state of the tubes from the control room when *Thetis* refused to submerge.

Now a torpedo tube, obviously, has two doors. The rear door is operated manually from the tube space and is opened to load the torpedo. To prevent water getting into the submarine while this is being done you need to shut off the forward end of the tube from the sea and this is the function of the bow-cap. On a T class submarine, the bow-cap was operated by telemotor pressure. A control panel with an indicator lever showed whether the bow cap was open or shut. When the rear door of No. 5 tube was opened, water had jetted in at sea pressure and kept on coming, thus indicating very clearly that the bow-cap also was open. In other words, the tube itself was open to the sea.

In order for him to proceed with the business of saving his submarine and his crew, Bolus naturally needed as much information as he could get about events in the tube space immediately prior to *Thetis* nose-dive. This meant careful questioning of those who had been involved. The general atmosphere on board at this point was certainly not one of panic, but there was some apprehension and Woods and his party were in a state of shock. Bolus was completely in command of the situation which he handled with firmness, confidence and sensitivity. It quickly became evident that a very serious mistake had been made. However, it was vital to get accurate information about the condition of the two flooded compartments and to maintain a positive morale among all members of the crew. Blaming people was not going to get us any farther on.

After his initial inspection of the situation forward, Bolus asked me to join him. I picked up a torch and made my way to the forward escape chamber. *Thetis* had two such chambers, one located aft and the other actually built into bulkhead No. 40 against which we were leaning. It could be entered either from the spot where we stood or from the torpedo stowage space. There were two doors, one on each side of the bulkhead. We needed to get a look inside the stowage space to see what was happening to the water level.

Bolus ordered the escape chamber door to be opened and I stepped inside. I raised my torch to the scuttles on the far side and peered through. The compartment was two-thirds full and the water level was still rising. This meant that the stowage compartment and the tube space were still connected somehow, possibly through the imperfectly closed watertight door or through the ventilation system. It was not a very encouraging sight. Debris floated on the surface, casting odd shadows. The movement of the water played tricks with the beam of my torch as I scanned the darkened interior. The enemy was within. Over a hundred and fifty tons of it.

18

The Longest Night

NAVAL TRAINING TEACHES men to respond positively and practically in times of danger. There was certainly danger. We were surrounded by it and it had poured into our cosy little submarine world with a violence which reminded us all just how fragile a craft we were in. The delicate balance between air and water which, under normal circumstances, maintained our buoyancy had been destroyed. We knew that both compartments were flooded and that *Thetis* could not surface in that condition. We knew that the only way of getting the water out of those compartments was by blowing it out. With number 5 tube open to the sea, pumping would be no good at all. As the torpedo stowage compartment gradually filled, the angle of incline eased still further. *Thetis* eventually came to rest at an angle of 6 degrees bow down. This made working conditions a lot easier.

We had two indicator buoys, one forward and one aft. They were operated manually by levers inside the submarine. When released, the flagged buoys would rise to the surface, still attached to the submarine by long wires, to mark its position. We also had two underwater guns which could fire off coloured smoke candles – red ones in an emergency – which would float to the surface and warn watchers that there was a problem. These were all part of the safety equipment listed on our diving programme for testing. When it became clear that no amount of blowing the tanks was going to help us, Bolus ordered the indicator buoys to be released and a red smoke candle was fired. It was by now about quarter to four in the afternoon and our tug would not be expecting us to surface for another hour. We therefore needed to let her know that we were in trouble. These mechanical devices were the only means of communication we had since we were of course out of radio contact and *Grebecock* had no underwater sound detection apparatus. In any case our ASDIC had been put out of action as we hit bottom. We could not receive through the hydrophones either. Although they had been protected by the ballast tanks at the time of impact, the subsequent short-circuiting of the electrics forward had rendered them inoperable.

While these failures were serious, we knew that as soon as *Grebecock* spotted our buoys and the smoke signal she would realize we were in difficulties and Lieutenant Coltart would put out the alert. What we did not know was that the wire on our after buoy had wrapped itself round our tail and the other one had become detached and been carried off in the strong current. What is more, *Grebecock* herself had moved some way away from the diving area and lost sight of our position. The smoke signal was not seen either. Our isolation was complete.

While Woods and his torpedo crew recovered and dried out a bit, we turned our attention to the salvage blow in the bulkhead. This was a high pressure air line through which air could be blown forward into the stowage space in the event of flooding. There was a one-way valve on our side with the open end leading directly into the forward compartment. For a second or two we felt relief kindling sparks of excitement. Surfacing with the aid of the salvage blow seemed a feasible operation. The equipment was in place and HP air was available. We went through the procedure step by step.

After some discussion the idea was abandoned. We had forgotten the torpedo embarkation hatch. This was the large hinged hatch in the top of the submarine through which torpedoes were lowered into their cradles in the stowage space. It shut down onto a rubber seating. Mr Bailey pointed out that it was designed to be held in place by seawater. The greater the depth, the firmer the seal. If we put HP air in through the salvage blow it would start to lift the hatch off its seating. Our precious air would bubble ineffectually away and we would still be left with two compartments full of water. The Captain meanwhile had asked for a report on the air situation. Our supply had been depleted by blowing the main tanks. He therefore decided that all remaining air should be conserved until we could be certain we would get positive benefit from it. The salvage blow was out on two counts.

There are only two ways of getting water away from a submarine – blowing and pumping. We were forced to reconsider the latter. Somebody suggested that if only we could get a man in escape apparatus into the flooded compartment he could shut the rear door of No. 5 tube and then we would be able to pump out. Once again, the equipment was available and in place. The man could be put into the stowage space wearing his DSEA through the forward escape chamber, which of course was freely accessible from our side of the bulkhead. The door would be shut and clipped. He would be flooded up to sea pressure, releasing the air compressed in the chamber through the manually operated outboard vent in the hatch. He would then be able to open the further door and gain access to the stowage compartment. It would be an awkward and painstaking journey negotiating all the debris floating about. He would have only a torch beam to help him pick his way through the dim waterlogged cavern. He would also have to negotiate the second watertight door into the tube space. There was approximately thirty minutes of oxygen available in a Davis Submerged Escape Apparatus and he would be carrying out physically demanding tasks. Nevertheless it seemed worth trying and First Lieutenant Chapman volunteered to go. He put on his DSEA and entered the chamber. The door was secured and he was flooded up. He was almost submerged when he signalled, obviously in some distress. The chamber had to be drained down before he could be rescued and the water had to be got rid of without it reaching the batteries. The only way to do this was to carry it aft along a chain of men passing buckets. There was over a ton of water to shift.

Chapman finally staggered out of the chamber, very faint and dizzy. His physical distress, caused by the high pressure he had been subjected to, was compounded by his emotional state of considerable agitation that he could not carry out the job in hand. This upset him very much. Lieutenant Woods then offered to take his place in the chamber but Bolus was unwilling to let a single man undertake the operation. If he managed to enter the stowage space but then failed to get back into the chamber it would remain flooded and useless. There was no way of shutting the further door remotely from our side of the bulkhead. Woods still wanted to try, despite the fact that he may well have been going to his death. Mitchell volunteered to go with him and was ordered to stay in the chamber so that if Woods did not return he would be able to shut the door, thus enabling the operators to drain down.

The same procedure was repeated, this time with the two of them. It had the same outcome. When the water got to about eye height Mitchell signalled that he was suffering acute pain in his ears and the chamber was drained down for a second time. Another ton of water to dispose of. Another chain of buckets stretching aft. Although in a sense it was better for the men to have something to do than to be sitting around idle and worried, the physical exertion of shifting all this water was using up our finite supply of air. Woods felt he was capable of having another try. He seemed driven by some superhuman force to effect a positive result from this calamitous state of affairs. At the time, I was quite unaware why this should have been so. Bolus agreed to a third attempt but again insisted on two men going. Second Coxswain Smithers volunteered but this attempt also ended in failure for the same reasons. Once more the chamber was drained down, once more over a ton of water was disposed of, but this time Bolus said, 'No more.' It was clear that no man would be able to stand the conditions, aggravated by the darkness and piercing cold, while he went forward to carry out the various operations necessary, even if he could tolerate being flooded up in the chamber. The plan was abandoned. It was seven p.m.

As we moved back to the control room I suggested to Bolus that, since we had experts in so many technical matters on board, it might be a good idea to call those people together to benefit from their knowledge and hear any suggestions they might be able to make. Bolus was all in favour and immediately assembled his Commissioned Engineer Officer Glenn, the

Admiralty Constructor, Cammell Laird's principal engineer and one or two others. He also invited me to take a part in their consultations, partly out of courtesy I suppose since I was the senior officer on board, and partly because they thought my experience might help them. The question was what to do next. The discussion which followed was remarkable in its way. Clear, practical suggestions were coming from all sides, despite the fact that everyone was under severe strain. Each man had a contribution to make and each man considered what the next had to say with great care and attention. After a while there was a pause.

'What do you think?' said Bolus, turning to me.

'I agree absolutely with everything you've done so far,' I replied. 'It's clearly hopeless to try for access into the tube compartment so I think we have to let that one go. Our only way of emptying the compartment is to get sufficient air to blow it out and that, we have now decided, has to come from the surface. That hatch needs to be secured from the outside to stop it lifting which means putting something across it, a strongback of some sort, and we obviously can't do that ourselves. All this points to our dependence on help from the surface so the only thing we can do now is wait to be found. That will not be long. Our diving signal went off at just after half past one and *Grebecock* will have picked up our markers by now.'

My position in this little group was very curious. They behaved exactly as though I were one of the ship's officers despite the fact that I was not in uniform and had no authority of command whatsoever. I am sure that if I had said, 'Jump!' they would have jumped, but *Thetis* did not belong to the Admiralty, she belonged to Cammell Laird. Cammell Laird had organized the trials in Liverpool Bay with a naval crew under the command of Guy Bolus. I was merely a passenger in plain clothes whose advice was being sought. My advice in this case would probably have proved sensible had our markers indeed been sighted and our position known.

By eight that evening we had had no indication of any movement on the surface. *Grebecock* would obviously have been aware by then that all was not well and we should have heard from someone. If nobody had contacted us it could only be because they didn't know where we were. We were in no position to speculate on the whys and wherefores of that. It was getting a bit stuffy in the submarine – remember we had far less air available than normal because we had lost two compartments-full and we were carrying double our normal complement. We had also carried out an ineffectual HP blow. The idea of using DSEA to escape through the escape chambers came up again but I cautioned against going any further along that line for the moment.

'Look,' I said, 'we know from the experience of Chapman, Woods and the others that successful escape from this depth is not feasible. In any case there is little point in escaping or even getting a body to the surface if nobody sees it. We are still not sure that anyone knows where we are, and the tides in the bay are strong. Anyone getting out now would simply be swept away and that would not get us any farther forward. The only thing we can be sure of is that people are looking for us and that we will be found.'

'So what we should be doing,' responded Bolus, 'is thinking in terms of a successful escape when we know there is someone nearby on the surface. We should be ready for that situation, which means somehow raising the stern of the boat to get the after escape chamber closer to the surface. We know we can't surface and we know we can't effect a successful escape from the forward chamber. We've proved that. We are going to need auxiliary air to get her off the bottom and we'll have to tell the rescuers exactly how to go about supplying that. We need to get a message to the surface.'

'If we can get an inclination of about 15 degrees,' the constructor calculated, 'our tail will actually be showing above the surface. That would put the after escape chamber only a matter of twenty feet or so below.'

The team of experts went over this plan several times, adjusting and refining it to take account of tidal variations in the Bay which would affect both depth of water and strength of stream. Commissioned Engineer Glenn sketched instructions for the surface rescue party on sheets of Admiralty message paper. He gave a brief description of the situation inside the submarine and then indicated where HP air connections could be made. He also showed where the strongback was needed to stop the torpedo embarkation hatch from lifting when air was blown in.

The Captain left the Control Room to move through the submarine and speak to all personnel. He found the men in good heart but needing something to do. Just sitting on the bottom waiting was very hard for them. Chapman, Woods and the others who had tried to get into the torpedo compartment were feeling a bit better. The pain in the ears and across the chest had diminished but they were still cold.

The team worked out detailed plans to lighten the tail of the submarine. This meant getting rid of all the oil and water in the after end. There were two tricky things to negotiate here. One was the fact that the fuel supply and water systems were entirely separate. The only way of getting the oil out was through the water system so the one had to be joined to the other. The second was the question of air. Air would be needed to blow the system but air was also needed inside the submarine. Things had reached the stage by about eight in the evening where breathing was still comfortable if one rested. Any physical exertion tended to produce panting. Those men not required to take a part in the tail-raising preparations were thus at least able to breathe in relative comfort whilst the Cammell Lairders who worked through the night found themselves stopping to recover more and more frequently.

Bolus again took up the business of getting a message to the surface. We had been listening for explosive charges near us but had still heard no sound from above. As far as we knew there was no one there. Even if we could have got a message to the surface — and we considered various methods of doing this — it might not be seen. In a fairly short time dusk would fall so Bolus quite sensibly decided to spend the night hours getting the tail up and then release a message at daybreak. Between eight that night and four the next morning there was considerable activity aboard *Thetis*.

The Cammell Lairders were magnificent. They had no machinery to help them in their job of making a new pipe to connect up the two systems. Everything had to be done by hand. It took far longer than planned. As the minutes ticked by breathing became a positive effort. We used the air compressors to try and reduce the pressure a bit and freshen the atmosphere but it was not long before they ran hot and had to be stopped. Men were forced to pause and drag in great gulps of air. But they persisted with their task. There was no food either. It had all been lost in the torpedo stowage compartment. By midnight the job was done and we heard air hissing through the inboard vents which meant that fuel from the first lot of tanks was going overboard. Once those were emptied the pipe had to be taken off and reconnected to the next lot. The tail started to rise and by dawn we were pretty sure that we could get the tail to the surface. It was another two hours before we knew the tail was showing.

We had now been underwater for sixteen hours or so. With a normal crew, *Thetis* could stay below for 24 hours quite comfortably. We were 103. We had lost quite a bit of air anyway and some personnel had been engaging in violent physical activity. The decision had been taken to use our remaining HP air to raise the tail. The air inside the submarine was very foul and we were all showing signs of distress. Some people put on their escape apparatus in order to get a draught of oxygen but I think Bolus was discouraging that because he wanted them to conserve what slim resources they had left for the actual escape. Up until this point I should say that we had all been quite capable of coherent thought, but Bolus realized how critical the situation had become and therefore put it to us that someone should go up to the surface with the rescue plans without delay.

'It will have to be someone with comprehensive knowledge of the situation on board and solid submarine experience,' he said. 'That means a member of our group. What we need is someone who can, if necessary, get action at the highest level without having to go through all the red tape. Time is now of the essence. I cannot go. I will await instructions from the surface. I can't *order* anyone to go. We still don't know whether or not we've been located but with the tail above water we must be soon.'

The description fitted me. I said I'd have a shot at it. 'There is the risk

173

that I will be swept away and drowned. These are tidal waters and the currents are strong. The message is the all-important thing. It must be found so I want it done up in a watertight packet and strapped to my wrist just in case. Now, the other thing is that I haven't used a DSEA for quite some time so I'd like a volunteer to go with me in the escape chamber.' It was agreed among the group that I should go and Bolus asked for a volunteer to go with me. Three men responded, Lieutenant Woods and two seamen, but I selected Woods for his greater knowledge of the submarine. I still didn't realize at that time that Woods knew he'd been responsible for opening the rear door of the tube which had resulted in *Thetis* going to the bottom. This would not be revealed until some weeks later. In a way he was ready to volunteer for anything to redeem this error. He had already volunteered to try to get forward to shut the rear door of No. 5 tube twice and suffered considerably in the attempts. The poor man must have been desperate to do anything he could to help his shipmates who were now in dire distress. As I say, I was unaware of this at the time but looking back on it I am sure that is why Woods was so quick to volunteer, even after his terrible experience in the forward escape chamber.

Woods and Lieutenant Chapman, who was going to operate the escape chamber for us, took final instructions from the Captain and then clambered aft. Since we had raised the tail to enable this escape, *Thetis* was once again canted at a steep angle. Just before I left the control room I told Bolus that I would attempt to hold onto the tail or the aft indicator buoy once I reached the surface until someone came along to pick me up.

'I'll let you know the instant I can what ships are in the area and we'll get the rescue plan into immediate operation,' I assured him. 'Meanwhile carry on sending men up in pairs. Best to put one rating with each Cammell Lairder because they won't be familiar with the equipment.'

'Right you are, Sir. Expect the next two men as soon as we've drained down from your escape. Goodbye, Sir. And good luck.' 'Goodbye, Guy.' With complete composure and absolute correctness he reached for his cap and saluted me. We shook hands and that, sadly, was the last I saw of a fine and courageous submarine officer.

19

The Escape Party

CARBON DIOXIDE POISONING acts on the mind in a strange way. Picture a wheel with spokes radiating out from the central hub and imagine the spaces between the spokes each contain a separate thought. Under normal circumstances you can rotate this wheel at will and engage whichever 'thought space' you need. You might want the one which is playing a game of golf, say, or you might want the one for doing the monthly accounts. Once you have finished with one thought you can disengage the wheel and move it round to the next one. You can slip it in and out of gear to engage the right thought automatically. You don't even realize you are doing it. Occasionally, very occasionally, it slips out of gear without you noticing and then you feel as though you've been day-dreaming. But even then you still have control over the thoughts and you can get back into gear, rotate the wheel and see where you are.

With CO_2 poisoning you lose control of the wheel altogether. You become disengaged from the thought you want and the wheel more or less spins at random. You may think about a number of different things before you finally drift back to the original thought. What is more you don't realize you have been for a little spin and you have no idea how long it has taken.

It took me three-quarters of an hour to climb aft through the submarine to the escape chamber. I didn't know that at the time. It just seemed a bit of a sweat. It wasn't far from the control room through the engine room to the chamber but the submarine was at a 35 degree angle and I was panting uphill. I remember passing men who sat with their heads in their hands and others who lay back sprawled against the bulkheads. No one broke down. No one was out of control. There were hands outstretched to pull Chapman, Woods and I through and even words of encouragement for the escape party as it made its laborious way aft. I cannot speak too highly of those on board. Their cheerfulness and dignity in the face of great adversity and discomfort were remarkable. Conditions had become so bad now that men's eyes watered almost continuously and they yawned and retched from lack of air. Soon it would be over. All we needed was to get that HP airline on from the surface.

Our party needed to rest for some moments before the escape itself could be undertaken. Once we felt able to proceed, Woods and I broke the lead seals on the DSEA boxes and put on our escape apparatus. By today's standards, when men can escape in totally sealed suits which will ensure their survival on the surface for up to twelve hours even in Arctic conditions, the Davis kit was pretty primitive. But it was all we had and, one must remember, the science of escape had not then been very thoroughly investigated. We didn't know that it was possible to escape from a depth of 100 feet without any apparatus at all, for example. Most submariners were completely unfamiliar with the way their bodies would react in water of any depth and were therefore unable to help themselves. Today, training in the 'escape tank' is all part and parcel of the business of being a submariner. Men are taught not to be afraid of the water. They are taught to feel at ease in it and how to use it to their best advantage, even when they may be tens of feet below the surface.

The Davis Submerged Escape Apparatus was a rubber bag attached to a harness with an oxygen flask which we carried on our chests. It was connected to a mouthpiece with a small cock which we could open and shut. We also had a nose clip and a pair of red rubber goggles. The nose clip helped to equalize the pressure in the eustacian tubes behind the ear drums and prevent damage under pressure. Rather like 'popping' the ears to clear them when you are on board an aircraft. There were two valves on the bag, one which allowed oxygen to flow into it from the flask and another which acted as an exhaust and allowed for the expansion of gas under pressure. When we had sufficient oxygen to inflate the bag partially, we could shut the intake valve and breathe from the bag which doubled as a buoyancy aid. There was also an apron which acted as a drogue to slow descent.

As one ascends, of course, the volume of gas both in one's lungs and in the bag expands. Hence the need for an exhaust valve. Our escape was only being made from an effective depth of something less than thirty feet, including the height of the escape chamber, but the greatest pressure change actually occurs between this depth and surface. In round figures air pressure is 15 lbs per square inch at sea level. For every 10 metres of depth you add on another 15 lbs or 'bar' as it is called. (Think of the weather forecasts you hear broadcast on radio and television. They often give you the air pressure at the centre of a very low depression in millibars or thousandths of a bar.) It is easy to see that at ten metres the pressure doubles, is half as much as that again at twenty metres and so on, therefore the rate of expansion of air in the lungs changes accordingly on the way back up.

When we wanted to replenish the oxygen supply we just opened the valve on the bottom right-hand side of the bag which was a very simple artificial lung. Woods refreshed my memory on the use of the apparatus and Chapman ran through the escape chamber routine. He checked that the upper hatch was shut, then opened the small lower door and Woods and I stepped inside.

176

With a final 'All right, Sir?' 'All right, Lieutenant,' the door was shut and clipped tight. We prepared ourselves for Chapman to flood up.

We stood face to face, almost touching each other, inside a seven-foot-tall cylinder which ran from the deck up to the pressure hull above our heads. A grim sort of intimacy. The interior was coated in white paint and the floor was tiled. At the top there was a hatch about thirty inches in diameter with an outboard vent in it which we would open manually. The hatch would hinge up vertically when the clip was released after we had equalized the pressure from within. The spring would give it a bit of help. The hatch could be opened and shut remotely from inside the submarine. After our escape Chapman would shut the hatch and the chamber would be drained down. He would then check the state of the hatch visually, open the bottom door and the next two escapees would be loaded inside.

We signalled Chapman to start flooding up and in swirled the water, cold, dark and foul-smelling. It was not a pleasant experience standing there waiting until the level rose high enough for us to climb the ladder on the wall of the chamber and equalize the pressure. When it got to about chest height I thought I'd better try breathing through the escape apparatus so I opened the valve on my bag to clear it of air and get oxygen in from the bottle. I put the mouthpiece in and started to breathe. Nothing happened. No air came through. The water was still rising and Chapman was keeping an eye on things through the glass scuttles. I banged on the inside of the escape chamber to signal that I was in trouble and Chapman immediately stopped flooding and started draining down. Meanwhile Woods helped me to check my apparatus and discovered that I had not opened the cock on the mouthpiece so, although there was oxygen in the bag, it could get no further. Had I drifted off into a day-dream? Had the wheel of consciousness ceased to turn for a few vital seconds? It was impossible to judge at the time but, with hindsight, perhaps that is what happened. I adjusted the cock and took a few experimental breaths. Everything was all right. I was very thankful to both Chapman and Woods for recognizing my difficulty and rescuing me from it. We signalled to Chapman and he flooded us up a second time.

As icy water hissed and gurgled in and as the tank filled I grasped the rungs of the ladder and more or less floated up to the top. I was still not too sure whether in fact I was going to be able to do what I had outlined to Bolus. It would be a question of swimming for a bit to reach the tail or the buoy and then getting a purchase. If I failed, at least the DSEA would give me some buoyancy so, if the worst came to the worst, there was a fair chance of my body being found in time and the message being recovered. As the pressure increased I had the sensation of two thumbs pressing hard into the bones on each side of my nose. It was intensely cold. Just as we were about to knock the clip off the hatch and pop out we heard the loud bangs of explosive charges close at hand. We had been found. It was too late to abort the escape.

Suddenly we were out, into the blackness. It felt like being fired through Chaos. I practically hit the boat that was waiting for us as I surfaced.

Almost at once we were hauled on board a whaler which had hitched itself onto our tail. The crew wrapped blankets around us and rowed us across to the destroyer which had found us, HMS *Brazen*. I sent for Lieutenant Coltart who by this time had transferred from *Grebecock* to the *Vigilant* – a twin-screw steamship belonging to the Mersey Dock Board. She was fitted out for salvage work and carried a complete set of diving gear. Her Captain, Hart, had received a call from the C-in-C Plymouth at about half past eight the previous evening saying that he feared an accident had happened to the *Thetis* and asking him to render assistance. He responded at once and proceeded out to rendezvous with the *Grebecock* carrying with him Lt-Commander Bittleston, the Naval Liaison Officer at Liverpool, the Wreck Master, a diver and a representative from Cammell Laird.

I indicated the watertight packet strapped to my arm and somebody helped get it off. I passed the contents over to Coltart and briefed him on the general situation; then I set about signalling from *Brazen* for the equipment Commissioned Engineer Glenn had asked for. Woods and I had escaped at about a quarter to nine in the morning. Within a very few minutes I found myself shivering and shaking under a pile of blankets on a bunk but I did manage to alert Coltart to men escaping in pairs from the aft escape chamber before I was taken below. *Vigilant* put down a boat and the men immediately hove up to *Thetis*' tail and began tapping in Morse, 'Come out.'

It took me about half an hour or so to regain my equilibrium. I suppose it was the CO_2 gas coming out of my system. I felt spasms of wooziness and sudden unexpected loss of control over my limbs. There was no doctor on board *Brazen* because she had been on a normal passage from the Clyde down to Portsmouth when the search and rescue alert had gone out to all ships in the area. As my strength returned I was impatient to be out of my bunk and up on deck again to see what could be done. I got a message off to the C-in-C Plymouth which read as follows: '9.43 a.m. Immediate. Intercept. Please pass general situation to Rear Admiral (Submarines) and Cammell Laird. *Thetis* is flooded to 40 Bulkhead. No. 5 tube bowcap and rear door presumed open. Port door of 25 bulkhead is believed to have only one clip on both compartments therefore being common. S/M is lying with bows on bottom in 130 feet and by pumping fuel the stern has now been raised above water. Air is urgently needed and crew are expecting diver to connect armoured hose to whistle or gun recuperator when they will endeavour to lighten bow with salvage blow on 40 bulkhead. Before this can be done, forehatch must be strengthened with strongback as it is feared any pressure in torpedo compartment will lift hatch off its seating. All on board are alive and endeavouring to escape by after DSEA which is near the surface but air in submarine is getting very foul.' *Brazen* kitted me out with dry clothes and as the Captain, Lt-Commander Mills, and I stood watching *Thetis'* tail, two men came up, Arnold and Shaw.

It was by now more than an hour since Woods and I had got out. We assumed that Chapman, who had been so calm and efficient in dealing with our escape, would be putting men out in pairs as we had discussed. It was worrying that so long had gone by before Arnold, a leading stoker (who subsequently lost two brothers in submarines), and Shaw, a Cammell Lairder, appeared. They were picked up in the whaler which had been standing anxiously by keeping a sharp lookout.

The waters of Liverpool Bay are deep and murky. The tide was running at about two and a half knots on the flood when Woods and I escaped. The easterly direction of the flood was actually helping to keep *Thetis'* tail above the surface. It would not slacken until high water at about half past eleven. *Vigilant's* diver had no experience of working at great depth. During the slack water period he was able to go down and make fast guide ropes to locate the fore hatch where the strongback had to go and the gun recuperator valve where the HP airline would be attached but he could achieve no more than that. The next opportunity would be low water at half past five that afternoon. Much too late.

The long delay before Arnold and Shaw's appearance was explained by two tragic failures. Apparently after Woods and I had gone, the chamber was drained down and prepared for the next two. It seemed to take much longer than usual. Things were moving in slow motion. This was partly due to the angle of the submarine. The next pair strapped on their DSEAs and stepped inside. Chapman flooded them up but something went wrong. Some error was made − possibly as a result of the unco-ordinating effects of the CO_2 − and they drowned in the chamber. A second pair replaced them but one of these also drowned. The other was taken out of the chamber. This must have been a terrible blow to Chapman and those preparing to be next out. Valuable time was lost while the chamber was drained and the bodies brought out. It took fifteen minutes to effect an escape and prepare the chamber for readiness under normal conditions. In the almost unbreathable atmosphere aboard *Thetis*, with her awkward bow angle, it took far longer. Morale must have been devastated. Nevertheless, Arnold and Shaw stood before us now. They had succeeded. They said that conditions on *Thetis* were pretty much the same as when we had left but that the need for an external air supply was acute. Time was so short now that we should expect men to appear in groups of four.

None did. All the time that we watched and waited we discussed what other measures we could take to help those still on board the submarine. It was not long before Captain Nicholson arrived in the destroyer HMS *Somali* with the 6th Destroyer Flotilla. He had been fully briefed on the situation. I transferred to the *Somali* and turned rescue operations over to him. Woods arrived on board and reported that no more escapees had been sighted and that he felt the situation on board *Thetis* must by now be desperate.

With a great wedge of tail sticking out of the water it seemed incomprehensible to the general public that we could not have simply cut a hole and reached inside to pull everyone out. But it was not so easy. There were so many variables. To start off with, *Thetis* was in a very unstable position, balanced like a harpoon which had found its mark by sheer fluke and which clung to it at a precarious angle. We feared that at any moment there might be a leak in the bow and she would go under again. Air bubbles had been seen coming from amidships. We wanted to be able to hold her up if we could. Once men started work on her tail, water could easily flood in. She was only showing sixteen feet or so above the surface.

The second problem facing the rescuers was *Thetis'* construction. The pressure hull of a submarine doesn't just open up like a tin of sardines. Its thickness and strength are designed to withstand great pressure. We did not have cutting gear to hand that was man enough for such a task. We felt utterly impotent.

There was one possibility worth considering, though admittedly it was a bit far-fetched. In the tail there was a thing called a Z tank. This was an internal ballasting tank. The wall, although of strong steel, was not as tough as the pressure hull. There was an external manhole cover allowing access to this tank through a second steel plate. The manhole cover was showing above the surface. Everyone realized that action had to be taken immediately if those left on board were to survive and so, bearing in mind the limited resources at our immediate disposal, the decision was taken to try and cut a hole in the wall of the Z tank with oxyacetylene equipment.

Captains Nicholson and Hart conferred and decided to get the stern high enough out of the water to carry out the plan. We watched as a three-and-a-half-inch wire was passed around her tail and made fast to *Vigilant*'s bows. Two tugs were made fast astern of *Vigilant* and started to tow. *Thetis'* propellers came clear of the surface. The Wreck Master from *Vigilant* climbed on to the stern, removed the outer cover plate and started to loosen the bolts of the inner manhole cover. It was now twenty-four hours since *Thetis* had completed surface trials and prepared to dive.

As the Wreck Master painstakingly unscrewed the bolts, air started to hiss out of *Thetis'* tail under pressure. Alarmed by this, Mr Brock tightened them up again and requested further instructions. He was told to carry on unscrewing the bolts which he did until *Thetis* suddenly started to move.

The tide by now had turned and was beginning to set to westward. Instead of helping to hold the tail up, it was now forcing it down. Mr Brock's position was extremely dangerous and he was ordered off the tail. Just as he got back into the boat alongside, *Thetis* pivoted on her nose and her stern swung round to follow the ebbing tide. Once more *Vigilant* and her tugs hauled away. The tidal stream was gathering force by now and suddenly the strain on the wire became intolerable. Before we could do anything more it parted. *Thetis* dipped underwater and disappeared.

There had been no chance to open up the Z tank. Although the outer manhole cover had been loosened we had been unable to get oxyacetylene gear aboard to tackle the inner bulkhead. But water must have got in somewhere. I think that there was probably one last desperate try with the escape chamber, that in their befuddled state either those escaping or those operating the chamber made an error and that the bottom door was opened while the top hatch was still open to the sea. Water then gushed in and took them down. I understand that a body was found inside the chamber when the salvage operation was carried out and that the submarine was completely flooded.

I don't like to think the men suffered a great deal. The air supply would have been exhausted. I think that people's minds, poisoned by CO_2, would have wandered like mine had done and that they would not have recognized the dire peril they were in, any more than I had as I stumbled aft. They were, most probably, unconscious by that time. We heard that there had been a faint response to tapping on the hull soon after Arnold and Shaw had escaped but that this had stopped. I believe that death came when the submarine was flooded and that all those on board met a peaceful end.

I cannot describe my feelings as I stood on *Somali*'s deck that dreadful afternoon.

We did not understand why it had taken so long to locate *Thetis*, but we had brought out what we genuinely believed to be a workable escape plan. There were delays and frustrations in getting the appropriate surface equipment to the correct location. In spite of all the gallant efforts made by *Thetis*' crew, ninety-nine men lay at the bottom of Liverpool Bay.

The Controller of the Navy, Admiral Frazer, arrived from London and he and I talked about what had happened. All those involved in surface operations recognized with deep regret that there was nothing more to be done. It was a matter of salvage now, not rescue, and that could be taken at its own speed.

In fact it took several months. Within a few hours of *Thetis*' final farewell I wrote a report. At the time it was written there were many questions which I could not answer because there were a number of separate events, both surface and submarine, which contributed to the accident and the ultimate loss of life. These did not become apparent until the subsequent enquiry. My account was of the things I knew to be true, from my presence aboard *Thetis* that day, and was addressed to the Admiralty to inform them of those details. It was completed on board HMS *Somali* before I left Liverpool Bay.

When Admiral Frazer had ascertained that no further action could be taken to save lives, he decided to return to London the following day and invited me to travel with him. We went down by train and my wife was at Euston to meet me. She, of course, was mighty relieved to see me alive and well but our reunion was very much tempered by the knowledge that ninety-nine other families would not be sharing our relief.

During the following days and weeks my wife gave great help and support to the bereaved by visiting, fund-raising for the families and writing numerous letters. I received a great deal of correspondence from wives, parents, relatives and girlfriends of the submariners who had not returned. Without exception they expressed gratitude for the attempts at rescue and an almost unbearably touching resignation to the loss of their menfolk in service to King and country. I found this very hard to endure. To survive when his shipmates have perished leaves a man struggling with strange emotions.

20

The Tribunal

I STAYED IN LONDON that night, running the gauntlet of the press who were out in force. The *Thetis* disaster was a terrible shock to the whole country. It seemed almost beyond the nation's comprehension that nothing could have been done for the men on board when the tail of the submarine was visible, sticking up out of the water. People had a quite understandable desire for knowledge, for explanation and then for justification of the awful incident. There was also the lamentable thirst for a 'sensational' story, an apparently inevitable concomitant of media reportage.

All I would say, indeed all I could say in the immediate aftermath of the tragedy, was 'No comment.' It was clear there would have to be an enquiry and the public would get to know what had happened from the facts brought out there. My report would be material evidence and although I had been in a state of exhaustion and shock when I had put it down, it did at least have the merit of being written within a very few hours of the actual events, by someone who was there and by someone who had as broad a knowledge and understanding of the situation as Lt-Commander Guy Bolus.

So very much of what was written and said about what 'really' happened on board the *Thetis* in the ensuing weeks and months was patched together from hearsay and speculation. Even after the enquiry, reporters were still after 'eye-witness' accounts. I refused to speak, out of respect for the bereaved who must have suffered untold anguish whenever another newspaper or magazine article appeared. I could only have told one small part of the story because my direct involvement with the accident ended after the enquiry. There were questions raised which I could not answer because they centred on technical aspects of the submarine's construction. There were other matters concerning the organization of the search and rescue operation over which I had no influence whatsoever and of which I had no knowledge. It was also a painful subject for me personally. Guy Bolus and I had believed that, given the fact that my body and the attached rescue instructions were found, the submarine would have been saved.

After my night in London I went on down to Blockhouse to resume duties as Captain (S) 5th Flotilla. Years seemed to have gone by since my last trip through those gates. The first signal to arrive at Blockhouse, alerting Captain (S) to the fact that something was amiss in Liverpool Bay, had been delivered about teatime on 1 June by a boy on a bicycle. It had taken one and a half hours to reach the submarine base from Lieutenant Coltart aboard *Grebecock* and eventually arrived at Gosport post office in the form of a telegram. Since it merely requested confirmation of the duration of *Thetis'* dive it did not appear urgent to those whose hands it passed through. The telegram boy got a puncture on his way down to Haslar Jetty Road and took his time about repairing it, dawdling in the fly-blown afternoon sun. At that time the headquarters of submarine operations in the United Kingdom had no direct link with Liverpool. It seems unbelievable but that is how it was. There was no teleprinter link to Blockhouse until 1940. The question of communications formed a major part of the enquiry, since valuable time was lost through delays of one sort or another.

Parliament said that it wanted an enquiry which should be headed by a judge. This was to be a tribunal, not a court, and its purpose was to ascertain what had happened, not to apportion blame. The judge would sit with assessors beside him to determine the facts of the case. Responsibility and compensation would be sorted out elsewhere. There had only been two previous cases where this procedure had been adopted. The first was the *R101* which had exploded in flames on its maiden flight to India in 1930 with the loss of 48 lives and the second a leakage of confidential budget information involving the former Chancellor of the Exchequer, J. H. Thomas.

Parliament arranged this and Sir Alfred Townsend Bucknill, a High Court Judge, was told off to hear the *Thetis* case. The Attorney General, Sir Donald Somervell, OBE, KC, MP, and the Solicitor General, Mr H. U. Willink, KC, had the task of presenting the case to the judge. Somervell and Willink came down to Blockhouse to go over a submarine of the same class as *Thetis*. I took them aboard, explaining what was what and demonstrating what all the technical terms referred to as we moved through the boat. They were particularly interested in the tube space, quite naturally, and were painstaking in achieving their objective of technical understanding of the operation of the bow-cap. They wanted to see the rear door mechanism. They also questioned me closely about the checking routine employed to establish whether or not a tube contained any water.

I demonstrated the two levers fitted to the rear door of No. 5 tube. The smaller one operated a test cock. The larger one was the operating lever controlling the door itself. I moved the test cock lever so that it pointed downwards in the 'shut' position. This not only shut the cock but also acted as a locking device on the rear door. With the test cock shut, the rear door could not be opened. This was clear enough and Somervell then asked me to go through a standard check. I directed his attention to the levers which operated the bow-caps and the indicator board which showed their state.

The first thing to be done was to ascertain whether the bow-cap was open or shut before proceeding.

With the bow-cap shut, I then started to move the smaller of the two levers through 180 degrees towards the 'open' position.

'What is the function of this?' asked Willink, pointing to the small hole, about three-eighths of an inch across, in the attachment of the lever to the rear door.

'This allows the operator to know the contents of the tube,' I replied. 'When the lever is at about nine o'clock, it lines up with a small hole in the rear door of the tube itself. If there is water in the tube above the level of the holes it will come out through them. If the tube is only partially full, the water will just trickle down the door. If, however, the water inside is under pressure, it will spurt out in a fine jet. This acts as a double check on the bow-cap indicator in case of telemotor power failure.'

'I see,' said Willink, taking a few notes. 'And what if there is no water in the tube? Does nothing happen at all?'

I explained that if the tube contained only air, there would be a slight but noticeable puff of escaping air as the two holes coincided. Willink made another note and then returned to his previous question.

'And what would it signify, Captain Oram, if there were no positive result at all from the alignment of holes in this test cock?'

'It could signify a blockage of some sort preventing any egress at all from the tube.'

'Under those circumstances, what would you expect the operator to do?'

I took a four-inch-long brass pin from its housing in the lever attachment and, moving the test cock lever to its nine-o'clock position, inserted the pin through the hole.

'This is the rimer,' I told them. 'As you can see, it is attached by a chain and is long enough to pass through the holes in both lever attachment and rear door into the tube. If there is any obstruction, the rimer should be capable of removing it. Once this had been done, the operator would return the pin to its housing, move the lever on through to the vertical position, thus putting the two small holes out of direct alignment but still allowing a very small seepage of water if any remained in the tube. At the "open" position the safety lock would be released and the rear door could be opened.'

'Is there any other means at all of ascertaining the state of the interior of the tube?'

'Yes, there is. Obviously the tube must be empty before a torpedo is loaded. There are drain cocks at either end of the tube, just above the WRT tank which show whether there is any residual water in the tube or not.'

'What is the WRT tank?' interjected Somervell.

'This is the "Water Round Torpedo" tank which is connected to the tube above by a pipe with a cock. The tank has a valve in it which opens directly into the sea. Having loaded a torpedo into the tube, the operator shuts the rear door and then floods the tube by blowing water from the WRT tank into it before the bow-cap is opened. If the torpedo were not surrounded with water whilst still inside the tube, the boat would nose-dive the minute the bow-cap was opened due to the change in pressure and consequent inrush of seawater. Once all is ready, the torpedo is fired by a blast of compressed air from the rear part of the tube. A lever which depends from the top of the tube triggers the torpedo engine as it exits and from there on its depth and direction are controlled by its own rudders and gyroscope.'

'Thank you Captain Oram. Your explanations have been of the utmost help.'

The next time I saw Somervell and Willink was at the Tribunal hearing in July when I was called as a witness. It was set up so that the lawyers heard the evidence and from the answers the witnesses gave, the judge had to decide what was fact and what was not. I was amazed at the skill with which these two lawyers were able to quote things which I had told them in the submarine some weeks before. They were able to present the judge with very clear answers through their examination of witnesses.

The assessors sitting alongside Justice Bucknill were a Naval Officer called Menzies who was a Submarine Captain and the Professor of Naval Architecture at Liverpool University. There was also a senior representative of Trinity House. These three took no part in the questioning but every now and then Bucknill would appeal to them for an expert opinion or clarification.

Naturally, since this was the first time anyone had publicized what had happened to the boat, there was a great deal of interest from the press, from the Navy and from me. I was interested because I was hearing things for the first time which explained why *Thetis* had suddenly nose-dived that fateful afternoon. I was still unaware of the detail of what had happened in the tube space and more particularly, of Woods' part in it. I did not know, for example, that Woods had carried out his inspection of the tubes on his own initiative and that he had not told the control room of his intention to open the rear door of No. 5. I did not know that he had not heard Bolus' order from the control room requesting a report on the state of Nos. 5 and 6 tubes. Had he done so, this might have relieved his burden of responsibility. As the tribunal continued it became clear that the loss of the submarine depended not on one single incident, but on a ghastly coincidence of events starting with the perfectly innocuous absence, on holiday, of a supervisor contracted to oversee the painting of the submarine which naturally included the interior of all tubes. His jaunty wave as he hopped on his bicycle and pedalled out through the dockyard gates to his wife and family marked the start of a series of small errors. Each had been avoidable, each had been capable of verification. The tragedy was that the final decisive action which sent her to the bottom – the opening of the rear door – was unnecessary. There were enough indications to show that all was not well with No. 5 tube even though one vital check had not been carried out. If you are uncertain about the state of a tube, the one action you do not take to verify its condition is the opening of the rear door.

People realized that this was not a court of law to settle any damages or compensation but they knew that at a later stage there would be cases for compensation and anyone who was connected with *Thetis* was represented. Cammell Laird, their subcontractors, the trade unions, the Admiralty, representatives of the bereaved families and the Mersey Pilot all had counsel there.

When I walked into the room to give my evidence I was confronted by a series of very sharp-faced barristers firing questions at me. The judge pulled them up once or twice for putting things to me like, 'Captain, if you had been in the *Grebecock*, would you have done this or would you have done that?' Justice Bucknill jumped in pretty sharpish when anything like that happened, saying, 'It's no use asking this witness this question because he was in the submarine, not in the *Grebecock* and therefore he cannot answer it. We are here to establish fact, not to apportion blame.' He repeated this last statement several times.

After all the available evidence had been given, the hearing was adjourned to await the results of efforts to raise the vessel. War broke out in September and I was appointed to command the cruiser *Cairo* on convoy duties in the North Sea.

Thetis was dry-docked in November and further investigations were carried out. Both the hatch and the lower door of the after escape chamber were found to be open. The wire from *Vigilant* might well have held the tail up for those few vital minutes more but a sudden inrush of water combined with the turning tide had finally sent her to the bottom just when we had been so near to relieving the acute distress of those left inside.

Upon inspection, the small hole in the rear door of No. 5 tube was found to be blocked with bituminastic. This obstruction was successfully cleared by using the rimer, in the usual way, from the outside. It could only be assumed that the rimer had not been used on 1 June, or on any other occasion since the finishing of the interior of the tube by the subcontractors who carried out the job, Wailes Dove Bituminastic Ltd.

Surveyors examined the bow-caps and found the one on No. 5 tube to be fully open. The bow-caps of the other five tubes were shut and their bow-cap shutters were indented from contact with the ground. The bow-cap shutter of No. 5 tube bore no indentation. The business of how, why and more particularly when this bow-cap came to be open and why it remained so was never satisfactorily resolved.

Justice Bucknill completed his report of the Tribunal hearing in the early spring of 1940. It was presented to Parliament by Neville Chamberlain in April. Several cases for compensation went on but I was not aware of the details. I do know that the rather peculiar nature of the dual control which was exercised between the builders and the Navy at the time of any boat trial caused some problems. The builders were responsible for the submarine and her actions until such time as she was formally taken over by the Admiralty. The Captain carried out the builder's instructions and the crew was under his command. For administrative purposes they were on my books at Blockhouse but all I did was pay them or deal with disciplinary problems such as defaulters. I had no authority over the operation of the boat. That was entirely in the hands of the builders. This dual control was recognized as necessary and had always worked smoothly. It produced some nice legal difficulties for counsel representing interested parties though and these took a considerable time to unravel.

I was never called as a witness again. I had given my evidence and that was that. By the time the salvage operation had been completed and the remaining pieces of the jigsaw had been fitted into place the war was gathering momentum. Having got the *Cairo* and her crew of RNR and RNVR shaken down I was called, briefly, back to the Admiralty and then appointed as Flag Captain to Admiral Harwood in my old friend *Hawkins*. She was patrolling the South Atlantic, looking after convoy traffic.

The *Athlone Castle* carried me off on the first leg of the voyage to my new ship. She was not a troop transport. I was one of twenty passengers on a liner designed to accommodate four hundred. This meagre complement rattled about like peas on a drum and we spent the first few days exploring the ship's broad, deserted decks for rare glimpses of each other.

We groped past Spithead where a convoy lay huddled in the mist. The curtain was suddenly drawn back to reveal a cross-channel steamer laden with cheering and excited troops. They overtook us, bound for France. For a second or two we caught the enthusiasm of their ebullient shouts and waves. The curtain abruptly fell back, cutting off all contact and deepening the air of unreality and silence which cloaked our own vessel as she slipped stealthily oceanward and on to Cape Town.

By strange coincidence we put in on 1 June. I was relieved at the prospect of being able to get some up-to-date war news after the ridiculously cut-about stuff we had been fed on the voyage out, but my mood was sombre as I went alone to my cabin to prepare for docking. A year ago to the day I had found myself aground on the bottom of Liverpool Bay with one hundred and two shipmates. In the intervening months the war had thrown that dreadful scene into a shadow which, I suppose, was a perverse kind of blessing for the four of us who survived. For those who still mourned, the wounds bled cruelly on under the keen blade of memory.

21

South Africa

I HAD SOMEHOW PICTURED Cape Town to be on the south coast of Africa facing south. It came as something of a shock to find it on the west coast, facing north! There were more surprises to come.

During a breakneck car journey to Simonstown, my fearless young WVS chauffeuse entertained me in her clipped twang with the latest 'war' story. The 2nd Australian Force had apparently just passed through, having been diverted from its original Palestinian destination to England. Half a dozen ships, headed by the *Queen Mary*, brought in thousands of troops. They swarmed ashore, broke their leave, broke up the hinterland, scandalized everyone and finally departed. Most residents were presently exhausted and could find very little amusing in this inter-colonial visit. My driver, possibly in an attempt to divert my attention from her enthusiastic cornering, described how two of the marauding Aussies had stolen a horse. Walking the poor creature into the General Post Office, they had stuck a stamp on its neck and instructed the dumbfounded postmistress to, 'Mail this to Austrylia, Leddy.' Whether this was the only story worth relating or whether the strain of my presence proved too much I am not sure, but my driver then relapsed into silence and switched on the radio. As we lurched up to Admiralty House just after dark I suddenly heard Big Ben booming and felt very homesick.

The pretty old Dutch house, whose gardens ran down to a private beach of fine white sand, was to be my home for the next three weeks. In the absence of a C-in-C, the Commodore-in-Charge occupied the official residence. It had been the home of admirals since 1790 and most of them peered critically out from sombre frames as I ascended the staircase gallery to bed that night.

I was due to join the *Alcantara*, an armed merchant carrier, which would take me across the Southern Ocean to *Hawkins* at a secret rendezvous. It was irritating to learn, almost before I had set foot on South African soil, that *Alcantara*'s refit was taking longer than anticipated and that we should not be sailing until towards the end of the month. Despite the prospect of a three-week delay, I was anxious to get on with such things as could be accomplished during this enforced shore leave. Accordingly I set off for the hospital the following morning to visit the Captain I was taking over from and see how the poor fellow was. I felt great sympathy towards him since he was obviously grappling with disappointment over the decision to relieve him of the *Hawkins* command. I had also expected to find him at death's door, since reports reaching me had indicated that he had been invalided off suffering with bronchial pneumonia. The doctors evidently suspected a patch on the lung.

I was happily surprised to see him up and about and preparing to go off for the day. He seemed very bright and breezy, having been told that his X-rays were clear and the prognosis good. He said he was expecting to rejoin his ship in about two months. I kept my own counsel, reasoning inwardly that doctors often keep a great deal to themselves.

My predecessor in the *Hawkins* did much to ease our interview, over which I had been slightly concerned, and I spent a pleasant time with him learning a great deal of the ship and her work. I was destined to be at sea almost continuously. We would go in for a few hours to deserted anchorages out of sight of land to oil once a fortnight. Then off again. Every two months there would be a twenty-four-hour visit to Buenos Aires or Montevideo – a period entirely taken up by official calls and banquets. Just my cup of tea! Then once more to sea. Communications with the outside world were regular, with mails out about every fourteen days and mails in every three weeks or so. One gnawing anxiety of mine was thankfully stilled during this initial briefing on the pleasantly airy hospital verandah by the intelligence that the C-in-C, Rear Admiral Sir Henry Harwood, was charming and easy to work with. He was understandably, though, getting very tired of the station having been there for four years but would probably be taken home in the trusty *Hawkins* once his relief arrived, whoever *that* might be. There was no inkling as yet. Still, from my point of view it was good to hear that I would be 'broken in' under an amiable admiral.

As I left the convalescent patient to his day out, I wondered what my four young midshipmen were making of things. They had travelled down by train to the *Alcantara*, taking my heavy luggage with them. Their feeling of anticlimax was probably even more pronounced than mine at learning of the delay. What was more, they had spent the voyage out in a state of heightened anticipation. Off into another hemisphere to join their first naval ship. And what glorious sight greeted their enthusiastic young eyes? An armed merchant carrier – in a filthy mess and surrounded by noise and discomfort. Not quite the Spithead Review!

My three weeks 'leave' went by quite quickly. There were various preparations to be made, of course, and a great deal to be learned about both South Africa and South America, where I was shortly to fetch up. Meanwhile various entertainments were provided by my hosts and I also spent a weekend shooting on a farm at Stellenrust on the other side of the

Drakenstein Mountains. It was owned by the local 'Mr Harrod' who also happened to be Minister of Commerce in Smuts' government. I would dearly have loved to have met Smuts during my stay, but he was away in Pretoria. He was, of course, a great scholar, botanist and General as well as politician and farmer. My hostess, who was an enthusiastic gardener, had been sorely troubled by baboons eating her young carrots and once sought Smuts' professional advice on the problem. He looked at her gravely and then with twinkling eyes pronounced, 'I like baboons. Grow more carrots!' This gift for creative compromise kept Smuts afloat on very stormy waters for longer than many doom-laden prophets thought possible.

The Stellenrust farmstead was forty miles distant from Cape Town in the region called Cape Colony. It was looked after by Mr Harrod's son and daughter-in-law who explained that most of the agriculture near Cape Town was 'cheque-book farming' because rents were so high. Harrod père had bought this particular piece of land about fifteen years previously and ran it partly as a hobby and partly to give employment. Life was relatively luxurious as a consequence. The nearest 'dorp' was the university town of Stellenbosch, picturesquely old Dutch and a hotbed of fervent nationalism. The activists in the Party had certainly stirred up strong feelings and their names and exploits were on every tongue. After one short week in the country I was in no position to comment on any of the local political views expressed but I determined to remain as open-minded as possible. Piecing together what I was hearing with the information already gleaned from passengers on the voyage out, I saw a picture emerging of a quietly simmering cauldron on whose steaming surface isolated warning bubbles were beginning to break.

I had been astonished by my fellow-passengers on the voyage out with their all-too-vivid tales of South African nationalists who put Party before Empire and who were outspoken in their hatred of the British. I, like many other Englishmen at the time, considered South Africa as one of the Dominions owing unquestioning loyalty to the Crown. Of course, one had heard of Mr Hertzog and his Nationalist Party but one imagined it to be the equivalent of the Labour Party — a worthy but outnumbered opposition.

My pitifully naive perception of the situation was given a severe jolt as first impressions of this extraordinary country — soon to become a vital strategic post, as Suez and the Mediterranean were closed to us — proved to be vastly different to my imagined state of affairs. The core of the whole problem was the 200-year-old rivalry between the English and the Dutch. In the first place, the Dutch took the Cape and made a colony. The English then captured it. Both lived in it. Gradually the Dutch farmers — dissatisfied with the competitive conditions in Cape Colony — trekked up-country and, after enduring great hardships, established themselves in what became the

Transvaal and the Orange Free State. This left Cape Colony with a mixed population of English and Dutch who were, on the whole, quite content to live peaceably side by side.

With the turning century, the alchemy changed. The Transvaal goldmines opened up in the 1890s. This honeypot drew a mixed population of adventurers from all over the world who swarmed in in no time at all to create the economic base on which modern South Africa relied. They were regarded by the Dutch, though, as 'Uitlanders' — outsiders.

Cecil Rhodes at this time conceived the idea of the Union of all South Africa under British Dominion. The up-country Dutch under Kruger wanted independence for the Transvaal and the Orange Free State, and the banishment of all Uitlanders from their hard-won territory. These two factions grew in strength and animosity. It was here that the young Smuts entered the stage as an ardent follower of Rhodes, in whose cause he made himself very unpopular with the Transvaal Dutch. Rhodes, however, was unscrupulous in his designs to add a United South Africa to the Empire even if, in so doing, he trampled on the rights of the Dutch. Before long Smuts found himself violently opposed to Rhodes and, equally violently, threw himself into the fight on the Dutch side under Kruger. Rhodes, after the failure of his extremely ill-advised raid into the Transvaal in 1896, withdrew from politics altogether. The Boer War which followed was long and bitter. Rhodes the Empire builder and his Queen — the last Empress — were both dead before it finished and the results of its cruel irresolution smouldered on for all to see, a far cry from that romantic dream of boyhood which had flashed into my consciousness in far-away Hyde Park.

The end found the Dutch sullen, unforgiving and disheartened. England, however, having won the war, gave South Africa self-government in five years and the Boer leaders, particularly Botha and Smuts, were content to govern their people under British rule. This was the state of affairs I encountered in 1940, but there was no doubt that, beneath the outwardly tranquil surface, all the old hatreds were boiling away. The loyalty of the Dutch South African was to South Africa alone. He was only willing to give loyalty to the Crown as long as Empire policy did not conflict with his ideas of what South African policy ought to be. At this point in history most people realized that the safety and status of an independent South Africa would be greatly endangered in a warring world. Better safe, as a part of the British Empire in return for token loyalty, than sorry and cast adrift alone on the tide of war.

The Nationalist Party, so I learned, was for independence at any cost and 'let the future look after itself!' They fostered nationalist feelings by insisting on a number of symbolic gestures. These included the rejection of the Union Jack in favour of a nationalist flag; the use of the Afrikaans language — a bastard form of Dutch — even though this meant bilingual legislation, and Government sitting in the Transvaal. This last necessitated a 'general post' between Cape Town and Pretoria every six months and doubtless caused an awful lot of grumbling and swearing in whichever language gave greater satisfaction. The Nationalist government in power before the war, under Herzog, succeeded in getting a South African appointed as Governor General — a break in the traditional practice of sending a royal representative. It was quite clear that the Nationalists hated the British and to spite us would cheer on our enemies. Security in this region was to become a major concern as the war developed.

Smuts led the party which considered its interests best served by hitching its wagon to Great Britain, while still being very pro-South Africa. When war broke out, the Nationalists confidently put a 'neutrality' motion before the House. Smuts, who had a sensitive finger on the pulse of the nation and the well-developed theatrical timing of an intuitive General in the field, rose dramatically to his feet and declared, 'We should fight. Who is with me?' Half the Government promptly walked over. This bold move cut the ground from under Herzog, and South Africa joined the Allies.

Smuts set his policy of entry into the war on a firm South African footing by pointing out that it was the avowed intention of Germany (and Italy too) to seize African colonies and that therefore this war threatened the Union itself. Many people believed that any attempt to bring the Union into the war would be most unwise and that precipitate action could cause the Nationalists to revolt. This would give Germany and her very active Quislings a foothold which might well finish in a bitter and bloody civil war, just at a time when the Empire could least afford such an embarrassment. Smuts, great statesman that he was, recognized his moment and did not hesitate to grasp the initiative from under the Nationalists' noses. For the time being he had control, but the position was a complex one.

The British South African was wholly loyal. The 'Smuts' Dutch South African was prepared to defend his country against all comers. The rabid Afrikaaner was concerned solely with South African independence and, in general, was obstructive to the war effort. As Prime Minister, Smuts faced an unenviable balancing act but his performance was masterly. He was gradually weaning the people away from an attitude of 'defend South Africa and to hell with the rest' to a broader understanding of events. This was leading many to realize that, by actively helping the Allies, they would be helping themselves.

The war in Europe added yet another ingredient to those already fermenting in the multi-racial cauldron. Whites accounted for a mere two and a half million in a predominantly black population. Less than a million of those were British South Africans. The majority were Afrikaaners who divided their allegiance between Smuts and Herzog, Smuts having the lion's share. The pure blacks – Zulus, Basutos and so on – lived peaceful lives, many of them working in the cities. There was a strong colour bar though, against blacks and mixed race people known as 'coloureds.' Within the non-white community the coloured seemed to consider himself superior to the pure black because he had white blood in him. The pure black, on the other hand, felt exactly the opposite, considering himself pure-bred. This led to all manner of practical difficulties and it was frequently impossible for the two to work side by side. And then of course there was gold – the lynch-pin of South African economic life. The country was nowhere near self-sufficient and imported most of her needs. Indeed, she was Great Britain's best customer. She paid her bills with gold, upon which she was more or less dependent for her livelihood. The gold was mined by blacks who worked for whites who themselves were divided and so the wheel continued to turn.

Midwinter gusts tugged at our jackets as the Commodore and I took a farewell stroll through the gardens of Admiralty House on the evening before my departure aboard the *Alcantara*. It was 24 June. The news from Europe had been worsening steadily. Italy had entered the war and the diversion of traffic away from the Mediterranean and Suez round the Cape had reinstated its shipping lanes as one of the world's main highways. Fortunately, the distance from our enemies was great and so this focal point was more or less immune from attack, but the odd sporadic attempt by an enemy submarine could not be discounted.

We had all been sickened, after several days of anxious waiting, to hear that the blow had fallen in France and that the country was overrun. Her apparent attempts at peace overtures with Germany made two things stand out quite clearly. First, Hitler's terms would certainly be the equivalent to complete capitulation including the French colonies and, second, the British Empire, without allies, was up against it. The position of the French Fleet was therefore a matter of great importance to us. The Commodore and I were of the same opinion that the maintenance of their ships divorced from their own dockyards would cause us great difficulties. My feeling was that if the French Navy was to break away and join us it would be wise policy to transfer them to our outlying stations and withdraw our own ships to the war area. In this way, outlying bases (such as this one) could take on maintenance tasks at a sensible and effective pace without being rushed into immediate requirements. Supplies of ammunition and stores could be built up gradually.

The strain thrown upon our own Navy was to prove very great. We had to maintain the blockade against Germany at all costs. The North Sea area had to be kept well in control against the possibility of invasion. Adequate protection had to be maintained for the American convoys and

195

anti-submarine work would have to be intensified. The Mediterannean would have to be closed in the west and rigidly controlled in the east. Where on earth were all the ships to come from? Looking out towards Simonstown that evening, where lights blazed, petrol was unrationed and there was hardly a uniform to be seen, we found it hard to believe there was a war on. But, faint and insistent, I could hear the sound of heads being scratched in the faraway Admiralty Operations Division. As we turned to go in for dinner I noticed a couple of tombstones, side by side. One commemorated the death of a midshipman, killed by falling from aloft in the *Maidstone* in 1820. The other was dedicated to the memory of 'Peter. The dear dog of Celia Goodenough.' I marvelled at the British who put up stones of equal size and dignity to mark the passing of midshipman or mongrel.

22

South American Patrol

MY LONG-ANTICIPATED REUNION with *Hawkins* did not go off quite as per signal. Far from rushing to embrace her long-lost sailor with outstretched arms, the lady kept him at arm's length for a full two days, and even then was reluctant to let him get anywhere near her! This was almost too much.

During our fairly deadly twelve-day passage of almost 3,700 miles from Cape Town across the South Atlantic I had been accommodated in a suite de luxe — the temporary home I suppose of wealthy Argentines or Brazilians at one time or another. No ghosts of former occupants disturbed my dreams, but on rising I was cautioned daily, in block capitals, in Spanish, German and Polish that the comfort of all on board depended on the state of the lavatories. I was further exhorted, in lower case, to co-operate in this worthy endeavour towards a sanitary world!

The *Alcantara* was a large lump of a thing, shorn of most of her finery. What remained was bedraggled and soiled by weeks of dockyard ministrations. As she rose to the sea for the first time since her refit, she suddenly came alive again. She and ships like her exemplified the change in life from peacetime to war. They were like citizen soldiers still in their plain clothes, hastily snatching a rifle and running to battle. This lady came of fighting stock though. The forerunner of her name was sunk in action with the German raider *Grief*. The only remnant of the old ship — the key to the Captain's cabin — lay like some religious relic in a glass case in her namesake.

Our final call before laying course across the ocean had been after dark into Cape Town to take on diesel. The Cape Town roads were very full of shipping waiting to discharge cargo or take on fuel and it was evident that something would have to be done to unclog this bottleneck, a problem which would inevitably worsen as the war progressed, to prevent this premier trade route from slowing to a dangerously vulnerable crawl. Our pilot, who of course handled merchant ships exclusively, took us up to the basin entrance at a speed which to my mind was excessive and allowed no margin for mistakes. A ship like the *Alcantara* had very little astern power and in consequence one could not treat her with the same dashing advance as a cruiser. On the other hand she wouldn't steer unless she had moderate headway. It is always interesting watching the handling of a ship, especially a vessel of an unfamiliar type. In ship handling I always adopted the principle that one has two propellers and a rudder and it is good seamanship at all times to allow for the failure of one of the three. Further, that whatever one is doing it ought to be possible to extricate the ship with the remaining two aided by an anchor in an emergency. If two of one's props collapse then it is a matter of fate. If she is kind one can get away without damage. Fate was not required to intervene in our case. There was no machinery failure and our excellent pilot swept us alongside with such panache that I felt sorry we had gone in under cover of darkness. His performance deserved full light and a 'full house' on the quayside.

The contrast between the heavy traffic of the roads and the open sea could not have been greater. We sighted not a single vessel on our crossing — small wonder that the *Graf Spee* had found it difficult to light on victims and had been forced to go to the Plate area, where Harwood so rightly figured she would eventually appear, but even that was pretty void due to the diminished trade between South America and Europe since the outbreak of war. With a safely executed crossing behind us we picked up the *Arndale*, our oiler, at the sea rendezvous at dawn on the appointed day. Together we went in to the secret anchorage, or rather we went part of the way when we met *Hawkins* who said the weather conditions were hopeless for transferring stores, this being a fairly typical winter's day for July in the South Atlantic, and sent us off to sea again. What a transformation from the *Hawkins* of nearly twenty years before, steaming so proudly up-river to the Flagship buoys at Shanghai with band playing and white sides gleaming. Now she presented herself in combat dress, grey and streaked with stains from the hawse pipes. Ugly black patches shone where many an oiler had brutishly rubbed the paint from her flanks at open sea anchorages. She seemed tiny and almost insignificant against the infinite horizon as she steamed past two miles away, an occasional wisp of spray sweeping over her foremost gun. Ships have their personalities — some are kindly, others cold. For me the '*L'Hawkins*' as a Saigon newspaper had christened her, showed a friendly and happy disposition. I had spent a very satisfying commission in her back in the 'twenties and hoped I should enjoy another such this time if only I could get aboard! Impatiently I turned in for my last night on the 'luxury liner' noting that the winter wind had shifted to the south and the temperature had dropped 15 degrees. It was feeling distinctly chilly.

Conditions did not improve any overnight and there was a good old chop going on a fairly lumpy swell by teatime the next day when the *Arndale* eventually got alongside us and 50 tons of stores and my luggage were safely transferred. The *Hawkins*, tantalizingly, did not put in an appearance, leaving me to spend a night on board the *Arndale* since *Alcantara* was off to patrol the Rio area. It wasn't a bad cabin, all things considered, but a bit of a come-down from the luxury accommodation of the past fortnight. However, the Mighty had yet further to fall, notwithstanding the calm, clear dawn which rather lulled us all into a false sense of security on the day of my eventual reunion with *Hawkins*. The secluded anchorage was, by necessity, far away from land and prying eyes. This privacy, however, did not come cheap and we paid our dues in perpetual anxiety on account of wind, swell and most uncertain tides. The appointed rendezvous was twenty miles from the nearest land and sixty from Montevideo. It had been chosen so that the normal traffic of the Plate passed well clear of our secret replenishments. From the *Arndale*'s bridge I spotted the top of a lighthouse. At last I could say I had seen America — my earlier sighting of Staten Island off Cape Horn in 1912 from the crosstrees of the *PJ* having been not, strictly speaking, continental! Then, out of nowhere, fog laid a clammy hand on us, the lighthouse evaporated as in some dream-like mirage and, more seriously, we were lost to *Hawkins*. My heart sank. However, in the afternoon she broke her radio silence and ordered us to close her in the secret anchorage. We arrived at 11 p.m. and a cutter was sent for me.

It was at this point that the genial C-in-C very nearly lost his next Flag Captain. The crew's boat-pulling was quite inadequate to the task it had been set. After three-quarters of an hour we had covered only half a mile, and most of that on a questionable course. The crew was exhausted and the tide and wind were taking us further and further away from our objective. In the nick of time some sharp-eyed lookout aboard *Hawkins* realized that we were drifting into the broad Atlantic and a power boat was sent to retrieve the new Captain from a watery grave.

It is not often one is greeted at midnight by a beaming hero bearing sandwiches, whisky and soda. Sir Henry's welcome was no mere formality. The cheerful victor of the Battle of the River Plate seemed genuinely pleased to see me. He soon banished all my feelings of irritation and cold with his great good humour. What is more he had the sensitivity to allow me to break away as soon as I had been adequately provisioned. I retreated into the snug warmth of my cabin where I found, like a welcoming beacon flashing signals of 'all's well' nigh on half way round the world, my mail. A sailor's life is one of great comradeship but also of great loneliness. The comradeship of life at sea has its own peculiar intimacy — deeper in a way than marriage can ever be because each man knows his life depends upon the man next to him. This is especially so in time of war and even more especially in submarines. The loneliness is being totally cut off from loved ones for endless periods of time. This privation is no respecter of rank. Rating and Rear-Admiral alike thirst for news from home. I slaked my thirst until 2 a.m. with six long letters for which I had waited eight even longer weeks.

Although it must have been a great relief to Sir Henry to know that he would shortly be relieved of this interminable patrolling in South American waters, my excitement and great pleasure at joining *Hawkins* to serve under him were tinged with disappointment that our time together would be so brief. I was to oversee a change of flag during my first patrol. Nevertheless, in the intervening weeks we established what I like to think of as a good rapport and the Admiral dubbed our evening meetings, in which we dissected the events of the day and prepared for whatever might launch itself over the horizon at us on the morrow with a companionable whisky and soda in his sea cabin, 'Oramnews.' The first of these occasions was a sombre one during which we heard, in an appalled silence, the wireless news of the British action against the French Fleet at Oran. What a miserably tragic twist of war's fortune that we, the champions of honourable sea warfare in which without cant we sincerely believed, were forced to attack our ally in harbour, to kill his men and to sink his ships. The C-in-C's face was grim as we parted company that evening. He said little but I guess our thoughts were running on parallel courses as we bade each other goodnight. What maggot of weakness, I wondered as I set about ordering my cabin and stowing my personal gear, could have eaten the heart out of the French people? Was it subtle enemy propaganda? Was it that they had become decadent with their surfeit of victory at Versailles? Was it their Latin nature causing total collapse after defeat or had their spirit never been in this war in the first place? Was the grandiloquent virtue of their statesmen without an echo from their people? I did not think the last could possibly have been true because the people of France appeared to have shown more spirit of resistance than their leaders. However, be all this as it may, the fact was that the leaders were now the puppet spokesmen of Hitler and France was in consequence our enemy. I would not have been surprised if Germany had ordered France to declare war on us – an order the Government would have been obliged to obey. I was at a total loss as to the possible reaction of the French people in such circumstances but thought it was a great pity that we had been forced to antagonize French public opinion by killing their sailors.

Not all our 'Oramnewses' dealt with matters of such gravity. Sir Henry said, with genuine feeling, that he would miss our chatty sessions when he finally left at the beginning of September. The feeling was a mutual one. The C-in-C's straightforwardness was something I immediately warmed to and admired. There were others who found his approach somewhat too 'natural' and direct, but he responded positively to directness in others and while one could, in a certain sense, describe him as a simple man, there was nothing simple at all about his intelligence and ability to tackle complex problems which he approached with, at times, a disconcerting clarity of vision and robust good humour. In consequence his judgements were invariably carefully thought out, unclouded by irritation and perfectly sound. I quickly learned that he was not a man to suffer fools gladly, but, as he himself admitted in an unguarded moment, his tender heart was apt to check the sting of his whip when he had to use it! His men perceived him as a modest, understanding and kindly leader who was sure of himself but who yet remained singularly unspoilt by the adulation showered upon him as the victor of the *Graf Spee*.

She lay just to the west of the entrance channel to Montevideo, a splendid monument to the determination of our ships. By the time we arrived to pay an official call for Sir Henry to say goodbye to his Uruguayan government friends, she had sunk into the mud leaving only her bridge and mast rearing drunkenly from the sea. Our visit lasted 24 hours precisely. Under the terms of the Hague Convention ships of war were only permitted to enter a neutral port for a stay of 24 hours once in 3 months for the purpose of fuelling. There was no mention of purely friendly visits which precluded the embarkation of either stores or fuel so we could theoretically have requested permission to enter more freely. In Uruguay this would probably have been granted, but by sticking strictly to the letter of the law we avoided German protests and thus the hardening of neutral diplomatic opinion against us.

My political and diplomatic history had been brought sharply up to date since I had sailed into South American waters where I learned that all Latin American countries were carefully trimming their sails to the belligerent wind. Germany's apparent invincibility and the accurate timekeeping of her schedule of conquest caused a feeling that she would win the war and, not unnaturally, Pan-Americans were eager not to antagonize a power which might shortly exercise dominion over them. The outcome, however, was not cut and dried. Recent evidence of British preparedness, Hitler's failure to be in London by July, the daily losses of German planes and reports of damage to German industries by the RAF were gradually convincing at least the Argentine that Britain was not done for yet. The majority certainly seemed to favour a British victory, although they were not wholeheartedly convinced of one.

Argentina had traditionally disputed the USA's evident desire to assume leadership of the American continent and the latter's size and military power put Argentina in a difficult and weak position. Hence she went to the Pan-American conference in a very canny frame of mind and, like the other delegates in Havana, emerged dizzied by the blasts of war. The enemy was certainly working hard in Argentina — 15,000 Germans in Misiones (a narrow spit of country in the north-east) having been very efficiently organized into making secret hoards of arms with the objective of welding Paraguay, Uruguay and southern Brazil into a German colonial possession. The Argentine's attempts to clear this up could only be described as mild, although some Germans were being brought to trial. Public opinion was not much impressed by this sort of behaviour and the Germans were in bad odour – a fact shown by the action of the pusillanimous government in arresting the editor of a peculiarly offensive German-run newspaper, *El Pampero*. The young Argentines, meanwhile, were feeling the growing pains of nationalism – a situation not unlike that which I had witnessed in China some years before. They disliked the spread-eagle of the USA, feared the shadow of the swastika and were irritable with Britain's hold over their economic life.

As I gradually took on board the complexities of the situation and began to develop some understanding of the delicately balanced local conditions, Sir Henry's recapitulation of our function in the South Atlantic assumed greater significance. It was not simply a question of staving off the boredom of a never-ending patrol which had, perforce, to continue both day and night almost without ceasing. At times we certainly began to feel like an old gramophone needle stuck in the same groove. *Hawkins* had notched up a most astonishing record of steaming and for an old lady of 21 years she was in remarkably fine fettle, but it was clear that a stand-off would soon become a necessity if serious mechanical failures were to be avoided. After leaving the Reserve Fleet in December, 1939, she had last seen England's shores in January, 1940, and since then had steamed 51,000 miles – the equivalent of maintaining a constant speed of ten and a half knots for six months. Both ship and company justly deserved a short rest for, out of 200 days, only twelve had been spent in harbour. *Hawkins* badly needed a face-lift and her company, on the principle that 'a change is as good as a rest' needed a boost. To try and alleviate the immediate strain on the crew I made various alterations to the ship's organization which had remained unchanged since her departure from England.

Men cannot keep alert without reasonable respite and to have had virtually the whole of the company in three watches for six months without any break other than one day a month in harbour was, I felt, very severe. Neither was it conducive to a successful outcome in the event of an engagement. The men needed more confidence in their own preparedness for such eventualities and their officers needed to be assured of 100% reliability. A slight but significant adjustment from three guns manned each night to two, and a third at one minute's notice relaxed the regime sufficiently for each man to get a full night once in three nights without obviously impairing our state of readiness. It also yielded a much-needed afternoon workforce hitherto denied to the Commander due to the whole ship's company having standing a watch each night. A drive to banish poor *Hawkins'* dirt and rust soon had the old lady starting to take pride in her appearance again, but weeks of toil were necessary to make up leeway.

Sir Henry emphasized that it was our job to keep the seas and that we should at all costs refrain from asking for benevolence unless we had some particular reason. Securing our shipping against raiders in the empty vastness of the South Atlantic was a bit like playing detective on a murder hunt with not even the convenience of a body on which to start. Reports from our merchant ships of smoke on the horizon might reach us up to a week after the event, by which time the raider, if raider he had been, was safely away and stalking fresh quarry in new waters. There were very good reasons for these time lapses. The merchant skipper was told to observe a strict wireless silence to avoid detection by Direction Finding. Obviously we could not hunt down raiders unless the victims and bystanders shouted the alarm. A merchant skipper needed to weigh the balance very carefully indeed before taking the decision to break his w/t silence. He, quite rightly, had the security of his own vessel in the forefront of his mind at all times, and to risk exposure to enemy fire for the sake of passing on information which would of course be of the greatest value to us in ultimately ridding the ocean of the threat was not a particularly attractive option to him.

Hawkins settled fairly easily into her new regime and everyone seemed to perk up as the cleaning brigade got to grips with things. We plodded steadily on, making ourselves readily visible as per instructions but rarely encountering anything of consequence ourselves. Then, splash! A large brick was hurled into our placid pool disturbing the peace of a Sunday evening. A series of signals reached us from a wounded and limping *Alcantara* south of Trinidad who had been hit and holed in the engine room a full thousand miles from our position. The raider had struck from eight miles outside her range and after opening fire had made off. *Alcantara* gave chase, closed the German and returned fire. The action continued for about an hour until a chance hit by a shell on *Alcantara*'s waterline flooded the engine room to two feet and blew out three of the four motors of the condenser extractors. With only one left to depend on, her speed was brought down to ten knots. The raider made off and after plugging the hole with hammocks, *Alcantara* gave up the chase and made for Rio. She reported that the enemy used shrapnel, but I thought she was more likely to have suffered the splinter damage which so many of our ships were experiencing. It was strange to think of the peaceful ambling old rocking horse with two 15-foot holes in her side and badly scarred with superficial damage. It was also maddening that she was prevented from finishing off the raider, but she made a valiant attempt.

Our casualties were two killed — one of them a Lieutenant who I had got to know on the voyage out from Cape Town — and seven wounded. This intelligence gave me pause for thought as I turned the pages of the Navy List that evening and saw, with piquant pleasure, my son's name beside my own for the first time. I felt great satisfaction on his behalf that the years of schooling had finally culminated in this achievement and could imagine his excitement at joining his first ship. Ironically, his first experience of Service life would be in the pursuit of man's crowning futility — war. But war offered youth opportunities so often denied in peacetime — the chance to give selfless service through courage, vision and the kind of idealism which all too frequently lies dormant until some predator rears up to snatch it away. Youth after war would be another matter. The dangers of rank disillusionment and the balance of young minds thrown out by too much experience of horror and too little of life would come in the confused and vicious seas following the gale.

Of German casualties we had no news, neither could we be one hundred percent sure that *Alcantara*'s fire had made its mark. We could only assume from the raider's behaviour that he had been hit hard and was, even as we pieced together the details of the action, slinking away to lick his wounds. It would have been folly for us to go chasing madly across the South Atlantic, so we sedately moved on to the area where our shipping plot showed the greatest density of traffic and awaited further news. That the wily fox had got into the pen and caught some chickens became increasingly apparent from the growing list of our ships overdue: two badly and four slightly. Our quarry had temporarily vanished over the horizon, but he was liable to pounce anywhere, unless of course *Alcantara* had disabled him, in which case he would be slinking off to regain Germany. We just did not know and, meanwhile, with the whole of the South American coast under our care, there were good reasons why we should have been in any one of a dozen different areas at once. We were further confused to get the QQQQ raider alarm signal from a vessel in a position NE of Ascension. *Alcantara*'s friend could not possibly have reached this position in the given time at a speed of less than 21 knots, so everything pointed to a second raider. As it happened, *Dorsetshire* was to the south and she was sent off to try and intercept, while *Cumberland* covered an unfrequented bit of sea on the off-chance that *Alcantara*'s raider would go to mid-Atlantic to repair himself. In the meantime we had to allow for the possibility that he would strike at our routes and so we remained poised between Rio and the Plate keeping our ears alert for a distress call. I did not anticipate another attack so swiftly, as a raider's main object was secrecy and once his position was given away his natural tendency was to make off to other waters. It was certainly a very effective type of warfare, even if in strike terms it was only partially successful. I felt the Germans had rather underestimated its efficacy in causing us to expend a massive amount of energy and spread our ships over the seven seas!

Having more or less written off the chances of a follow-up raid in my own mind I was called from my slumbers in a hurry a couple of nights later with the report, 'Darkened ship right ahead.' It was not unusual to find merchant ships darkened but one never knew. I reduced speed and sighted our friend about a mile away. All looked well and I was just about to ask his name when he spotted us, shied like a horse and steamed away stoking up for all he was worth. We flashed at him, but, getting no answer, and, by his silhouette, knowing him to be British, we went on our own course so as not to frighten him. Suddenly from the wireless office came a report that a ship was making the QQQQ call, giving a position 160 miles to the south of us. In spite of this position we had a strong suspicion that it was our friend shouting his dread news to the world. He thought *we* were the raiders! Fortunately we were able to confirm this by D/F bearings and we chased off into the darkness after him to put his fears at rest. We eventually caught him still straining every nerve to get away and flashed at him till he answered that he was the *Temple Moat*, whereupon we signalled 'Congratulations on your promptitude Stop I am British warship Stop Please cancel your distress call Stop Goodnight Ends'!

The, apparently, conflicting interests at work in the bosom of the merchant skipper, upon whom we were in so many ways utterly dependent both at home and at sea in this war, were not the only obstacles to be faced in the matter of communications. The Admiralty seemed to be achieving remarkable success in keeping us utterly cut off as we bobbed about between Rio and the Falklands. With the two raiders still at large we were very much on the alert, a condition which was hindered rather than helped by a change of code. Owing to the deterioration in the mail service, we did not receive our copy by the date on which it was brought into force. We consequently found ourselves in receipt of signals which we could not decode. The Naval Officer on the Falklands, being familiar with the vagaries of the mails, was astute enough to wonder whether we had got our copy and almost extricated us from our predicament by broadcasting a signal to the effect that he would pass on messages in another code if we wanted them. The silly mutt then went and sabotaged the whole thing by adding that for security reasons he would *not* send them on unless he got a signal from us saying that we wished him so to do! There we sat for several days, forced to maintain wireless silence, with untranslatable signals coming in all the time. A classic example of the importance of looking at a problem from both ends. The Falklands Officer had got it half-right and then ruined it by not thinking it through.

Fuelling visits were not requested unless unavoidable since Admiralty policy dictated that we should hold these up our sleeve so as to have a legal right to enter harbour after an action at a time when it might be vital to get re-fuelled and off to sea again. Sound advice, but it directed my concern once more to the question of maintaining morale and alertness among the ship's company who, with such short periods ashore at such long intervals on their weary unchanging patrol, found time dragging almost interminably.

In China we had been virtually unrestricted in such matters; on the other hand there had been no war to fight and the underlying strategy had been the motivation of men who were essentially playing war games. Here the war was real enough, no doubt of that, but any action we saw was likely to be sporadic and extremely unpredictable. Our job was none the less important for all that. Showing ourselves on the neutral route to and from the Plate, which lay fairly close along the shore east of Montevideo, would accomplish a threefold object: firstly we should be reported at intervals so that the enemy got the impression that we invariably haunted the normal trade route; secondly when we occasionally disappeared, we created an air of uncertainty and thirdly, by being constantly in the vicinity of the various routes followed by British ships entering or leaving the Plate, we were handy if a raider appeared. We consequently rang the changes on the first two, so arranging matters that we were never very far away from the focus of British activities. On some days we would be sighted by up to a dozen neutral ships whose brief appearances gave some reason for our existence during the uninviting days of cloud, high winds and unexpectedly tempestuous squalls which on occasions forced *Hawkins* to bury her nose deep into the giant waves and even submerged the stern, sometimes to a depth of as much as eight feet as she rose to meet the next challenge. With a jar of extinction the monsters would break impetuously forward, spray streaming wild like white hair blown in the wind and, standing hypnotised in my sea cabin, I would watch my scuttle become a living emerald.

Sir Henry's farewells were completed. A change of flag more or less in mid-ocean cloaked in the utmost secrecy presented us with some nice difficulties, but we heard in due course that our new C-in-C had left Cape Town in the *Queen of Bermuda* and would soon reach us via Tristan da Cunha where she was to embark a mad clergyman. We were under orders to remove him *by force if necessary* and return him to Durban where we should, at long last, get our much-needed refit. I don't think any of us really believed we would achieve the ultimate haven without disaster until we heard that musical echoing of the wedges being driven into the shores.

23

South African Convoys

OUR SIX WEEKS IN Durban slipped by in less than half that time, or so it seemed. *Hawkins* echoed to the clang and clatter of a thorough refit, although labour was becoming more and more difficult to find as the effects of the European war began to seep through to South Africa. One morning the usual dockyard symphony of irrepressibly tuneless whistling to metallic hammer blows was temporarily silenced by a visit from the Minister of the Interior who brought with him the Mayor. Their purpose, other than the sociable consumption of large pink gins, was unclear, but the Minister was very amiable and most interesting on the subject of Smuts's visit to Egypt, an event which had been carefully premeditated with complete secrecy.

Smuts, Eden and Wavell found themselves in complete agreement that the war would enter its Middle Eastern phase in the New Year of 1941. Wavell was apparently satisfied with the resistance he could muster in Egypt against an Italian thrust from Libya and was quite sanguine about the result. He was less confident about the double threat from both north and west but felt that, with the arrival of the promised reinforcements in a few months time, he would be able to cope. Winston Churchill was apparently in agreement with these three on the development of the war but a section of the British Cabinet still clung to the invasion bogey and was averse to weakening the strength of forces in Britain in any way.

I was in the offices of the *Natal Mercury* several evenings later watching the linotype machines rattling out the next morning's headlines when the news of Hertzog's resignation from the extreme Nationalist party came through. The editor was a friend who had invited me in to see the newspaper being made and to have a chat about the current goings on in the country. He was in the middle of a very entertaining description about the absurdity of the censorship regulations when he suddenly broke off and rapped out, 'Stop the front page!' A buzz of excitement went through the place as tomorrow's news was rewritten. Hertzog and Smuts represented two large sections of public opinion and each had a sizeable following. The outbreak of war had caused a small flow of Hertzogians to go over and follow Smuts's Imperial banner. It had also caused Hertzog's Nationalists to become more outspoken, to a degree which, in extreme cases, could definitely have been called pro-Nazi. This anti-British attitude did not find favour with all the

Nationalists and a gradual split in the party had been growing. The *Mercury's* editor explained that the Ossewa Brandwag — Watch on the Waggons — nominally a cultural organization, had in fact been thoroughly organized on a military basis. Hertzog's resignation would undoubtedly prompt the moderates in the party to follow suit, thus throwing the extreme Nationalists into the limelight. Hertzog's absence would strengthen the hand of Government in tightening up the Brandwag's activities.

At nine o'clock on a Sunday morning under a tear-filled sky the sailors cast a mournful eye at the retreating shore as we left harbour. For six quick weeks they had had fun, friendliness and freedom and the grey sea stretching to infinity appeared a poor cold companion as he slapped a spray over the bows. We were bound for the Cape and Simonstown once more, before heading off across the Southern Ocean to resume our patrol. There were no alarms on the passage south; the Agulhas Banks were for once unshrouded by the fog which so often rolled across those particularly treacherous shipping lanes, boiling up as if from some subterranean cauldron, and we went in and secured with little bother, other than the inconvenience of an overcrowded harbour. My preparations for dinner and bed were abruptly curtailed by that uncomfortable signal 'Raise steam with all dispatch.' Accordingly at 9.15 p.m. I crept out of harbour once more into a dark and cheerless night.

Our quarry was a Vichy French ship which, with other outlaws, was trying to run the blockade from Madagascar into Dakar or France. She had been sighted by the aircraft patrol 160 miles south of the Cape of Good Hope at 6.10 p.m. and I had orders to search and, if I found her, to bring her into Simonstown for examination. We were anxious to track her down because she had on board the ex-Governor and other prominent Frenchmen of pro-Ally feelings who were being forcibly repatriated; we were eager to rescue our gallant friends. It did cross my mind that if we came across them they might scuttle and there is precious little one can do to stop a scuttler except frighten him with big noises. Judging by the gale and heavy sea we met outside I imagined the thought of scuttling would be wholly abhorrent. A prevailing south-easterly which blew all summer long at that latitude had been howling for days. Whether its local appellation of 'Cape Doctor' described a cooling influence which kept the populace healthy or a psychological one which tore the nerves to shreds and filled the asylums I could not fathom. The saving grace was that it generally accompanied blue sky and warm sun.

The French ship must have taken fright at the aeroplane and sheered off to the southward for we saw nothing of her and so returned, after twenty-four hours of fruitless steaming, to Simonstown where I had to request another four days in the dockyard to attend to the de-gaussing coil which had been fitted in Durban. It had failed to survive the heavy seas we encountered on the way round and was tearing away all round the fo'cs'le. The delay was irritating and frustrating in that it was a false start for the men who had found it difficult enough leaving Durban and reconciling themselves to more long weeks of patrol. On the other hand it was a very good thing that the de-gausser had failed before we had left Africa's shores and not in mid-Atlantic. The men snatched at an unexpected few days ashore and I went off to play golf in a mood not ideally conducive to accurate putting.

I returned from my game to find a complete change of plan awaiting me. We would not be returning to the South American Division!

It transpired that this change was part of the Admiralty's scheme to dispose available forces for dealing with the increasing number of armed raiders on the high seas. There were reputed to be five in addition to the *Admiral Scheer* currently operating in the North and South Atlantic, also the Indian and Pacific Oceans. Consequently hunting groups were being established and troop convoys were being given close escort. This was a matter of prudence since they were such tempting bait. The fast convoys taking reinforcements to the Middle East had a formidable journey of just on 12,000 miles from Southampton to Suez – that is 30 days' continuous steaming for a 17-knot ship. Allowing time for fuelling, turning round and repairing, a ship would be occupied for three months in taking out a single load of troops and returning. This made me wonder whether it would not soon be forced upon us to push heavily escorted troop convoys through the Mediterranean.

The hunting groups, consisting of 8″ cruisers and aircraft carriers, were positioned at focal points – namely the Azores, Freetown, Plate and Cape. The convoy escorts were told off to work the North Atlantic, from Britain to Freetown, Freetown to Durban and Durban to Aden. This was our new brief and we were due to start work in 48 hours on the Freetown/Durban section. Trade convoys were to be escorted by AMCs when available and covered by R class battleships in the North Atlantic and the hunting groups elsewhere. On studying the Admiralty's scheme I discerned the hand of Sir Henry who, as Deputy Chief of Naval Staff, had a large say in matters of policy. The formation of hunting groups at focal points was always one of his convictions and he considered that if shipping were suitably and widely spread out, the sinkings would be negligible on the open seas. This would force the raiders to work in the focal areas where we could pick them off.

On sailing to assume our new role as escort I was surprised and pained to hear that we had thirteen absentees – nine seamen and four marines. The relaxation of Durban clearly had not satisfied their wants and they had cut themselves adrift in search of more. I suspected that the majority had not really intended to desert but, thinking we were returning to nine months' intense boredom off South America, they had decided to grasp the opportunity for a final fling. The ship having slipped off under new orders earlier than expected, they would now all have to go to prison. This was a shame since our new work offered more substantial fare than the Plate patrol. We would have to visit our southern terminal points – Durban and Simonstown – for fuel and an occasional day or so in harbour. The northern terminal at Freetown was a damp, hot hellhole from all accounts, but, taken by and large, we would be going into harbour about once a week, a vast improvement on South America if only the thirteen hotheads had trusted in fate to deal them out a better hand on this patrol and joined their ship on time. Our sea-time obviously depended on the number of troop convoys requiring our protection and there seemed little likelihood that it would be very much reduced. It did, however, have the definite advantage of gratifying and instantaneous feedback in that a convoy gave visual evidence of useful work accomplished. Off South America our existence often seemed aimless and our usefulness nebulous.

We met our first convoy at the northernmost limit of our beat just two hundred miles below the equator. It was an imposing party – ten ships of more than 20,000 tons escorted by the *Devonshire* and the *Cumberland* who sent a boat to *Hawkins* with our new orders. We manoeuvred gently into her place and she disappeared to the west to take over the C-in-C's pendant in our stead. A rather cheerful 'Give our love to Lobos' from our Navigator summed up the popular feeling as we saw someone else going off to what we knew was a deadly boring existence. For our part, we looked with pleasure and uplifted pride at our charges – it was nice to have some scenery in our view for a change. Assuming that the smallest of these giants took 1,500 men, we probably had a full Division of troops and their equipment in our care. The next stop was Durban and then on to Palestine, I imagined as reinforcements for our Middle Eastern defences. It was heartening to see this evidence of extensive preparation. We had already passed a similar convoy on its way to Egypt as we had come north to rendezvous with ours.

The manoeuvring of a large convoy was a clumsy business. The signal staff in the merchant ships were very limited and naturally had not the speed of a Navy signalman. To alter course by signal was a drawn-out affair but it could be accelerated by the Commodore's decision to go for an 'emergency' red light turn. This involved exhibiting a red light to warn of a 20-degree turn to take place at its extinguishment in the direction indicated by blasts on the fog horn. It could be executed fairly quickly but was limited to 20 degrees as the convoy 'wheeled' round because the columns would otherwise get too close to each other and come on to a possible collision course if a greater turn were made. Consequently after each emergency 20 degree turn there had to be a pause of up to 20 minutes for the convoy to avoid running itself down. The navigational turn of, say, 85 degrees therefore represented, in practical terms, four turns of 20 degrees taking an hour even by the red light system and a final 5 degree turn by signal. Laborious and painful!

After 5,000 miles of loving protection we had to kiss our convoy goodbye and spring ahead at 23 knots for a brief separation. Our long trek north to meet them and the comparatively high speed turnaround meant I was running short of fuel so that I had to get ahead to Simonstown, dash in and fuel and out again to pick up my charges and shepherd them on to Durban. Not an easy thing to do with a convoy which was making 7.5 knots. I silently cursed the poor staff work which had landed me in this predicament, with my tanks getting steadily emptier and the uncomfortable thought that we *might* meet the *Scheer*! It was all so totally unnecessary. The Admiralty had told me where to go to and the day on which I should leave. Operations Division should have worked out my fuel consumption and, if they had done so, they would have realized that covering that distance would leave me very small margin for fighting battles on the way and would not permit me to get to Durban at all without re-fuelling, hence my frenzied dash in and out to top up.

On arrival I found my delinquents waiting miserably for the wrath of Job to break over their heads and awful punishment to be meted out. Their reasons for absenting themselves were tragically futile: 'I'd lost my kit and got tired of borrowing, Sir'; 'I'd got no friends in my mess, Sir'; 'I had VD and missed my leave at Durban'; 'I was tired of being treated like a child and a housemaid, Sir.' The real reason running through all their stories was that the Navy had not come up to their expectations. The South American work was so boring that they simply could not face another nine months of it. Since the *Hawkins* was the only ship of which any of them had any experience, they thought that, if they missed her, they might get sent to another and more exciting one! There was nothing really wrong with any of them. Only eighteen months before they had been civilian workers in Glasgow, Dundee or Edinburgh – oddly enough they were all lowland Scots – knowing nothing of the sea or ships and, at their tender age, for none was over 21, practically nothing of life. Poor lads, it must have been a miserable and bewildering time for them. Three of them were young Marines, fine honest youngsters. They had been caught miles up country where they had been trying to enlist in the South African Army. Each had a grouse against the Navy, having tried to get out before the war to take up police work so as to be near their parents who were in distress. When their applications had fallen upon deaf ears they had developed a grudge against authority. This internal struggle boiled up to an uncontainable pressure which made them desert.

The question of punishment was largely determined by the shortages, constraints and pressures which were becoming a feature of everyday life in this war. Detention was the obvious answer but, as it so happened, the detention quarters were full to overflowing and the only alternative was to give them a shorter sentence of hard labour. This was felt to be a degrading and inappropriate punishment for RNVRs under 21 for their first offence – a feeling with which I concurred. On the other hand the men had to be punished in the interests of discipline and the sentence had to reflect the gravity of the offence as a deterrent to a practice which was all too common on this station. A compromise was eventually reached by giving them 42 days hard labour, suspended, which meant they were in effect bound over to be of good behaviour for six months. They were drafted back to *Hawkins*, a step I considered undesirable but against which I was not permitted to register any protest. I told each one that the punishment was made heavy to stop cowards leaving their ships which drew an indignant 'I'm not a coward, Sir!' from each in turn. My personnel problems were further embellished with very convincing blarney from three Northern Irishmen who presented themselves before me in response to recent reports of bombings in Belfast. In broad brogue they feared for the safety of their loved ones. The first declared that his wife was childlike and would do nothing without him beside her. The second complained with tears of emotion in his voice that he had not seen his son since the day of his christening and now the little lad was nearly 18 months old. The third was distraught that his wife would not put her safety above his own abiding passion – she refused to go to the country because she would not run the risk of moving his racing pigeons!

No doubt the approaching Christmas season had something to do with these piteous requests. I was more concerned with raiders. Wireless D/F bearings were indicating enemy units in the region Ascension/St Helena and we also had a report of a ship sunk by a 'battleship' near the equator. This last I thought was probably the *Scheer* who had gone to ground after an attack some weeks previously. We could be on converging courses! The tactics to be employed in such an event were complex. His 11″ guns could outrange ours by some 4 miles – a hazardous belt of water to traverse before we would even be able to hit him. Our primary function, when not occupied with convoys, was to 'report' to 'shadow' and to go on reporting. To do this we had about four knots of excess speed. The chances of being able to close down from 15 miles to 3 miles in the short space of tropical twilight were remote, unless, during the day, we could get him up against the western horizon. If, as a raider, he adopted conventional tactics, he would evade. That would lead to a long chase from astern in which *Hawkins* would never get within gun range – just the sort of negative scenario which would probably happen.

I turned my mind from the depressing permutations of action in the event of an encounter with the German to my seasonal duties which involved reading a prayer on Christmas morning, singing a carol with the ship's company and, after trying to alleviate the inevitable melancholy of being denied the joy of home and family at this time with a short address which leaned heavily on the laudable part everyone was playing in ridding the Empire of this threat to its freedom and securing a better future for all our loved ones, I desisted and handed out bottles of beer on behalf of the officers. This last was met with beaming smiles. My official tour of the mess decks – a somewhat embarrassing and difficult processional task – revealed an atmosphere of happy boisterousness and the usual coterie accompanied me with horseplay. It was all very good-humoured and there was much cheering and singing. Decorations were a bit sparse but most messes had improvised rather well – Bromo cut in tasteful shapes and chains was a favourite. The beer given by the officers was promptly arranged in patterns, and oranges and nuts spelt 'Merry Christmas.' Each man had a pound of turkey and a whack of rum-laced pudding together with twenty cigarettes given to him by the Navy League and cigars from the Women's Auxiliary at Cape Town. There was also an individual present for each boy – so on the whole everyone did well. We then piped 'Hands to dance and skylark' which resulted in an egg fight in the galley flat!

On New Year's morning we came upon a ship's lifeboat with nine poor weak survivors from the tanker *British Premier* which had been torpedoed by a submarine on Christmas Eve. The torpedoes had struck amidships and the oil which had poured out immediately caught fire, turning the sea into a raging flame. Our survivors – two engineers and some firemen – were aft and managed to cut away a lifeboat in which they frantically tried to get away from the burning oil but they soon realized that it was hopeless and jumped into the sea begging for a miracle. To their relief the stream of flame seemed to part and the boat drifted clear so that they were able to swim and climb into it. They managed to pick up a steward who was terribly burned. Apparently no other boats got away and it was assumed that the rest of the crew was trapped and died. For over a week they endured the heat of the sun by day and the cold of the night. There were no seamen among them to give them help or confidence, but they set a sail and travelled, as they thought, north-east because they knew from a casual conversation that the ship was about a day out from Freetown. The poor burned sailor was delirious until he died the day before we found them.

They rationed their food and water and said they could have gone on for another week but it was pathetic to see them feverishly and recklessly drinking their precious water as *Hawkins* approached. We picked them up and when they were safely out of the boat we asked them if there was anything in it they wanted before it was cast adrift. With troubled looks the senior asked anxiously if the bully beef was on board. This rather sad story showing complete disorientation was quite understandable. As soon as they had seen us closing they had had a good drink of water but were still desperately hungry so it was quite natural that they should concentrate their efforts on conserving their food which had, for eight days, literally been life itself.

More curious than the pitiful survivors' reactions was the state of induced loss of proportion engendered in the Commander and myself (so we discovered later) at the sight of the precious fresh water being callously drained from the breakers* before these were handed on board for our own use. An instinctive horror rose in both of us at the sight of such reckless waste and we were each moved by an impulse to stop the men emptying it away. These feelings were entirely the result of emotions raised by the intensity of feeling in the minds of our shipwrecked sailors. They quickly recovered and seemed none the the worse for their ordeal. One remained in bed with a burnt arm but the others soon started wandering slowly and happily about the ship. We were hearing and reading about the torpedoing of ships almost daily by this time, until the personal effects of their horror were lost upon the mind which grappled callously with the figures of tonnage sunk, disregarding the human suffering each hit caused. Possibly some prophylactic device of memory to stave off the madness of conflict. Six weeks later we heard our survivors had not been the only ones. Four more were picked up four hundred miles from the spot where we had come across ours. They had managed to live on a single nob of biscuits and rain water for forty-one days.

Almost every time I put in to refuel I would find a change of plan awaiting *Hawkins* with the result that we eventually fetched up in Aden, having been called upon to accompany *Formidable* on her mercy mission to replace the damaged *Illustrious*. I put to sea in a sombre frame of mind for this duty, having also received the intelligence that *Regulus* was overdue. Though so many years had passed since I had tended her first careful steps, it was all still very vivid in my mind and I could recall nearly all the details of the boat, details stamped into my memory by constant interest for months at Barrow and the many discussions in which almost every pipe and valve was argued over. I felt her loss very keenly, although, except for poor Currie, her Captain, I knew none of her company. She was a good submarine and in my subsequent fleeting contacts with her I had always heard her praised. Another link snapped with my submarine life.

As we rounded Guardafui which separates the Indian Ocean from the

---

* Long, flattened wooden casks containing fresh water which formed part of the standard survival equipment in small boats. The term dates from the time of Nelson and originates from the Spanish 'bareca' meaning a small barrel or keg.

Gulf of Aden and sighted the lighthouse, I glanced at the chart and was filled with horror. To be condemned to tend the light on this most desolate cape, perched high upon the edge of a precipitous cliff falling away to the sea and with hundreds of miles of barren rock at one's back, ranked as one of the three most forbidding duties in the world, according to my Navigator. To sit in a state of limp neurosis for six months of the year whilst the hot, damp, south-west monsoon spread a grey pall of cloud to smother one's puny purpose must surely have been to hit the depths of moribund dreariness. When I enquired what the other two duties were he responded, 'Piermaster at Wigan and Ferryman in the Falklands.'

After a brief call on SNORS*, an emaciated version of the man I had known two years previously — so much for Red Sea life — we dashed back down to Kenya and in baking sun panted into harbour after three days' high-speed steaming during which we broke our own record doing 607 miles in twenty-four hours. Steaming at 25 knots was a distressing experience for the old lady, afflicting her with an ague causing clouds of sulphurous particles to puff out of her funnels and a violent trembling. The ship's company went about its business with chattering teeth, trying vainly to extract the grit from its eyes. This merry St Vitus' Dance was enlivened by the loss of a large chunk from the blade of the port outer propeller. Otherwise our geriatric conveyance turned in a splendid performance to get us into Mombasa for the start of Operation Canvas.

* Senior Naval Officer, Red Sea.

24

Operation Canvas

THE ROUND OF CONFERENCES which had taken place at Cape Town before Christmas and in some of which I had participated, resulted in the reinforcement of the South African Army, bringing it to a state of readiness for the capture of Italian Somaliland. The troops waiting on the frontier were commanded by General Cunningham, the brother of the C-in-C Mediterranean. Naval co-operation was necessarily limited, but our normal functions of keeping the sea lines of communication open and denying them to the enemy would insure the Army against any sudden surprises which reinforcement of enemy positions by sea might cause. We were also able to assist by bombarding coastal batteries, running reconnaissance and attack missions with the Fleet Air Arm and by organizing and transporting stores and food to the Army by sea once a port had been taken. These and other points were discussed at a meeting in the *Shropshire* and, as a result, *Hawkins* and *Hermes* departed in company for an area to the eastward of Kisimayo where our arrival was timed to synchronize with the soldiers going over the border. Our position was selected to provide a suitable base from which *Hermes* could operate aircraft to detect the movements of enemy merchant ships escaping from Kisimayo. We assumed that escaping ships would have speeds of from 6 to 10 knots which, during a 10-hour night, would take them 60-100 miles off the coast by daylight. It was expected that they would sail at dusk so as to wrest maximum advantage from the hours of darkness, but to encourage this mode of thought the *Cape Town* had recently shown herself off Kisimayo giving the impression of a regular patrol. *Hermes'* aircraft were able to operate a search up to a depth of 100 miles. Just before dawn on Day 1 of the operation the first flight took off from *Hermes* and, filled with high hope, we waited for their reports.

The sun rose opalescent out of a sea as flat as my chart, spreading a saffron crimson path to the east and lighting our first target. We dashed off in pursuit and as we got closer we saw that an aircraft had picked her up and was circling round. A little later the aircraft made me a signal that the ship had stopped and was lowering boats. Suspecting this to be a prelude to scuttling I told the aircraft to fire at the boats to discourage such bold thoughts — which it did. The ship proved to be the Italian SS *Adria* to which I sent a boarding party who formally captured her and — to the accompaniment of shouts of joy from the sailors — we saw the White Ensign replace the Italian flag. The Italians accepted their fate with resignation, though the sight of jack tar with a rifle — carried with an amateur and easy nonchalance reminiscent of Mr Chamberlain's umbrella — was unnerving enough to send them scurrying round the deck in acute alarm. I sent one of my lieutenants, McVey, over with a prize crew and shortly afterwards I left him to take his new command into Mombasa. My instinct about the *Adria*'s intentions had been spot on. We found an explosive charge placed ready and the Captain said they were about to sink the ship when the aircraft made them think differently. One Italian had been wounded by a stray bullet and we took him on board. He later died and was buried at sea.

The aircraft had by now reported another ship 30 miles to the westward and so, satisfied about the *Adria*, I set off in pursuit. Unlike her sister, the SS *Savoia* made no attempt to scuttle and an occasional burst of fire from the aircraft kept the crew entirely submissive. Once more a boarding party went over and captured the ship and in a short time she too was off to Mombasa in charge of Lieutenant Pugh. And so, in six short hours, two ships had sailed into our trap with a naivete that was too good to be true — but this was not all. Later in the day I suddenly got a wireless signal from *Adria* to say that he had encountered another Italian, the SS *Erminia Mazela*, and that he was taking her with him to Mombasa! We were completely in the dark as to how he had managed this but the result was so eminently satisfactory that it filled us with high spirits.

Having had such success on Day 1, we decided to draw the same covert once more but held little hope of a kill. To our joy within half an hour an aircraft reported another ship, the SS *Manon*, a very grimy collier, which we duly captured and sent off to Mombasa. The crew was very dispirited and seemed relieved to be taken. They told us there was an acute food shortage in Kisimayo and they had put to sea virtually without food, without orders and almost without hope. The only thing they did have was coal — but they only had enough of that for eight days. In the meantime one of our aircraft had been busy and had located two more ships. By 1100 we had them in sight, with the aircraft circling and behaving in a threatening manner. The first we came to was a liner, the SS *Leonardo Da Vinci*, who hoisted a tablecloth by way of capitulation as soon as we approached. Our success rate was becoming embarrassing. I now had six officers and seventy-five men out of the ship in prize crews and I was beginning to run short of personnel, so I told *Hermes* to take the Italian while *Hawkins* went off after the second, a German.

The *Uckermark* (as she proved to be) had shown more spirit than her Italian companion and, in spite of bursts of machine-gun fire and a bomb dropped nearby, the crew had exploded a scuttling charge and had abandoned their ship. By the time *Hawkins* closed her she already had a slight list and the boats were a mile away. She was obviously sinking so I decided that the only hope of salvation was to get the German Captain and Engineer back on board their ship and to try and frighten them into showing our boarding party the steps to be taken to check the inrush of water. I therefore went straight for the boats and picked up the crew of 46, from which the officers were segregated and brought to me.

Most of them were cowed and frightened except one Nazi-looking purser whom I would readily have put back in his boat and cut adrift. I had to curb my temper but my sadistic impulse received slight assuagement by ordering the man to take his hat off when he spoke to me! The Captain and Chief Engineer accepted my order to return with resignation and a shrug of the shoulders. They both retorted that the ship was bound to sink but that if I insisted on their being there so be it. I did insist and so it was. The boarding party, helped by the German Engineer, managed to shut a door to the shaft tunnel which so slowed the flooding that the ship floated for two days, but her Captain had been right. She eventually went down when a bulkhead cracked while she was under tow by the *Ceres*. I sent the German crew off as prisoners under a guard in the *Leonardo Da Vinci* to Mombasa.

The third day of Canvas gave us the last of our successes. An aircraft from *Hermes* sighted a small merchant ship just south of Brava and let her have a stick of six bombs out of which three hit, and the ship, which was carrying Italian troops, was hastily run ashore. All the other birds had flown except three who were found scuttled in Kisimayo. A couple got away to the north but the *Shropshire* managed to disable one off Mogadishu. The final tally out of the fourteen ships which had been photographed in Kisimayo a month before was five captured, four scuttled, one ashore, one damaged at Mogadishu and one unknown. Two Germans had got away before the operation started. We were quite pleased with our performance which yielded a healthy addition to our total tonnage to be used for war purposes. For all this though, we still had not fired our guns in anger!

As Canvas moved into its second and final phase, it became apparent that the Italians had evacuated to Mogadishu. The Army was therefore able to get ahead of its programme and by Day Five they had occupied Kisimayo in preparation for a crossing of the Juba River where the Italians were making a stand. This defrauded us of a bombardment of the shore batteries, since they had been abandoned, and the men felt much aggrieved to be done out of their bit of thunder and glory. They had to wait some considerable time and even then it was not, strictly speaking, 'enemy action' although I suppose one could loosely have called it that. When we had taken the *Uckermark* the boarding party had removed what useful equipment it could before she finally sank. Among the booty was the ship's cat, a ginger lady who was immediately dubbed 'the Nazi-Blonde.' Her arrival was soon noticed by our own ship's tom, Tiger, whose ardent lovemaking distressed everyone and put severe strain on any of his remaining nine lives. With a promptitude worthy of her Teutonic upbringing the lady presented us with three ginger kittens whose arrival we celebrated by a 7.5″ shoot, the only gunfire we had contributed to the entire operation! Mother and children fortunately survived the shock. Father, the miserable mouser, deserted his responsibilities by missing the ship at Durban.

By way of compensation we got another Chaplain who, as a new broom, set about brushing our souls vigorously by insisting that he needed 'sit down' church. This raised the intolerant spirit of the Commander to snort about the impracticability of such fancies in war, at sea. It was left to me to try and calm the bellicose waters with a little sweet oil. We began with a workable compromise. It was agreed that 'church' would replace 'prayers' but that for the time being it would be conducted in a designated area on deck. The Chaplain's first such act of worship was attended by Neptune, base pagan, who rose from his slumbrous depths and, filling his lungs with a large monsoon, covered our small area of church with spray! With resource and sagacity we repaired, with a much reduced congregation, to my lower cabin. Neptune, not to be thwarted, hove his great body about until our frail shell rocked wildly in his tempest. This swept all tranquillity from our simple devotions and solemnity fled through the scuttle. Not even our Chaplain could have expected us to respond 'O Lord, make haste to he-el-el-elp us!' with any degree of beauty as we lurched in an uneasy roll. When it was over, Neptune, with a great guffaw which all but threw us on our beam ends, retired to his amphitheatre and left us in a perfectly calm sea!

By comparison with the 'holy terror' whom we had been instructed to remove from Tristan da Cunha whilst attached to the South American Division, our new Man of God was an absolute tyrant. I had actually grown quite fond of the da Cunhan, a wiry, bearded little man who spent hours on the deck peering through binoculars at sea birds. His conversation was lively and very much to the point, but never offensive. This man was made of sterner stuff and evidently intended to do battle against the sea, the flesh and the Commander as evidenced by the playing of his 'trump' card. This took the form of a letter addressed to me, referring me to an Admiralty Order which began: 'IN THE CONVICTION THAT the present war is a struggle between Good and Evil...Their Lordships, all appreciating the necessity for Sunday work, emphasise the need for Divine Service and prayer...and direct that in all Battleships and Cruisers.....a space to be set aside for the worship of God.'

This communication raised the Commander to fresh heights, or perhaps it would be more appropriate to say lowered him to new depths of scorn and guile and, with contumely, he challenged the Man of God to find a single space wherein we could swing the Nazi Blonde! I really felt that one war was quite enough for us to cope with and that we could do without religious strife so threw my weight on to side of Godliness in an attempt to stabilize the situation. In consequence, to the fury of Beelzebub's Lieutenant, my spare cabin was dismantled preparatory to painting and conversion for use as a chapel. Our inaugural 'Sit Down Church' was an unusual experience musically as the Chaplain, whose powerful convictions were not matched by his voice, was deprived of the loudspeaker which Neptune slyly sabotaged at the last moment. Above the parson's head swung a little yellow canary in his cage – unnoticed and forgotten by the refurbishment party until we burst into our opening hymn. He was thrilled! Never had his soul received such tremendous stimulation, never had his larynx been in better form, and, throwing out his proud chest, he shrilled in a paean of rolls and trills. Between the more choral parts of our service he felt the need of sustenance and busily scattered seed upon the Chaplain's head but, with the first bar of music, he sprang again into action and shamed our guttural growls with the purity of his piping. I heard not a word from our Man of God after this performance. When I looked in at the door of my lower cabin one evening later in the week I saw the 'Hawkins Swing Kings' at rehearsal. At the back sat a sallow able seaman drummer, an unlovely creature even to his mother, who beat his tintinabula with febrile vacancy. The balance of sacred and secular power had clearly been restored.

The final paragraph to our part of Operation Canvas was written with the exploits of Lieutenant McVey, the hero of a unique action. His prize, the *Adria*, was steaming towards Mombasa when he sighted another Italian ship. Quickly lowering his white ensign, McVey edged across until he could pass under her stern to read the name *Erminia Mazela*. He then ranged up alongside and showed his true colours – a revelation which spread panic and led to a rush for the boats. McVey thereupon fired a rifle across the bows but this passed unnoticed so he fired a rifle at the ship's side. The resulting loud twang reverberated into the Italian consciousness so that the ship's company rushed for cover. After this display of force the victim became quite docile and fell in behind her captor without argument. It must have been many a year since a prize had captured a prize. It conjured visions of vicious hand-to-hand fighting in the Napoleonic Wars. McVey's description of events left no room for romantic illusion – the deed in this case was negligible since there was neither opposition nor risk and, as he put it, the whole thing was child's play but it did offer a heaven-sent opportunity to tickle the public fancy with a dashing account of derring-do. McVey, an RNR Officer, had done well.* He might have considered that with a handful of men he could achieve nothing. As it was he tried and succeeded and the fact that his victim collapsed in fear did not detract in any way from his personal decision to seize a ripe opportunity firmly.

Our patrol and convoy duties continued. The old lady bore up well but she was in desperate need of radical overhaul and sailors were in need of relief. After forty exchanges with other ships we finally received the signal to summon us home, but not before I had to deal with a case of bigamy!

A Leading Seaman from *Hawkins* was one of a gang who frequented the residence of a certain family at Durban. This family was under suspicion for Fifth Columnry and so for a time it was my duty to read the fervent letters of the constant sailors with the result that, unbeknownst to them, I got to know them quite well. Unfortunately, the nicest character of this happy little band was criminally indiscreet in one of his missives and I had to send him to prison for three months. The most lascivious one was also the most cunning and had managed, thus far, to live a nefarious life without infringing the law. The last member was a liar and a fool and, to my astonishment, a potential bigamist.

His lawful wife, who was something of a termagant, had written letters appealing and letters infuriated to me on the subject of her neglectful husband. I, on my part, sat closeted on several occasions with the guilty spouse in an atmosphere redolent with supplication. This produced no useful result other than the self-evident fact that he and his wife were incompatible and that she was, even as we spoke, engaged in divorcing him. I sorrowfully wrote to the lady only to receive an indignant telegram accusing me of putting ideas into her husband's head! It transpired that he had written too with a tale of scandalous life on board this hell-ship which had sent his wife hot-foot to her MP — the Commodore of the barracks, and as far as I knew the Air High Marshal himself — for the lady was a batwoman in the WAAF! Her main cause for dissatisfaction lay with the simple sailor's avowed intention of deserting if the ship was ordered home as he could not stick the 'intolerable conditions on board.' This was naive of him but had apparently worked wonders in the bosom of his wife! I was next surprised to read in the Durban paper that a marriage had been arranged between this hapless Leading Seaman and a daughter of the house of spies. No amount of questioning on my part could unravel the web of cross and double-cross this wretched son of Belial was playing. He persisted with the story that his lawful wife was divorcing him. She harangued me from the Northern Hemisphere saying she was not. I kept these explosive documents well locked up and said nothing but I put my spies on the errant husband. To my consternation they confirmed that wedding plans were well advanced and the ceremony was due to take place in three days' time.

* He was subsequently Mentioned in Despatches.

With pontificate ceremony I saw this much entangled man – in the presence of a witness – and taxed him with the rumour which he flatly denied, protesting it was ridiculous as he was a married man and could not therefore marry again. Having got this admission out of him, I wagged a forbidding finger as I recited the gravity of the offence of bigamy in the eyes of the civil law. Although it was outside my jurisdiction I deemed it prudent to inform the Cape Town police who did precisely nothing. Three days later, having sedulously spread the propaganda that his divorce had been made absolute, the miscreant got married with bridesmaids and all by special licence at Rosebank Methodist Church. It was impossible to imagine what sort of game the idiot was playing unless he was planning a sudden getaway up-country and a new start under a false name. I had no legitimate grounds for keeping him under restraint since he had committed no offence against Naval Law. The police said they could not act until it could be proved that his first wife had been alive on the day of alleged bigamous marriage. I was called urgently from my cabin in the middle of all this by a messenger reporting a suspected act of sabotage. What a relief! I quickly handed the whole thing over to a higher authority and went in search of saboteurs.

Our preparations for the return to England were well under way and we were taking on stores and passengers all the time. A regular ticking noise in the canteen store had been reported from an adjoining locker flat. A feverish breaking of locks and scrabbling amongst cases of cigarettes uncovered no infernal machine. In the middle of the hunt the noise mysteriously stopped, putting the wind badly up everyone. The Doctor was summoned with his stethoscope but even he, with infinite care, could not find no more trace. The noise had been regular and clocklike and it obviously originated from somewhere. Did its cessation indicate safety or was it an ingenious intermittent mechanism that recommenced after an interval and would shortly explode? Temporarily baffled, we placed a sentry to keep eerie watch for the ghostly sound and uneasily turned in. In the encouraging light of morning we grappled with our problem and found that several of the cases of cigarettes had been recently embarked from Cape Town. Ah! Ossewa Brandwag? We would tear them open and expose their knavish trick! Then the noise suddenly started again – just as the *Devonshire*, after a night in harbour, switched on her echo-sounding machine preparatory to going to sea!

We filled up with passengers – sick men, poor men, criminals, reliefs – and with stores, spare gear and a multitude of food parcels which contained oranges, lemons, wines, cheeses, soap and gammons for our beleaguered families at home. I missed the trial of my bigamist who did attempt to desert and was captured owing to the arrival, on the eve of our departure from South Africa, of further cargo of £3,000,000! It lumbered through the dock gates in plain vans guarded by tough-looking men with bulges in their pockets. There were four hundred and forty-nine gold bars − each worth £7000 − entrusted to me for safe (sic) passage to England. We were putting it gingerly away in the Admiral's store, the best we felt we could do for an opulent passenger, when we were struck by sinking qualms that the deck might give way under his 15 tons of weight and shoot him into the bilges! I didn't quite know what would happen if I lost one of my precious burdens − it would certainly have taken the government a very long time to stop it out of my pay! The more I thought about the hideous responsibility, the more convinced I became that I should be given one half of one per cent as a pourboire.

Finally we got away, albeit on three legs, and the old grey mare started her last 6,000 miles by striking a smart 24 knots on the way to Table Bay. We went on to the de-gaussing range to get the correct settings for our coils before entering mined waters. Our final sight of Cape Town was under a full moon with all her lights twinkling as we set course for home. They were the last lights we should see until the war was over but we were all more than ready to wrap ourselves in physical blackout in return for the inner light of excitement and happiness. We had hardly put our nose round the corner into the Atlantic when we felt the chill blast of enemy action. Off Walvis Bay, just 24 hours ahead of our position, the SS *Bradford City* sent a distress call saying that she had been torpedoed by a submarine and that survivors were making for the coast 300 miles away in their boats. This was followed by a second signal saying that all had been located by one of our aircraft and food had been dropped. The news of disaster so close at hand threw us into a frenzy of zig-zagging and every whale and porpoise became a portent.

We steamed doggedly northward for twenty-eight days. Through the dark misty dawn of a November Sunday morning I turned to the south coast of England to make Start Point which suddenly reared its dim shape high above me. The old lady fairly flew up channel through the icy wind, passing the lighthouses like milestones as she spread her broad white wake like a carpet upon the bitter green sea. Alive with the sharp weather and with our own keen anticipation, the ship's company stamped and blew and became turkey-red in joviality as the hour-glass of absence hurried its last few grains into past forgetfulness.

Off Portland two 'Hunt' class destroyers, like a couple of hounds, came bounding at us with such an eager greeting that they seemed bent on leaping onboard before nosing down to their protective work. Off St Albans two Spitfires swooped about our ears like agitated albatrosses. Off The Needles minesweepers trotted to meet us towing their inconsequential balloons like children on a cold day. Then suddenly we were home. Mist merged into dusk as we came quietly into Portsmouth − a deserted, tattered home, wrapped in a Sunday silence and showing no signs of life save the flickering gulls and one small boy who threw up his arms and gave us a piping cheer from the Point.

25

Harbour Stations

HAWKINS' DEFECT list was pages long after virtually non-stop steaming for over 160,000 miles. The bearings had gone in pretty well every pump in the ship and all the wireless gear had worn out. The stays on the masts needed replacing, in fact almost everything was beyond redemption. I tucked her up in dry dock with a care and maintenance crew, where she stayed for about six months undergoing a complete refit. I went on leave but found it difficult to relax because I was waking every morning at dawn to go on the bridge.

The war still had more than two years to run. It was a tense time. The *Prince of Wales* and the *Repulse* were lost in the China Sea. With the scanty information available we did not understand how these two great ships could have gone so quickly. All we knew was that they had been sunk up towards the Vietnamese coast with devastating loss of life. The only assumption we could make at the time was that they had ventured further than they should have done without air cover and that the Japanese had sent dive bombers and torpedoes and sunk them both. It seemed inconceivable that the Japanese could have carried out the operation so far from land but they had done it and we learned, to our great cost, the power of air warfare against ships.

I had no idea that my next job would be but I knew that, having had command at sea, it would probably have to be work ashore and so I resigned myself to the idea of this. After two or three weeks I got a personal letter from an old shipmate called Wee Mcgrigor, a member of the Naval Staff at the Admiralty, bidding me to come and see him as he had a job of work that he wanted me to do. Wee Mcgrigor, who was below average height, was a big man in heart and brain and he had all the characteristics of a Scottish terrier in that once he got his teeth into something he never let go. I was intrigued by his letter and arrived in his office to be greeted on rather more formal terms than our relationship had previously been conducted during our years together at Fort Blockhouse. Wee Mcgrigor was now an Admiral and an important personage in the Admiralty hierarchy as Assistant Chief of the Naval Staff (Weapons), a post which carried a great deal of authority although he did not actually serve on the Admiralty Board.

He asked me whether I had been satisfied while at sea with the amount of information about war in other theatres. Lack of detail and, more importantly, up to date information had been a major problem and I was eager to grasp the opportunity of airing this topic which was a major headache for all COs trying to fight a war in radio silence with nothing but the daily bulletins which one knew in any case had been manufactured for propaganda purposes. Unless the Commander-in-Chief took the trouble to send out information, one had nothing to go on and felt very much isolated for weeks on end. My views obviously coincided with his own. 'Right,' he said, slapping the table in front of him and taking a firm terrier-like hold of the problem. 'That's exactly why I've sent for you, Joe. I agree with you that something must be done about it and your two years at sea put you in an ideal position to sort it out. I want you to come here to the Admiralty and sift through the C-in-C's reports. If you pick up anything which you think would have been useful to you at sea as a Captain, and of course you will, then we must see about ways of promulgating this information to your brother Captains who are actually at sea at this moment.'

All naval activities were controlled by the Admiralty Board which comprised a politician as First Lord sitting in the Cabinet responsible for the Navy and all its works. Then there was a First Sea Lord, the professional head of the Navy who was a senior Admiral of great experience. There were four other Sea Lords each with different responsibilities: personnel; ships and dockyards; stores and equipment; air-aircraft carriers and their aircraft. Finally there was a Civil Lord in charge of buildings and a Parliamentary Secretary who was a member of the House of Commons. The Board of Admiralty was served by a staff composed mainly of experienced Naval Officers to advise on all aspects of the service. Collectively they were known as The Naval Staff and the First Sea Lord had the subtitle of Chief of Naval Staff.

The Staff itself was divided into two parts: one was concerned with the active operations of the war and comprised divisions responsible for plans, intelligence and operations. The other half dealt with the policy to be followed in the material world. This comprised divisions responsible for advising on specific subjects like gunnery, torpedoes, navigation, signals etc. These two halves were in the general charge of Rear-Admirals and my friend Wee Mac was in charge of the material side. The Board of Admiralty was the authority which gave the go-ahead on the advice of the Naval Staff. It could only get its money through Parliament, in other words the First Lord, who was a politician – Alexander during my time there. The Naval Staff could only advise on matters of policy. The implementation of the policy was dealt with by the large Admiralty Departments. The people who worked in these departments were specialists in given areas and were not uniformed personnel. The Director of Naval Construction for instance designed our ships and had the authority to approve designs that were put up by shipbuilders. He was in charge of a big drawing office and had a core of naval constructors with specialist degrees who carried out the work.

The system, although complex in its formulation, was in fact extremely effective. During the war, Admirals and Captains experienced tactical moves by the enemy which varied daily so they had to adjust the disposition of their own ships to counter the action. This was normally reported by the Commanders-in-Chief and picked up by the Naval Staff who took any action which they thought necessary. There was a superb example of the procedure in action when war broke out in 1939. We knew that the enemy had a magnetic mine which could be dropped onto the sea bed and activated by the magnetism in a ship passing above it. Our first intelligence of this menace had come as shipping off the east coast was sunk for no apparent reason. I had witnessed this in the *Cairo* in the early days and we were mystified as to how the mines operated until we actually got hold of one. Our need was fulfilled one day when an obliging enemy aircraft dropped one of his new toys in the Thames estuary where it fell in the mud without exploding and lay there waiting for a brave group of uniformed officers from the *Vernon* torpedo school to come and take it away. Having made it safe, they dismantled it to ascertain the method of construction and then set about utilising Departmental expertise to come up with the appropriate counter-measure. The result was a de-gaussing wire which, in crude terms, cancelled out the magnetism of the ship so that she did not activate the mine when she passed over it. It was fortunate that this unexploded gift had been dropped into our laps so early in the war. On the advice of the Naval Staff, policy was put in place to fit all ships with de-gaussing coils and within two years this had been achieved. There were literally hundreds of similar examples going on all the time. The Naval Staff was kept busy seeking out and recording all matters which required a policy decision. The Departments then set about implementing them as fast as they could.

My two years patrolling and escorting with the *Hawkins* had contributed in one small way to improve the flow of information needed by captains at sea. Vessel identification during time of war was a difficulty, as I had discovered on more than one occasion by myself being unable to discover who I had in my sights or, in the case of the terrified *Temple Moat*, being mistaken for the enemy. Boarding, the ultimate choice in a doubtful situation, took considerable time and was impracticable if one was escorting a convoy. If the sea was rough, it was totally impossible. What we needed was a photographic card index of the ships of the world. Given this, one could penetrate all but the most skilful disguises affected by the artful raider – from a respectful distance! Such an identification aid could, of course, have been constructed before the war, but it wasn't. Once hostilities had broken out, the taking of good photographs of all neutral and allied ships, free or in the hands of the enemy, became impossible and we were forced to rely on a selection of photographs in *Talbot Booth** or on verbal descriptions which were often clumsy, gauche and of little real value. I was not alone in finding an omission in the matter of visual identification of ships so several of us set about devising a method by which the silhouette characteristics could be written and signalled in a short coded form**. This served to standardize the viewpoint of observers who had to report the appearance of a merchant ship, and greatly simplified the promulgation of information. It also had the advantage in practice that from a quick record of a ship's features, an accurate silhouette could be built up later. Within a relatively short space of time we collected over a hundred silhouettes and the C-in-C eventually agreed to all ships and ports pooling the silhouette information that they gathered to be passed on to warships from a central library.

My researches into the reports received from Commanders-in-Chief at the Admiralty revealed a wealth of useful detail which was not being fed back into the system in digestible form, if at all. It became quite clear that minor, but often important, information gaps could be plugged to enable general improvements and modifications to be made to weaponry, procedures, ship deployment and all manner of operational necessities crucial to the efficiency of naval activities and hence the winning of the war. By the introduction of a simple device which was called Fighting Experience, the key findings of active COs at sea were collated together and re-circulated with immediate dispatch to their colleagues in all theatres of war. This had the effect not only of keeping everyone much better informed but of reducing the feeling of isolation and boosting morale.

Once the flow of information had been unclogged, I moved on the exalted position of Director of Training and Staff Duties — a job which I knew absolutely nothing about and therefore had to spend the first few weeks ferreting round to find out what it meant.

The first batch of promotions announced after the outbreak of war made a great break in precedent. Hitherto, captains had been swept off the top of the list — the grain falling into the Flag and the chaff blowing to the four winds. In 1940, for the first time ever, promotion was by selection from any

* *Talbot Booth* was the merchant vessels' equivalent of *Jane's Fighting Ships* which was carried by all warships during hostilities.

**This code was first employed by the R.A.F. Flying Boats based on Colombo in August, 1941, when they used it successfully to identify a suspicious vessel in the Maldives. She turned out to be the Panamanian S.S. *Mascot*, a vessel of unusual design whose silhouette was quickly and accurately built up using the code, copies of which were subsequently circulated to all ships on the East Indies Station for a more general trial.

captains in the top 5 years of the 'zone.' The objective was to find younger Admirals; in this it succeeded, but what it really meant in practical terms was that it opened the system up to allow outstanding COs to be brought to Flag rank before the war was over. This was a welcome step but it did not go far enough. The real source of blockage was at the top of the Admirals' list itself. If the Admirals and Vice Admirals had been pruned by one third, there would have been ten vacancies for *selected* Rear Admirals and an equal number of extra Flags could have been given to chosen Captains. Drastic measures perhaps, but these were drastic times and one could not postpone the winning of the war until suitable COs reached the top of the list! I felt that all but the very best should have made way for first-class younger men to have the opportunities that seniors had had for many years.

Manning the constant flow of new ships being brought into the service gave us a different set of problems. In gross numbers there were more than enough men available but we suffered an acute shortage of trained men of experience. Before the outbreak of war in 1939, half the Navy had been under 21. To these was added an influx of civilian youth. Thus in the midst of a war whose duration was unknown, the Navy found that the sea experience of fifty per cent of its crews did not pre-date the outbreak of hostilities. This meant that Naval ships could not spare any of their limited number of trained men for vessels brought into the service, for they relied on them for their own efficiency. The war sailor could not yet be sent for training to take on higher responsibilities because he had not been long enough at sea to qualify as a man of experience. The supply of trained men for new ships practically ran dry. An analysis of the experience of my ship's company in *Hawkins* showed that it was the first ship for 420 of them. If I added those who had been at sea for less than two years I came to the somewhat alarming conclusion that nearly 4/5ths of my crew were immature sailors. In effect the ship was steamed and defended by a cross-section of British provincial life with a handful of South Africans thrown in as leaven. The Jolly Jack of peacetime was a rare bird indeed, so rare that one was tempted to pipe a tear of affection for the breed, now a practically extinct prototype. The wartime sailor, faithfully modelling himself upon his glamorous predecessor, was conscious of some ready-made aura which attached to it in his own interpretation of the part. He was often dismayed to find that the dazzling mythology surrounding all this sea business did not quite come up to expectation. There was much to be said for the 'new boys' though. The model set for them to follow was good and by his exacting standards we were able to run our complicated machines on a very weak mixture of RN spirit!

To meet this shortage of experience, ships at sea were subjected to constant dilution, constant training under difficult war conditions, ship's companies growing ever more youthful and fewer and fewer solid men of experience to give stability. This was the price we paid for retrenchment in time of peace. The Geddes Axe and all the other cutbacks were now being felt with a vengeance. It was not simply a question of having a job any more, it was the very question of survival. In the Second World War the Navy was forced to expand in two years to a size which had taken four and a half years of intense effort in the First World War.

By 1942 the Navy was being built up for the Normandy Landings. There was no shortage of raw material for ratings: in the case of officers, things were rather different. Having learnt a lesson in the First World War that it was dangerous to use professional sailors for work outside their normal duties of running merchant ships, we concentrated much more on RNVR and conscripts between 1939 and 1945. The customary procedure for selecting conscripts with officer-like potential was for ships to recommend men who showed the requisite signs. They would be recommended by their Captain and from these a certain number were selected for actual officer training.

This system had a number of serious defects. Basically, the standard of selection was very irregular in the sense that candidates were put forward by virtually any CO from a thoroughly experienced officer in command of a battleship down to a quite junior officer in charge of a small vessel. The thing was flawed from the start. Nevertheless a large number of officers were appointed to the training establishment at Hove called the *King Alfred* which opened its doors to them in 1940. As the demand for young officers increased, so the numbers of young men aged about 19 passing through *King Alfred* accelerated from an intake of twenty-five a week at the beginning to something like a hundred towards the end. The course lasted about two months and operated in a way which gave no particular cause for alarm until, in 1942 as DTSD, I noticed a report from the Captain of *King Alfred* which pointed out that in the previous year the wastage rate had reached the disturbing figure of 33%.

Naval conscripts came through the door as ordinary men off the street — they might equally well have been educated at Eton or Borstal — that was of no consequence. They then went into a basic training establishment — *Collingwood* at Portsmouth, *Ganges* at Harwich and so on — where they were given twelve weeks' indoctrination. None of these chaps had even put on a uniform before. Everything was completely strange to them and at the end of twelve weeks the best that one could hope to have done for them was to have given them basic disciplinary training and a little primitive seamanship. After that they were drafted to barracks where they remained until drafted to Naval employment. This meant that a recruit might be sent to any type of vessel or even in some cases to shore service.

The Naval barracks in the home ports were at this time filled with a mixture of every type of rating ranging from the long service RN to the young 18-year-old recruit straight from the basic training establishment and the throughput was at a fairly high rate. Under these circumstances barracks became notorious as hotbeds of graft and undisciplined behaviour. People pinched things and tried to get away with just about anything they could. In this ragged mêlée the raw recruit was confused as to his position and did not really settle down until appointed to a ship where he became a part of a disciplined ship's company. While serving in a ship at sea he was under the observation of experienced officers who, if they recognized officer-like potential in a man, would recommend him for consideration for a commission and those men so recommended were eventually drafted to *King Alfred* to do the three-month course prior to being actually commissioned.

A report showing a 33% wastage rate therefore represented a serious drain on manpower because men had to come from the seven seas back to the barracks for training and if they failed that was wasted time. It also meant that roughly thirty men each week were being returned to the lower deck thoroughly disappointed at not having been chosen to become officers. My job as DTSD was defining itself very clearly.

I was sitting pondering this problem in The United Services Club one evening when I happened to pick up *Picture Post* and noticed some photographs of an Army training establishment at Watford which subsequently became known as the War Office Selection Board. I read with growing interest in the accompanying article that men with officer-like potential were given a special training and tests there before being commissioned. The problem was very similar to the one which we were facing at *King Alfred* so I trotted across to the Director of Military Training and asked to go and visit the people at Watford to find out what they were doing. They were very obliging and I had a most instructive day.

The physical reality of the War Office Selection Board did not quite come up to the grandeur of its title – it was a lot of wooden huts actually – but what went on there was more to the point. The army did not put their people through the final battery of tests until they had served under regimental conditions for nearly a year. This meant that the tests themselves could be designed employing a certain amount of military skill because by that time the recruits had absorbed a small but significant amount. In the case of the Navy the situation was much more difficult because the men under basic training only did twelve weeks before being drafted away to ships all over the world. This pointed to the fact that if we were going to make an attempt at choosing suitable men for commissioned rank, it would have to be done within those twelve weeks when the young ratings were as green as a starboard light.

There were useful insights to be gained from the Watford experiment which might be applicable in our case and I decided that it would be desirable to set up a somewhat similar establishment within the Navy. The fault in the naval system was the irregular method of selecting ratings suitable for a commission. We were also up against 'Stripey' in the barracks who did a very efficient job of instructing his young and innocent charges in the ethos of how to get away with as little as possible without getting caught.

On thinking all this over I came to the conclusion that it was impossible to educate captains of all types of ships into any uniform system of selection and that any work we were going to do in the way of selecting potential officers would have to be done in the basic training establishment during the first twelve weeks of training. The Second Sea Lord, who was the Member of the Board responsible for personnel, lent a sympathetic ear to my findings and was quick to see the point. He gave me permission to go ahead with any trials which I saw fit and I arranged for him to appoint a Lieutenant to my division to do any field work that was necessary in one of the basic training establishments. In this I was extremely fortunate in having Charles Owen, a destroyer Officer who was temporarily on shore due to night blindness, to assist me in the work. His persuasive charm worked wonders on some of the crusty old Captains we had to approach after we had got the scheme operational. There was one in particular at the start for whom Charles never forgave me. I wrote to this old crab asking if I could go and see him on the matter of training and he agreed. Knowing that he might be prickly to handle and recognizing what a splendid public relations man I had in Charles, I took him along. At ten o'clock the following morning I was in the Captain's office outlining what it was that we wanted to do, with my innocent but charming Lieutenant parked outside. After a brief explanation I said, 'I wonder whether you would like to take on the job of doing this trial.'

'Yes, yes, I'll do it,' he grunted, 'but I'm not going to have my organization upset. No newfangled ideas here. I know what I want. I know how to choose a good officer.'

Recoiling slightly from the blast, I grovelled a bit and reassured him with, 'Oh, yes, I'm sure of that, we all know of your reputation but I wonder whether you could try this out.'

'Well, yes, all right. But I'm not going to be interfered with!' came the stern response.

'In that case, perhaps you'd like to meet my Lieutenant,' I pressed home my advantage.

'What's he got to do with it?'

'Well, I thought of leaving him here with you to save you the labour of looking into it.'

'No, no. I don't want to see him! He's your chappie. You do what you like with him.'

What I did was to leave poor Charles, rather like a father leaving his boy at prep school, to cope with the overfalls which were bound to give him a bit of a bumpy ride with a couple of thousand men under training with a dyed-in-the-wool obstructionist of a Captain. Somehow or other he worked a miracle, eventually charmed him into such vehement advocacy of what we were trying to do that he boasted about it all over the place and almost became an embarrassment to us by claiming far more for the scheme than we felt it deserved.

We naturally did not expect ready-made officers to be found in large quantities and we knew that most of the people that we would be considering would have had no contact or interest in the Navy or the sea. But we did know that within a short space of time these potential officers would be serving in an active capacity in tank landing craft and a whole host of new vessels under conditions of extreme difficulty. We needed men of intelligence with some inborn qualities of leadership, but at that early stage we did not set our sights too high.

The only time available for us to select future officers was the ten weeks following the initial obedience training at the basic training establishment. Any tests we were going to carry out would have to be done during this period. The Captain at the *King Alfred* reasoned that the failure rate was so high because the material sent to him was not up to the minimum standard required in three main areas: firstly, many of the those sent to him had not got the necessary mental capacity to absorb the basic navigational requirements for an officer; secondly they were often too confused by the sudden and dramatic change in their lives brought about by joining the Navy to display any powers of leadership which they might possess and, thirdly, quite a large proportion seemed to have no desire to become officers and showed no ambition to pass out successfully from their course.

The appointment of extra schoolmasters to give instruction in simple mathematics would solve the first problem. In the second case it seemed to me that they needed shaking out of themselves and indoctrinating with naval thoughts and habits. The third reason was interesting and most unexpected and it was rooted in the unwholesome atmosphere of the barracks under the influence of 'Stripey' a dearly loved and dependable character in peacetime but with a definite inclination to get out of doing a job if he could. He was also a master of 'the book' and knew his way intimately round all the rules and regulations.

We got our new officer selection scheme approved and over a period of a year the dropout rate finally went down to 2%. A great deal of the credit was due to my Lieutenant and the skill and judgement that he displayed in building the organization which followed. It relied on close observation of the candidates at all stages and people had to be trained how to do this.

They became known as Testing Officers who worked with small groups of men. We found that ultimately the members of each group were the best judges of leadership amongst their peers since the generation gap prevented more mature Testing Officers from getting a true picture of candidates' potential.

We invented tasks for them to do like giving them three planks and a bucket of explosive and telling them they had to get it across a chasm but the planks were too short. The group almost invariably tuned in to the true leader. In any group of eight it was the general rule, although we did emphasize to ourselves that it was wrong to make generalisations in these cases, that a false leader would jump up and say, 'Come on chaps! Let's get on with it!' and start giving orders. The others would listen for a while and then turn away from him to the true leader who had stood back to think about it. At the other end of the scale was the clown who, having built the bridge, had to be the first one across it. The culmination of the whole thing was to put them in a darkened room with a chart to simulate the bridge under blackout conditions and then have WRNS crawling round under the table letting off fire-crackers in buckets to see how they would perform in the stress of battle!

My own character training had been done in the *Port Jackson* forty years before. There I had started to learn about people, their strengths, weaknesses and real qualities. Most of all I had learned to recognize and value the old sailors' willingness to help — the rogue's yarn which runs through all true sailormen the world over.

ENVOI

JOE ORAM WAS released from Naval service on the eleventh of March 1946 with the rank of Captain. His contribution to both technical and operations sides of the submarine service are undeniable. Many innovative devices for the improvement of equipment and procedures which sprang from his fertile imagination were acknowledged officially by his superiors and adopted into Naval use. He had an original and farsighted way of solving problems — what would probably nowadays be referred to as 'lateral thinking' — an approach which did not always meet with a sympathetic hearing in the somewhat turgid hierarchy of Admiralty. Somehow or another he was, more often than not, lucky — or shrewd — enough eventually to find an enlightened champion who would allow a dummy run. The pudding was usually proved in the eating. When not, he was the first to describe the fiasco as 'a complete bloody cock-up'.

On retiring from the Navy, he offered his services to the government and was appointed to the Department of Sports Goods and Musical Instruments at the Board of Trade. He delighted in the absurdity of this appointment when re-telling the story later in life after experience as a 'head-hunter' in collaboration with Charles Owen, running one of the first such selection and recruitment agencies in the country.

After a series of moves and promotions, the Board of Trade provided him, quite accidentally, with a way-point for the return to training. It sent him to Cardiff as Controller for Wales where an invitation to a dinner party resulted in his being invited to become a founding member of a committee to establish an Outward Bound School in the city. Recognizing Joe Oram's passionate interest in the training and general development of young people and his talent for enabling them to get the best out of themselves, the organizers asked him to join the Board of the main school at Aberdovey. This 'made the wind creak in the rigging again,' as he put it when surveying the second half of his long life, 'a wind which seemed to have died completely when I left the service.'

The Warden at Aberdovey, possibly feeling the nearby sea and mountains were being somewhat overplayed in developing self discipline through risk and adventure, pointed out one day that there was just as much opportunity for Outward Bound to fulfil its aims in the city. Oram picked this idea up at once, got the Board to commission some research and City Challenge was born. On a visit to Edinburgh to see how the project was going, he described a conversation with a seventeen-year-old girl. 'What job that you've done since you've been here has made the biggest impression on you?' he enquired. The girl thought for a moment and said, 'Oh, the mental hospital.' 'I just don't understand that,' he admitted. 'I went there today too and I couldn't help it but I wanted to push the patients away from me.' The girl brightened immediately and with great kindness assured him, 'Oh I felt like that at the beginning but after a short time you get over it. I knew I could help them because they wanted love and I had love to give.'

After five years in Wales, he returned to England where he ran into his erstwhile Lieutenant, Charles Owen, and was introduced to the business of 'head-hunting'. Charles could never quite put his finger on the secret of Oram's success. His technique was unique but remarkably effective. He would pin a likely candidate to a chair in his office for what seemed like hours on end, apparently boring him to death on the subject of submarines. He would then take him out for a drink and make his assessment. It was invariably correct.

Oram was a longstanding member of the committee of the Cape Horners Society and in the early 'seventies became President. This kept him in touch with what he always regarded as the most formative part of his career — his sail training. He worked from an office at the Maritime Museum in Greenwich and took part with relish in the continual debate over definition of eligibility for membership. Should yachtsmen (and women) who had rounded the Horn be admitted or not? Some members believed not and fought fiercely for the exclusive right to belong to those who had stayed the course in a merchant vessel under sail. Oram pointed out the dodo-like consequences of this contention and eventually yachtspeople were granted entry, but not as full members. That privilege remained sacrosant for 'Abatrosses' (those who had commanded a merchant ship under sail) and 'Cape Horners' (the hapless crew).

At the age of ninety, Captain Oram decided to write the second volume for his autobiography. His memory was wonderfully acute, his sense of humour very much alive. He was still a superb teacher and most cogent commentator on current affairs and modern life. In many ways, he was still a man ahead of his time.

During the collaboration on the preparation of this book, it became clear that the *Thetis* accident had irrevocably changed him. He never betrayed any trace of bitterness or resentment at the behaviour of some of his fellow officers who effectively shunned him after the event, though he must surely have been deeply wounded by it. His desperation at being unsuccessful in his brave attempt to save the *Thetis* crew stayed with him for the rest of his life. He was only able to discuss it when 'the apple had ripened' and the time was right. Even almost fifty years afterwards, it was harrowing for him to relive the experience. He was not promoted to Rear-Admiral before retiring and one can only speculate on the reasons.

On 17 February, 1986, Captain Oram returned to HMS *Dolphin* as the guest of the then Commander, Alastair Johnson. A wardroom dinner was held in his honour after which he made a tour of the base he had commanded 48 years before. He showed particular interest in the Submarine Escape

Training Tank, putting one or two questions which rather caught the Instructor on the hop. Apart from the obvious advances in technology, little seemed to have changed for him and he slipped back into his Naval 'persona' with consummate ease.

In his heart, Captain Oram never left the sea. Having put in to port for the last time, he died peacefully on 29 May, 1986.

INDEX